Building Literate Communities

Building Literate Communities

In Conversation with Sheridan Blau

Edited by

Kathleen (Buchan) Kelly
Teachers College, Columbia University

Ruth Vinz
Teachers College, Columbia University

Paul M. Rogers
University of California, Santa Barbara

National Council of Teachers of English
340 N. Neil St., Suite #104, Champaign, IL 61820
www.ncte.org

Staff Editor: Cynthia Gomez
Manuscript Editor: Michael Ryan
Interior Design: Jenny Jensen Greenleaf
Typesetting: Barbara Frazier
Cover Design: Adrian Morgan

ISBN (print) 978-0-8141-0224-4
ISBN (epub) 978-0-8141-0225-1
ISBN (PDF) 978-0-8141-0226-8

It is the policy of NCTE in its journals and other publications to provide a forum for the open discussion of ideas concerning the content and the teaching of English and the language arts. Publicity accorded to any particular point of view does not imply endorsement by the Executive Committee, the Board of Directors, or the membership at large, except in announcements of policy, where such endorsement is clearly specified.

NCTE provides equal employment opportunity (EEO) to all staff members and applicants for employment without regard to race, color, religion, sex, national origin, age, physical, mental or perceived handicap/disability, sexual orientation including gender identity or expression, ancestry, genetic information, marital status, military status, unfavorable discharge from military service, pregnancy, citizenship status, personal appearance, matriculation or political affiliation, or any other protected status under applicable federal, state, and local laws.

Every effort has been made to provide current URLs and email addresses, but because of the rapidly changing nature of the web, some sites and addresses may no longer be accessible.

Library of Congress Control Number: 2024946804

"And whenever I write . . . I'm always looking for a way to—it's something like a graphic representation; it's a brief but memorable way of presenting a body of information so that it sticks; it's like making a poem . . . "

—BLAU INTERVIEW, 2021

To My Undergraduate Students

Growing younger every year,
You have now grown to be my grandchildren,
Innocent, respectfully amused at my musings and
Forgetfulness; sometimes yielding for a moment
To ideas and feelings from a time and place
Remote, yet resonant for you like a song
From a childhood lived in another century.

I love you easily when you enter
With me into the little church at Bemerton,
Where George Herbert preached in 1632
In the tinted light of windows glazed with stories
Of repentance, grace, and sacrifice,
Strange categories of feeling you now begin
To recognize as language you can use.

I can also love you on days when you refuse
To talk, smiling shyly at my rough questions:
What do you make of this? Doesn't this
Mean anything to you? What is it
You don't understand? Let me hear what puzzles you!
I am pushing you to see there is
No mystery to reading poems
Except the courage and humility
To say: this I don't get. Why does he say
This or that, and what can it mean?

Helping you to understand the paradox
That through our questions
We find most of what we need to know
And almost everything worth saying.

—Sheridan Blau, March 17, 2006

Contents

Foreword

Mentorship in the Fields of English Education

Patricia Lambert Stock

This collection of essays, which offers the breadth and scope of work done in the name of English education, was inspired by Sheridan Blau, teacher, scholar, and program builder, whose own work has influenced research and practice across the fields of English language, literature, and composition, what the editors of this collection have wisely dubbed "the fields of English education." As chapter authors celebrate Blau's contributions to their work and to scholarship and practice in their fields, they draw attention to a phenomenon that has been foundational in the establishment and development of the fields of English education: the professional activity known as mentoring.

Dictionary definitions vary slightly from one to another but essentially identify *mentoring* as a form of social learning in which a more experienced individual offers advice or guidance to a less experienced person, especially in a job or at school. A number of articles draw attention to the fact that mentorship can take many forms that cannot be succinctly defined or easily illustrated. A chapter of the story of my work in English education is a case in point, a case illustrating the generative role mentorship has played, not only for me but also in the development of scholarship, practice, and program building in the fields of English education.

Workshop as Mentor

Although I did not realize it at the time, my work in English education began to center on composition studies in 1978 when

I was teaching English in Pioneer High School in Ann Arbor, Michigan. In November of that year, I attended NCTE's Annual Convention in Kansas City. When I registered for the convention, I decided to attend a three-day, post-convention workshop on the teaching of writing. I was teaching a composition class for twelfth graders, and I wanted to learn more about the emerging writing-to-learn practices in the field that had been inspired by the British study, *The Development of Writing Abilities (11–18)*, conducted by James N. Britton, Tony Burgess, Nancy Martin, Alex McLeod, and Harold Rosen (1975). Ken Macrorie, whose name was a household word to every teacher of writing at this time, led the workshop. Ken's books, *Telling Writing* (1970) and *Uptaught* (1970), had already made their mark on the teaching of writing across the country, and I wanted to learn more about what he could teach me.

In the final session of the three-day-long workshop, which I found inspiring, I was awarded a collection of books about the teaching of writing by Bob Boynton, publisher of Ken's books. At the time, Bob was editor of professional books for teachers of the English language arts for Hayden Publishing Company. Three years later, in 1981, he established Boynton/Cook Publishers, which came to be widely recognized as the leading publisher of professional books for teachers of the English language arts. Throughout its existence, Bob was the heart and soul of Boynton/Cook Publishers. When he retired in 1987, Boynton/Cook joined the highly respected publishers Heinemann. Although I did not know it at the time, Bob Boynton and Ken Macrorie would mentor me as I made my way into the developing field of composition studies in English education.

Seven months after the workshop, in late June 1979, together with other teachers from schools, colleges, and universities throughout the state of Michigan, I attended the first in a series of annual summer conferences for teachers of writing sponsored by the English Composition Board (ECB), a unit established in 1977 in the College of Literature, Science, and the Arts in the University of Michigan to develop a writing-across-the-curriculum program, the first of its kind in a large research university. All of us who gathered on the campus in Ann Arbor that June wanted to learn more about the university's new writing program and about how to teach writing effectively in an era when teachers across the curriculum were about to be asked to teach writing-in the-disciplines (WID). In a closing plenary session after three days of intensive talk and writing, one of the conference leaders, Bernie Van't Hul, professor of English and developer and director of the new introductory composition course in the university, suggested we continue our conversation and our discussion of the teaching of writing.

When participants were invited to share thoughts about the conference and possible follow-up activities in a post-conference evaluation, I offered a description of a newsletter that I imagined might usefully serve the needs of practicing teachers of writing. To my surprise, several days later, I was invited to the university to talk more about my suggestions with Bernie and Dan Fader, director of the university's new writing program. I described what became "fforum: A Newsletter of the English Composition Board" and was invited to join the faculty of the ECB to develop and edit it and to teach composition. After several sleepless nights and long discussions with my husband, I made the career-changing decision to accept that invitation.

Having proposed that the ECB should ask the most influential thinkers in the field of writing instruction at the time—whose names and ideas had been topics of discussion during the conference—to write newsletter-length essays (2,000 words or so) to a group of 125 teachers in Michigan, I confronted the reality of what I had done. How would I contact those established scholars, to say nothing of asking them to write articles encapsulating the heart of their thinking for a fledgling newsletter to be mailed to 125 teachers? I was in unfamiliar territory. Uncertain of what to do, insecure, and scared, if the truth be known, my thoughts turned to the workshop I'd attended the previous November and to the only people I could imagine who might be positioned to help me, Ken Macrorie and Bob Boynton. I garnered my courage, found Hayden Publishing Company's phone number, and called Bob Boynton to ask for his advice. Bob answered his own phone. Kind and reassuring when I said things like, "I'm sure you don't remember me, but . . .," Bob responded, "Of course I remember you . . .," and proceeded to help me address the challenge I'd undertaken. That morning, Bob and I began a conversation that continued for almost forty years. After describing my situation, I asked Bob if he thought Ken Macrorie might be willing to write for the first issue of the newsletter. Without skipping a beat, he said he thought Ken would and gave me Ken's phone number. Phone call number two of my new career in composition studies was to Ken Macrorie, who also answered his phone, who also assured me he remembered me, and who said he was happy to write a 2,000-word essay for a brand-new newsletter to be mailed to 125 teachers. And the rest, as the saying goes, is history. Every one of the influential scholars I asked to write over the years I developed and edited "fforum" said "Yes." Among those generous English educators were Edward P. J. Corbett, Peter Elbow, Jimmy Britton, Nancy Martin, Donald Graves, Donald Murray, Ann Berthoff, James Moffett, Sheridan Baker, Toby Fulwiler, Art Young, Lee Odell, Cy Knoblauch, David Bartholomae, Stephen Bernhardt, and William Coles, to name but a few.

What began as a newsletter for 125 teachers in Michigan gained a circulation of more than 2,000 teachers across the country in three short years, leading me in 1982 to ask Bob Boynton if he had any interest in publishing a book of some of the essays. Once again, Bob said "Yes." *fforum: Essays on Theory and Practice in the Teaching of Writing*, my first book, was published in 1983. Among the readership it found were classes of university students who were preparing to teach writing. The support that Bob Boynton and Ken Macrorie offered me as I charted a new course in English education is but one example of the how acts of mentorship contributed not only to an individual's career but also to the development of scholarship and practice in the fields of English education.

Another Workshop: Another Story of Mentorship in English Education

Rolling back the tape of events that led me to relocate my work in English education from secondary school teaching to teaching and program building at the university level and to conducting research in composition studies, teacher education, and practitioner research, I pick up a strand of story that features two distinguished English educators who also mentored me: Bernie Van't Hul and Sheridan Blau. As I focus on particular moments in this strand of my story, I'll begin again in a workshop as I draw attention to scholarship and practice undergoing development.

In the spring of 1979, fellow English teachers and I gathered in a classroom in Pioneer High School for a professional development workshop that had been billed as an introduction to the University of Michigan's new composition program. The workshop was to be led by Bernard Van't Hul, professor of English and director of Introductory Composition in the university. I'll take a minute to describe the workshop Bernie offered that spring morning for two reasons: First, the workshop influenced the practice of many teachers who participated in it over the years that Bernie and others offered it; and second, it's the seed of a significant strand of my research and publication.

That morning when Bernie offered the workshop in Pioneer High School, he captured my colleagues' and my attention immediately with an anecdote, an encapsulated tale of one man's humble beginnings, unanticipated good fortune, great expectations; of another man's denied passion; of crime and its consequences. Leaving the end of the story hanging in mid-air, Bernie concluded the anecdote with a question worded something like this: "As a result of the events that I have just told you, what kinds of things are going to be written?"

My colleagues and I smiled at the skillful way Bernie had used the anecdote to draw us into the workshop. As we named the types of writing that would necessarily follow the intriguing events he reported, Bernie filled the chalkboard in the front of the room with our responses: newspaper articles, legal briefs, letters. . . . When there was no more room on the board, he distributed some of the genres of writing that we had named: an autopsy surgeon's report, a legal brief, a front-page newspaper article, a magazine article. As we read excerpts from these writings and began to discuss the nature and logic of their generic features, my colleagues and I agreed that they were quite different from one another. Bernie had positioned us to see for ourselves that although English teachers are customarily charged with responsibility for teaching students to write effectively, English teachers are not necessarily prepared to teach students how to compose some of the genres of writing we were examining that day.

The final piece of writing that Bernie shared with us was Robert Browning's dramatic monologue "Porphyria's Lover," which tells the tale Bernie used to introduce the workshop. Acknowledging his indebtedness to Cleanth Brooks, John Thibaut Purser, and Robert Penn Warren for the pieces of writing he used "to open his workshop" Bernie indicated that his argument—and therefore his use of the writing samples—was quite different from the argument that Brooks, Purser, and Warren wished to advance when they crafted the writing samples and published them in the "General Introduction" (1–8) to their well-known textbook *An Approach to Literature* (1964). Their purpose was not to illustrate that what counts as effective writing differs in different discourses; their purpose was to *make a distinction* between writing and literature (emphasis mine here in print; Bernie's in the workshop). A gifted teacher, Bernie used the various pieces of writing, including the one that Brooks, Purser, and Warren identified as literature, to argue for the set of theoretical principles he had developed to guide the teaching of writing in the University of Michigan's new writing program.

Charged with the task of transforming the university's freshman English course (in which students were asked to write about British and American literature) into an introductory composition course in which students were to be prepared to write in disciplines and fields across the curriculum, Bernie turned the attention of University of Michigan faculty, teaching assistants, students, and an audience of college, community college, and secondary school teachers across the country (thanks to workshops sponsored by the Andrew W. Mellon Foundation) from models of American and British literature and surface features of writing to classical rhetoric and effectiveness of language use. He made his message memorable with the acronym MAPS, which he meant to serve as a reminder that all language use (spoken and written) is more or less effective depending on the how well it does the following things: fulfills the generic expectations for the Medium or Mode (genre) in which it is composed, addresses the needs of the Audience and Purpose for which it is composed, and satisfies the demands of the Situation in which it is composed. Because his goal was to change teaching practices, Bernie chose the workshop format to demonstrate and model both the theory he was advancing and the practices he was proposing. According to Bernie, his theoretical construct MAPS was "warmed over Aristotle," Aristotle's rhetorical theory rekindled in light of twentieth-century scholarship in linguistics.

I began to share Bernie's anecdote and adapted writing samples with my students the next day. When I moved from teaching secondary school English to teaching college composition and teacher education, I shared the workshop anecdote and writing samples with countless composition students, preparing teachers, and inservice teachers who, in turn, have shared the materials with their students and colleagues.

Years after that spring morning in 1979, Sheridan Blau, in his role as director of the South Coast Writing Project (SCWriP), the National Writing Project site at the University of California-Santa Barbara, invited me to offer a workshop at the project's annual reunion. When I asked Sheridan what issues were on the minds of practicing teachers of writing at the time, he indicated that teachers in the area were concerned about preparing students to write effectively in different content areas (science, social studies, etc.). I decided to open the workshop by reenacting Bernie's workshop as faithfully as possible. Because those who would attend the reunion were K–university teachers of all subject areas, I also decided that while we'd begin our work by examining the difference among literacies of different disciplines, we'd roll back to concentrate on how different disciplines' literacies develop in the first place.

In a workshop that I entitled "Experience to Exposition: An Exploration of Genres of Learning," I shared the anecdote and writing samples that Bernie had shared with my colleagues and me in the spring of 1979. However, just as Bernie's purpose in telling the anecdote and exploring the genres of writing that he credited to Brooks, Purser, and Warren was not their purpose in developing and publishing the materials, mine was not his. Just as his built upon Brooks, Purser, and Warren's work, revising and extending it in the light of rhetorical and linguistic theory for the purpose of improving the teaching of writing-in-the-disciplines

(WID) in the late 1970s, I built upon Bernie's work, extending it in the light of research developed in the writing-to-learn (WTL) strand of the Writing Across the Curriculum (WAC) movement.

The purpose of the workshop I offered in Santa Barbara that summer, and for years thereafter in University of California and California State University writing projects from San Diego to Chico, was to circulate strategies used in my teaching to prepare students to enter discipline-based and field-based conversations. These strategies invite students to write about and relate experiences they bring with them to subjects they are beginning to study in school. Bernie's anecdote and the materials he developed to raise questions about generic expectations for effective writing serve as a generative starting place for my workshop. Building upon that foundation in my workshop, I am able to pose questions like these: Given the fact that what counts as effective writing differs remarkably in different cultures, disciplines, and fields, how can teachers best prepare students to think, talk, read, write, raise questions, and participate actively in those various cultural, disciplinary, and field-based communities? How can teachers prepare students to see how the vocabulary, questions, research, and discourse of disciplines develop in the first place? How can teachers enable students to use disciplinary discourse themselves as a model for understanding how others have done so? In other words, how can teachers prepare students to enter new studies, understanding that they will be learning languages and practices that others have had a head start in developing but confident that they can catch up because they themselves have already developed a study, its special language, concepts, and methods of creating knowledge?

To allow workshop participants to develop their own answers to framing questions, I invited us to use a variety of genres of learning about a subject of study, such as children's play, to which participants of different ages and backgrounds bring some experience, a subject that will grow increasingly complex during the course of the workshop. As participants write to (re)collect, sort, analyze, and synthesize information about the topic of children's play, to begin to read what others have to say on the subject, and to express their developing understandings, we discuss both what and how we are learning about the subject and the ways in which we might adapt the learning activities we are practicing in the workshop for our students and the subjects we teach.

For many of the reading, writing, and discussion activities that I introduce in this workshop, designed to invite newcomers to: develop a field of study, dramatize how a discourse develops, see how questions for further exploration and plans for how to conduct research into those questions develop, I am also indebted to Amherst College's legendary teacher of composition, Theodore Baird. Although I never met Baird, his practices for teaching writing and thinking, like Bernie Van't Hul's, have been circulated by his students and their students; Bernie's in workshops and Baird's in print (e.g., Bartholomae & Petrosky, 1987; Coles, 1978; White, 1973). Baird's theory and practice of teaching composition may well be thought of as classic in the body of knowledge that has shaped the teaching of writing since the second half of the twentieth century. In their writing, Baird's students demonstrate the impact on learning of a composition course that asks students to use writing, discussion, and course-required reading, including emerging collections of their own writing, to explore and develop knowledge about a complex topic of inquiry.

I've described this workshop and how it unfolds in detail in a chapter of *Entering the Conversations: Practicing Literacy in the Disciplines* (2014), a book that I co-wrote with Trace Schillinger and Andrew Stock. In the book, Trace and Andrew describe teaching practices that they too had published previously for peer review, refinement, and community use in workshop form in NWP sites and professional conferences. In richly detailed accounts, they describe how they use roleplaying as a strategy for engaging students in required subjects in their curricula. Andrew describes how his fifth-grade students learn the discourse and subject matter of ecosystem studies and US and Canadian geography and government by developing its discourse and knowledge as they themselves play the roles of wildlife biologists and legislators crafting wildlife protection laws. Trace describes how she prepares eighth graders in an interdisciplinary humanities course to study the American Revolution by positioning them to engage in a revolution of their own making, as revolutionaries, anti-revolutionaries, and pro and con media groups covering the revolution. As Andrew's and Trace's students become players in the subject matter they are studying, they develop a discourse for discussing and writing about it and methods of exploring the questions and issues that they themselves raise in the process, including reading primary texts and already published scholarship in the fields.

Although it was Bernie who first inspired my interest in the workshop, it was my work in the National Writing Project, as a site director and a member of the project's national advisory board in the 1990s, that deepened my interest in it as a venue in which teachers shared their successful practices with one another, not just for community use but also for peer review, criticism, and refinement. When the NWP was founded at the University of California (Berkeley) in 1974, teaching workshops, one of the three constitutive activities of the project's summer institutes for teachers, were understood as accomplished teachers' demonstrations of their most successful practices for teaching writing. But it became clear to many of us involved in the project over time that they were something more than just demonstrations of practice. They were examinations of practice by communities of professional practitioners, many of whom often went on to revise and reform the practices being made public for their own teaching purposes. They were, in effect, publications of practice for peer review, refinement, and community use, or, to put it in academic terms, they were a developing scholarship of teaching practice.

When, on Sheridan's recommendation, other NWP site directors across California invited me, year after year, to offer the same workshop I had developed for Sheridan's site's annual reunion, and when fellows from previous years came back to participate in the workshop again, my interest in the workshop grew. I conducted studies of what I had come to recognize as a research genre in which teachers published their best practices for peer review and community use in the service of building a scholarship of teaching. And I began to write about my developing thinking on the subject (Stock, "Toward a Theory of Genre in Teacher Research: Contributions from a Reflective Practitioner," 2001). Publication of this article and talks I'd begun to give on the subject led me—with support from Michigan State University and the National Writing Project—to conduct a multiyear study of the workshop as a genre of practitioner research and publication, as a means of building a scholarship of teaching practice. Working as a participant-observer at five National Writing Project sites during the summers of 2005 and 2006, attending follow-up observations of site reunions, observing a number of participants introduce practices they experienced in the summer in their own classrooms, I traced—over twenty years—the impact of a workshop that I attended in the early 1990s in Oakland County, Michigan, on classroom teaching (elementary through university courses), state- and national-level projects, and published articles.

When that work-in-progress was reported in an invited research session at the annual meeting of the American Education Research Association (AERA) in 2007, it was well received. One of the comments made at the session drew attention to the fact that research in education seldom documents the generative effects of practices that reach across many venues and over a substantial period of time. And that which may be said of the workshop publication of teaching practices, for the scholarship of teaching they produce, may well be said also of the role that mentorship has played in the development of scholarship, teaching, and program building in the fields of English education.

A Closing Word about Mentorship in the Fields of English Education

I began this essay by noting that acts of mentorship—how they take shape, what their impacts are—defy succinct definition. I also claimed that countless generous acts of mentoring have contributed immeasurably to scholarship, practice, and program building in the fields of English education. To make my case, I followed advice generally attributed to Anton Chekov: I tried to show, not tell.

I tried to show how Bob Boynton in his work as publisher of emerging scholarship in the teaching of the English language arts always had time to entertain new ideas and support ideas he found promising. I tried to show how Ken Macrorie, who taught, wrote, conducted workshops, and was nothing short of a hero in English education when I met him, answered a telephone call, said, "Yes," and became the first published author in a project that went on to launch my work and to have broad impact on the teaching of writing at the time.

I tried to show how Bernie Van't Hul's workshop inspired my teaching. I didn't tell how his teaching, the introductory composition course he developed in the University of Michigan's new writing program, a course that I had the opportunity to teach, the English 125 books of classroom materials he published annually for use in the course, and the professional development workshops for teachers of the course that he offered weekly had an invaluable impact on my teaching and my scholarship in the years to follow. I didn't tell how when I joined the university's English Composition Board to edit *fforum*, Bernie was an invaluable advisor, how his erudite, tongue-in-cheek artwork enriched it delightfully. Throughout his career, Bernie was first and foremost a teacher, an extraordinary teacher. To me, he was that and more: an extraordinary mentor.

I tried to show how Sheridan Blau, whose career-long work across the fields of English education inspired this collection of essays, encouraged me to probe my developing interest in the workshop as a research genre by inviting me to offer dozens of workshops in multiple venues and to follow the uses to which they were put by teachers who participated in them. I didn't tell how he encouraged me to undertake the years-long study I conducted of workshops offered by practicing teachers in National Writing Project summer institutes and conferences and the short- and long-term impacts of those workshops. And I didn't draw attention to the fact that, in doing so, Sheridan invited me to develop a strand of scholarship into a practice that figures prominently in his own teaching, scholarship, and program building. As articles in this collection attest, Sheridan has not only offered countless workshops for practicing teachers and published books and articles about workshops, but he has also created venues in which hundreds of teachers have published their best practices for peer review, refinement, adaptation, and use.

In many fields, scholars speak about those who influenced, supported, and—in many cases—advanced their work as giants in the field on whose shoulders they stand. In the fields of English education, particularly in language and writing studies, which are themselves constitutive forces in all other branches of learning, the terms we most often use to describe such individuals are typically more modest. We usually speak of those who paved pathways for us and our work by describing them as mentors who were interested in our emerging work as they observed, learned, or read about it. We speak about them as mentors who answered calls, who offered helping hands, who extended invitations, all in the service of building a community of colleagues committed to doing good work well. And when the occasion presents itself, we honor them.

Works Cited

Bartholomae, D., & Petrosky, A. (1987). *Ways of reading: An anthology for writers*. St. Martin's Press.

Britton, J., Burgess, T., Martin, N., McLeod, A., & Rosen, H. (1975). *The development of writing abilities (11–18)*. Macmillan.

Brooks, C., Purser, J. T., & Warren, R. P. (1964). *An approach to literature*. Appleton Century Crofts.

Browning, R. (2010). Porphyria [Porphyria's lover]. In J. Woolford, D. Karlin, & J. Phelan (Eds.), *Robert Browning: Selected poems* (pp. 70–73). Routledge. (Original work published 1836)

Coles, W. (1978). *The plural I: The teaching of writing*. Holt, Rinehart and Winston.

Macrorie, K. (1970). *Telling writing*. Hayden.

Macrorie, K. (1970). *Uptaught*. Boynton/Cook.

Stock, P. (Ed.). (1983). *fforum: Essays on theory and practice in the teaching of writing*. Boynton/Cook.

Stock. P. (2001). Toward a theory of genre in teacher research: Contributions from a reflective practitioner. *English Education, 33*(2), 100–114.

Stock, P., Schillinger, T., & Stock, A. (2014). *Entering the conversations: Practicing literacy in the disciplines*. National Council of Teachers of English.

Introduction

As a Whitmanesque enactment of "Every atom belonging to me as good belongs to you," we come to the heart of Sheridan Blau's belief that the flow of ideas, the pursuit of what eludes us, and the wonders of learning are best explored in company with others. Deeply rooted in the belief that communities of teachers cultivate a more expansive vision of literate engagement together rather than through self-assertation, Sheridan creates and advocates for spaces for inquiry and practice in multi-venues from workshops, classes, dinner conversations, conferences, NCTE, and National Writing Project sites. *Building Literate Communities: In Conversation with Sheridan Blau* is a collection of chapters written by authors who reflect on and extend Sheridan's life-work contributions and, in doing so, reveal his and their intellectual genealogies. What becomes obvious in this collection is that an intense, careful, and outward scrutiny does not reach any forms of certainty in self or group knowledge but rather is the grist for fleeting and unstable insights and provocative questions that lead to the next explorations and dissatisfactions with "what is."

Yearning is often present and palpable when in company with Sheridan. Just around the corner of an idea he is articulating or writing is another question, another provocation, or a statement that might cause mild bemusement or outright objection. Whatever the reaction, where you/we/us might find ourselves is caught in a web, a new unsettled space for inquiry, or, as Whitman might describe metaphorically, a new "fold of the future."

Our intention is not to provide an uncritical celebration through these chapters but to see the substantive ways in which these contributors build on Sheridan's questions and doubts, how they often go astray, learning as they go, following his provocation to begin by taking up the questions, tensions, and dilemmas in their own ways. Throughout, we find evidence of Sheridan's influence and leadership in the field. His ever-present invitation to thinkers to see what they *can do* informs his work and this volume. Whether through the small and more intimate acts—in classroom interactions, as mentor to a new teacher, as coauthor for an article or book—or working from within organizations—National Writing Project, NCTE, SCWriP, UCSB, and Teachers College—each of these chapter authors acknowledges the extent to which Sheridan's interactions have influenced their lives as professionals, writers, readers, scholars, subject matter experts, and creators of pedagogical knowledge. Collegiality is engendered but not as a result of agreements and consensus. The critical work of creating dis-comfort and dis-ease, often clothed in ambivalently and reluctantly acknowledged uncertainties, is filled with a bounty of possibilities, curiosities, and joy.

We hope you find these chapters wildly generative in their diverse accounts of teaching, learning, and life, and in the shared project of making our educational world a thriving place to live and flourish. We hope. Hope is a noun and a verb. As a noun, it is manifest in the concreteness of persons, places, or things. As a verb, it flies, hovers, lifts, soars, and acts itself into meaning in the world. The early Germanic word for hope is "hoppen" and most likely is derived from the word "hop," to literally take a "small" flight. In each of the chapters collected here, which we invite you to read in any order you desire, you will see each writer's flight through hope, desire, and tenacious exploration. In summing up Sheridan's role in all that is reflected in these chapters, perhaps central is a simple pedagogical principle that applies to his classroom teaching as well as his interactions as mentor and colleague in the building of literate communities. Antoine de Saint-Exupéry explains it beautifully:

> *If you want to build a ship don't drum up people together to collect wood and don't assign them tasks and work, but rather teach them to long for the endless immensity of the sea.*
>
> —*Citadelle,* 1948

"Nobody can learn for you. Nobody can teach you. And you have everything you need right from the start."

—Blau interview, 2021

Chapter One

Invisible Writing: Suppressing to Enhance

Peter Elbow

All existing things must "pay penalty and retribution to one another for their injustice, according to the disposition of time."

—Anaximander

Humans struggled a long time to make speech visible—that is, to invent writing. Why would Sheridan ever want to make writing invisible again? The answer involves a birth story. James Britton (1970) convinced himself that invisible writing is impossible; he experimented and found that if he couldn't see the words he was writing, he couldn't write. But Sheridan—trying to confirm this result—found himself *disconfirming* it. Britton had based his negative finding on a sample of just one: himself. Sheridan tested using many people and many repetitions and found that invisible writing—suppressing your ability to see your words as you put them down—far from inhibiting your writing actually *enhanced* it, both the process of writing and the product or the text. What a lovely illustration of why scholars require disconfirmation of any new hypothesis.

The process here is very like the children's game "Whac-A-Mole": Suppress X, and you enhance Y. Knock something down *here* (the ability to see the words you write) and something else pops up *there* (ease and power in writing). What if we applied this principle to other dimensions of writing? Or even more widely to other realms? That's my goal in this essay: Suppressing X and enhancing Y.

A Case for Freewriting

Invisible writing (IW) enhances speed and fluency. When we can't see what we're writing, we can't stop; otherwise, we'll lose our place. So, invisible writing leads to freewriting. And when we freewrite, we can't plan—or at least plan farther ahead than the next sentence, which better not be too complicated. And when we can't plan, we get spontaneous syntax and vocabulary—the kind of language typical of ordinary speech.

I saw an interesting illustration of this when I was doing a workshop with graduate students in Finland. Their English, even for writing, was humblingly good. I wanted to invite them to compare what it was like to write in two languages. After we did that, I asked them which language they preferred for writing. As always, I like to peddle the virtues of writing in one's home language. But they mostly agreed they preferred writing in English—a foreign language. They said that in English, they didn't so much notice their mistakes! It's the awareness of mistakes and our need to correct them that inhibits our writing and makes us feel stupid. In freewriting and invisible writing, we just turn off any worry about mistakes.

Intonation Units

The linguist Wally Chafe (1989) showed how ordinary spontaneous unplanned speech comes packaged in "intonation units": tiny bursts of nonstop language that always show rhythm and a point or two of stress. But when speakers are too vigilant against mistakes, they rein in their speech and ruin the rhythm of intonation units. This sabotages the music and energy they usually have in their normal unselfconscious speech.

This is a particular problem for speakers of nonstandard or nonsanctioned dialects.

Such speakers often run away from the natural music and rhythm in their unselfconscious speech. "Ain't nobody don't use double negatives." You don't get a pungent sentence like this if you are too vigilant against mistakes. Speakers of nonsanctioned versions of English have been told too often that their speech is wrong for writing (which is, of course, true for mainstream speakers, too). I like to sum up this problem by distinguishing between *uttering* and *constructing*. Uttered syntax ("Ain't nobody . . .") is almost always comfortably speakable and hearable; constructed syntax may be correct, but it is less likely to fit comfortably in the mouth and the ear.

Looking under the hood of ordinary speech, we find Chafe's intonation units and the sequences of stresses and pauses and pitches that are rhythmic and musical. To understand the power of intonation units in language, I coined the mantra "easy out, easy in." That is, when our speech is spontaneous or unplanned (easy out) it creates rhythms that find smooth pathways to the brain (easy in). This is why writing is easier to understand if it is built out of the intonation units of speech.

A good way to illustrate the virtue of intonation units is with song titles and lyrics. Songs highlight the natural sense of rhythm in ordinary spoken language: "She wheels her wheelbarrow [dee DA dee dee DA DA] through streets wide and narrow [dee DA dee dee DA DA]." Or from Broadway: "You must remember this" [dee DA dee dee dee DA], "a kiss is just a kiss" [dee DA dee dee dee DA]."

I bring up song titles and lyrics to confirm Sheridan's arguments about invisible writing: when we write invisibly and can't see our words, we are more likely to fall into unplanned language—which is built out of the intonation units of speech. I'm happy about these findings because what we see in the unplanned language of invisible writing holds also for the unplanned language of freewriting. When speech and writing are unplanned, they are easier for listeners and readers to understand. Invisible writing inevitably pops us into the musical language and syntax of unplanned speech.

The converse illustrates the point, especially in the case of academic writers and diligent students: When we write with extreme vigilance—too preoccupied with the danger of mistakes in grammar or "infelicities" of syntax—we can almost never produce the kind of syntax that is good for readers, music to our ears and suited to our brains. When writers are too preoccupied with the danger of error, they slip into defensive language.

Defensive driving may save lives, but defensive writing ruins the energy and rhythm of intonation units. We see here one of the many reasons why "academic writing" is so often difficult and unpleasant to read.

Felt Sense

When we write invisibly and can't see any words, our attention is forced inward. When we go inside, we open the door to writing from felt sense, a concept from Eugene Gendlin (1978), a phenomenological philosopher who died in 2017. I found his writing a bit difficult and muddy, but Sondra Perl and I were both won over by the importance of his heretofore unexplored insights. I was once lucky enough to be in one of his workshops, and I wrote the foreword to Perl's book *Felt Sense: Writing with the Body* (2004), derived from Gendlin. When we write from felt sense, we are not hurrying—not using freewriting or trying for spontaneous syntax. We allow writing to move more slowly and invite lingering.

So, now we are talking about two contrasting textures of writing: fast freewriting and a more lingering felt sense process of finding words. Both are invited by invisible writing and both are fruitful. Both help people find words, thoughts, and feelings they might not have otherwise found.

Let me point to another experience that many writers have: "I know what I want to say, I just can't find the words." Is there any claim more often scorned by writing teachers? When I was a student, I was told over and over, "You must get your meaning clear in your head before you write. Figure out what you really want to say before you start putting down words." Or "If you can't say it clearly, you don't really know it." Statements like that often lead students to give up. Teacher scorn was one of the reasons for the title for my first book, *Writing Without Teachers* (1973).

Metaphor

When we write without being able to see our words and write more from inside—from feelings and the body—we are more likely to fall into metaphor. Metaphor is a prime example of nonlinear, nonlogical thinking, and metaphor is fertile for creativity. Metaphor follows from feeling a resemblance.

Aristotle was dead wrong to say metaphor can't be taught; it can. The point is that it doesn't need teaching; few people can avoid falling into metaphor when they engage in unguarded speech. And this doesn't count the unconscious metaphors built into our language, as in phrases like high aspirations and low motives—nor the metaphorical etymologies buried in the words that we stand under when we understand something as Lakoff and Johnson (1980) elaborate in *Metaphors We Live By*.

When I finally finished my course work for my PhD—this time at Brandeis after having had to quit grad school at Harvard and teach for seven years—I was preoccupied with metaphor: metaphor as a mode of thinking, not metaphor as linguistic decoration or ornamentation. I credit Bob Greenway, tireless, brilliant first dean at Franconia College, for planting the seed of my interest in metaphor.

To work with metaphor, we start with the feeling of resemblance that we all commonly experience: "X seems sort of like Y, but I can't quite say why." Here is where Gendlin (1962, 1978) can help us with writing, even though writing was not the focus of his work (besides doing philosophy, he also did personal counseling and even therapy). He suggests that we direct the flashlight of our attention with a wider beam. Instead of attending only to words, linger and go inward and attend to our physical body. Pause and wait and try to notice *where in our body* we *feel* that resemblance.

We can then invite that feeling of resemblance to lead us to a word or a phrase for *how* the two things resemble each other. Of course, that word or phrase will almost never seem like a precise or accurate description of the resemblance. But we can linger on that felt gap between the word and the physical feeling of resemblance, and we can invite that gap to lead us to a slight change in the physical feeling. But then, putting attention on the slight change in physical feeling invites a slight change in the word or phrase. Following the same process—attending repeatedly to the gaps between the words and the physical feelings—we can continue to invite readjustments to both feelings and words.

In short, he's suggesting an ongoing dialectical alternation: The physical feeling invites a slight change in the word, but then a bit of dissatisfaction with the word nudges us into a slight adjustment to the physical feeling. All the while, we're trying to work our way closer to two things: a *feeling* that clicks as right and a *word* that clicks as right. But we almost never get there, so we are almost always left with productive gaps.

What I love about Gendlin is how he honors the feeling of *wrongness*. It's that feeling—"wrong again, I *knew* I was no good at finding words"—that can stop us from writing. What a relief to find *value* in that wrongness—wrongness as the motor that pushes us forward to better words and more productive feelings. It's also important that he disagrees with the common idea that words are more precise than feelings. Feelings usually seem so vague. But he insists that the feelings of resemblance (or any feelings of meaningful relationship)—and it's crucial for him that we locate these feelings in the body—are in fact "precise" and "intricate" (his words). He insists that these feelings are more intricate and more precise than words. I know from my experience—and Sondra Perl speaks of it, too—that these feelings and this process are invaluable for writers.

In short, when you write from felt bodily sense, there's a chance of getting outside of the field of verbal language and getting closer to the mystery or transcendent dimensions of creation. When we are trying to say something, where do we find the words? It's a mystery. Gendlin (1991) at least gives us some hints. He writes:

> In all speech the words must come. If they don't come, we cannot make them. We have to wait. Also, if the wrong ones come, we can only say "just a minute"—and wait, then try again. We recognize this kind of coming: it is characteristic of all bodily comings. It is how sleep comes, and tears, the

> appetites, and orgasm. Emotions must also come to you—you can't produce one at will. So also, the muse cannot be forced or invented. She must come. We *can* make ourselves receptive, but we don't control her coming. (p. 105)

Suppressing Vision Can Enhance Other Bodily Dimensions

When we follow Sheridan and write while unable to see the words, it heightens our awareness of how other parts of the body can play a role in writing. (Think about columnist Don Marquis's [1927] invention of Archy the cockroach, who wrote such wonderful columns for the *New York Sun* by hurling himself head first onto the keys of the abandoned typewriter in the newsroom.) Almost everything I've written about writing calls attention to the role of the body in writing.

It's amazing the number of ways humans now can write. Most obviously, now that we have dictation software, we can think ourselves back to early Greece when rhetoricians sometimes recited their text and used slaves to transcribe ("Take a letter, Miss McGillicuddy"). It seems as though our contemporary culture of literacy has sought to suppress the record of how much important writing even in the modern period was produced by dictation. Henry James used an amanuensis and dictated a huge proportion of his work. Interestingly, as he made more use of dictation over the course of his career, his prose got more intricately tangled. Richard Feynman's famous lectures on physics were the product of dictation through a writing block. His friends and colleagues had to tape his lectures and sometimes lock him in a room and not let him out until he produced. When I was exploring voice in writing (see Elbow, *Landmark Essays on Voice and Writing*, 1995), I came to learn how many "writers" weren't primarily writers. They were *dictators* of much of their important work. Mark Twain famously praised writing by dictation:

> You will never know how much enjoyment you have lost until you get to dictating your autobiography; then you will realize, with a pang, that you might have been doing it all your life if you had only had the knack to think of it. And you will be astonished (& charmed) to see how like talk it is, and how real

> it sounds, how well & compactly & sequentially it constructs itself, & what dewy & breezy & woodsy freshness it has, & what a darling & worshipful absence of the signs of starch, and flatiron, & labor & fuss & the other artificialities! Mrs. Clemens is an exacting critic, but I have not talked a sentence yet that she has wanted altered. There are little slips here & there, little inexactnesses, & many desertions of a thought before the end of it has been reached, but these are not blemishes, they are merits, and their removal would take away the naturalness of the flow & banish the very thing—the nameless something—which differentiates real narrative from artificial narrative & makes the one so vastly better than the other—the subtle something which makes good talk so much better than the best imitations of it that can be done with a pen. (Clemens, pp. 370–371)

I explore dictation and the music of speech more in my *Vernacular Eloquence*. When I first went to high school and even college, not everyone had a typewriter, but teachers appreciated typed papers. Hallmates used to borrow my typewriter. At one point, I resorted to blank caps for the keys since I could touch-type, but not many others could.

What strikes me now is the difference between writing by hand and typing. Most poets I know write by hand, at least for the early stages of composition. Typing destroys the sensory connection between a word with its letters and our mouth—that connection that is so crucial in the case of poetry and spoken language. "Voice in writing" may be a powerful metaphor, but it doesn't match the *actual physical* relationship we have to words when we actually speak them.

Suppression as Whac-A-Mole in Realms Other Than Writing

The Whac-A-Mole process is most obvious in the vegetable realm when pruning leads to new growth and energy. But it applies widely.

Suppressing Writing Enhances Spoken Dialogue. Plato (274c), channeling Socrates, argued *against* the ChatGPT of his era: writing. Presciently, he claimed that writing would be devastating for human memory; people in oral cultures have astoundingly strong memories. Most of all, he insisted that it was unnatural to send words out into the world as orphans (his term): that is, words unattached to the mouth of a live speaker—and not just a live speaker but a speaker *in dialogue* with another live speaker.

In dialogue, the speaker can be held responsible for the meaning of his words. Plato felt that language was not really language unless it was in dialogue. If this sounds extreme, remember that when Aristotle, even later and further from magical thinking, defined humans as "social animals," he meant that a solitary human was not actually a human. Plato warned correctly that written words—because they are orphans and have no parent present—would always be prone to misinterpretation.

Suppressing Voice Enhances Silence. Because of my extensive work on voice in writing, I was invited to co-lead a weekend gathering on "Writing and Voice" at Pendle Hill, a Quaker retreat center not far from Philadelphia. In his invitation to me, the director said, "You lead the voice part, and I'll lead the silence part." During the weekend, we did a lot of writing and a lot of sitting in silence. We all noticed that everyone's writing took on more resonance and voice *after* a period of silence. George Steiner's *Language and Silence* (1967) is remarkably insightful for a more detailed examination.

Suppressing Images Enhances the Beauty of Written Script. This is exactly what happened in early Muslim culture. Images were forbidden (see also the prohibition against "graven images" in the Ten Commandments), and this led to extraordinary beauty in the Arabic script itself.

Suppressing the Body and Other Physical Qualities Enhances Mental, Creative, and Moral Qualities. Since pre-classical Greece, there's been the prominent myth of the blind poet and the blind seer. Because she can't see outwardly, the seer can peer inwardly more deeply or into the future. Beethoven, as he grew older, sicker, and more deaf, displayed an extraordinary flowering of creativity and depth in his famous late works. His deepest and most mystical works came after he was completely deaf. We see the same deepening in Shakespeare and his mystical late plays. Edward Said (2006) devoted a book, *On Late Style*, to the remarkable enhancement of depth that often appears in artists as they age and lose physical power.

Consider Franklin Delano Roosevelt. As he became more crippled and more ill, he powerfully led the country through the frightening years of World War II. (We're liable to forget that the outcome was far from certain.) He had to take more risks and find more courage. Helen Keller, blind, deaf, and highly impaired in speech, wrested courage and insight from her condition of almost total isolation from the world.

Invisible Writing by Students

I remember hearing about a teacher who said to his student about his paper: "You know, I'm obviously the first person who's ever seen these words. It's clear that you wrote them, but just as clear that you've never really looked at them. You'd never have turned them in if you had."

I noticed a major effect on my students' writing when I started using publication as an important part of my teaching. I required every student to make enough copies of their papers for every student in the class. I counted this as an official cost for the course. They brought the copies to my desk on the due day, and I brought a big stapler so I could make the class anthology. Of course, this happens more easily now online, but it was a more powerful an instructive ritual when it involved a thick stack of papers and a stapler on my desk. In that earlier situation, a class publication had more *éclat*.

At first, I only did it at the end of the semester. The goal was celebration and sharing. Later, I did it for every major paper. Of course, plenty of students didn't read them all—or at least not after the first time in the semester. But what I came to value was the way this practice made them *feel public*. Sometimes my next assignment was to figure out something interesting that they noticed in their classmates' essays or stories. This made a good occasion for working on quotation and footnoting.

The first time I did this, I noticed that some students got mad; they even felt kind of betrayed. They didn't expect their pals, real persons, to see their writing. They expected only the teacher to see their writing. This brought out an odd underground assumption lurking in the back of many students' minds: "This is not *real* writing and the teacher is not a *real* person. This is just a school assignment. I don't want my real friends to see work that I'm not proud of."

In James Baldwin's autobiography (1985), he describes working in a brothel where the white prostitutes didn't bother to cover their nudity in front of him. As a Black man, he realized that he didn't count as an actual man to them. I gradually realized that many students didn't mind handing me a piece of writing that they didn't respect. It's only a piece of junk that I have to hand in to the stupid teacher. Publication made their writing more real by the logic that school writing is not real writing.

As I used this technique, I learned that I couldn't put out the class magazine at the beginning of the class period. Once they picked up the magazine, they were lost for the next thirty minutes or more. But when they picked up the magazines, what do you think they did? You guessed it. They turned to *their own paper.* It may have been nothing but an exact photocopy of what they had just turned in, but now they were seeing it *through the eyes* of their classmates. It looked different now.

Interestingly, this practice had a big effect on copyediting. I had found it a hopeless battle to get them to care about proofreading. Nowadays, computers clean up a lot—and students often think that's enough, when of course it is not. But when the students read through the eyes of their classmates, they see mistakes they actually didn't see before.

Writing was extremely invisible during my two years as a student at Oxford. My tutor never saw an essay I produced. Every week I *read* it to him, but he never saw it. (And he never had to take home essays to comment on.) The only visible writing I did at Oxford, and it was the only writing that carried any important stakes, was on nine three-hour exams over four-and-a-half days at the end of two years. And because they were exams, you weren't much penalized for grammar and spelling mistakes and poor prose as long as the content and thinking were sound (though of course better writing makes an argument more convincing).

It wasn't until late in my teaching career that I finally began to use invisible writing this way—and it was a way that Don Murray (1998) had always talked about. He made all his students read their papers aloud to him. This odd use of invisible writing (odd at least in the American context) made a big impact on my teaching for my last few years when I finally used this practice. I didn't have time to listen to every draft or final draft. I used it for half the class and reverted to the normal system for the other half—switching halves on the next paper. This system took a lot more of my time, but I made up the time by not taking those essays home to read and comment on.

As Murray emphasized, the main thing about this system is how the very act of reading aloud—especially in the presence of the teacher—gives students *literal audible feedback*. They *hear* problems that they don't see. When I said that students had never seen the papers they turned in, it was kind of a metaphor. But it is literally true that most had never *heard* their own writing. Often, they were surprised and floored by what they heard: "Oh that's awful, I've got to change that sentence." Or "Uh oh, that idea contradicts the idea earlier in the paper." For it's not just words that are more vivid when read aloud, it's thoughts, too: one more virtue of invisible writing or words read aloud.

Concluding Meta Observation

Methodologically, Sheridan serves as a bridge between the subjectivity characteristic of Britton and me and the objectivity characteristic of Flower and Hayes. In a larger sense, when invisible writing forces our attention inward to meaning and felt sense, it plays a trick on our attention. It forces us to *be more aware* of *where our attention is going*. In that way, it helps us learn to *control* our attention. It's not quite Zen, but it's a step in that direction. By the same token, by forcing us inward with nothing to look at as we write, it also takes us a step closer to the mystery of creation itself—creation at the heart of writing, creation *ex nihilo*.

Sheridan's experiments with invisible writing were also experiments with empiricism. Experimenting over and over, he tried consciously to control the variables. He brings some genuine methodological validity to insights from the process movement and also to the single dimension of writing that is most mysterious yet most important: invention.

My wife makes fun of me for spending so much time celebrating freewriting. "Face it, Peter, you spend 99 percent of your time revising. Why don't you talk more about that?" But I don't have much of a contribution to make about revising (though now I'll make some claims for the chapters about it in *Vernacular Eloquence*). Invisible writing, like freewriting, doesn't get whole essays written. Neither yields more than relatively short pieces. But like freewriting, invisible writing can get us going at the start of things and can extricate us from mud holes that threaten to swamp a substantial project.

Works Cited

Baldwin, J. (1985). *Go tell it on the mountain.* Dell.

Britton, J. (1970). *Language and learning.* University of Miami Press.

Chafe, W. (1988). Linking intonation units in spoken English. In J. Haiman & S. A. Thompson (Eds.), *Clause combining in grammar and discourse* (pp. 1–28). John Benjamins.

Clemens, S. L. (1967). *Selected Mark Twain-Howells letters: 1872–1910* (F. Anderson, W. Gibson, & H. Smith, Eds.). Belknap Press.

Elbow, P. (1976). *Writing without teachers.* Oxford University Press.

Elbow, P. (Ed.). (1995). *Landmark essays on voice and writing.* Routledge.

Feynman, R., Leighton, R., & Sands, M. (1964). *The Feynman lectures on physics.* Addison-Wesley.

Gendlin, E. (1962). *Experiencing and the creation of meaning.* Free Press of Glencoe.

Gendlin, E. (1978). *Focusing.* Everest House.

Gendlin, E. (1991). Thinking beyond patterns: Body, language, and situations. In B. Ouden & M. Moen (Eds.). *The presence of feeling in thought* (pp. 21–151). Peter Lang.

Lakoff, G., & Johnson, M. (1980). *Metaphors we live by.* University of Chicago Press.

Marquis, Don. (1927). *Archy and Mehitabel.* Doubleday.

Murray, D. M. (2014). The maker's eye: Revising your own manuscripts. *Writing about Writing: A College Reader*, 610-14.

Perl, S. (2004). *Felt sense: Writing with the body.* Heinemann.

Plato. (1995). *Phaedrus* (A. Nehamas & P. Woodruff, Trans.). Hackett Publishing Company. (Original work published ca. 375–365 BCE)

Said, E. (2006). *On late style: Music and literature against the grain.* Pantheon Books.

Steiner, G. (1967). *Language and silence: Essays on language, literature and the inhuman.* Atheneum.

Chapter Two

What Is the So What *of Literacy Instruction? Lessons Learned from Sheridan Blau*

Carol Booth Olson

Sheridan Blau has been a longtime friend of the UC Irvine Writing Project (UCIWP) and a frequent guest speaker at our Invitational Summer Institute from the inception of his Writing Project site in 1979 up to the onset of the pandemic in 2020. His presentations never ceased to be one of the highlights of our summer institute as he exposed us to his deep thinking about the theory and practice of teaching literature and experimented with the workshops that would become the centerpiece of his award-winning book *The Literature Workshop: Teaching Texts and Their Readers* (Blau, 2003). However, his most profound influence on our site was as a mentor and respondent to a smaller group of WP fellows participating in an advanced institute beginning in 1982 that continues to this day. As we worked to develop a theoretical foundation for our Thinking/Writing Project, which later became the Pathway to Academic Success Project, Sheridan was crafting his own conceptual frame for the process of meaning construction, which he called Humane Literacy and subsequently renamed Disciplined Literacy. As he explored the question, "What is the *so what* of literacy instruction?" he taught us a number of valuable lessons that gave us food for thought, inspired us to interrogate our own assumptions, led us to the work of other scholars, and helped us to conceptualize and frame our own work as a Writing Project site.

In this chapter, I will explore some of the key principles, core beliefs, and lessons learned from Sheridan. These include:

- The goal of instruction is to cultivate and nurture humane literacy in our students, including textual, cultural, and personal literacy.
- Readers and writers engage in similar processes of meaning construction involving the drafting and redrafting of ideas.
- The teaching of literature should not be about transmission but transaction; the locus of authority should be shifted from the teacher to the student.
- The process of meaning construction takes place within a rich social and cultural context of a community of learners.
- Learning is both affective and cognitive; revising meaning involves commitment and detachment.
- Students should engage in metacognitive processing, treating their own products and processes as objects of inquiry.
- Teachers themselves must be models of humane literacy, willing to take risks, evolve, make mistakes, learn, and grow.

Although we have embraced these principles and integrated them into our own practice and research on the efficacy of those practices, there are notable differences in how we have enacted them and some key areas in which we disagree. The ways in which we diverge, theoretically and pedagogically, will also be discussed.

The goal of instruction is to cultivate and nurture humane literacy in our students, including textual, cultural, and personal literacy.

During the summer of 1982, thirty teacher/consultants who had been previously trained in the UCIWP Summer Institute returned to the campus for what would turn out to be the first of an ongoing series of Second Time Around Institutes. United by a common concern about the rather limited depth and range of critical thinking we were seeing in the writing of our students across grade levels, districts, and educational segments, we set out to explore ways to provide students with much-needed practice in thinking and writing—practice that would enable them to tap a fuller range of their cognitive potential. With a lot of hard work, some healthy disagreement, and a certain amount of serendipity, we managed to forge a vision in that first summer of an instructional model designed to foster critical thinking through writing that combined basic principles of learning theory, composing process research, and the practical strategies of the National Writing Project. Further, we developed a core of demonstration lessons designed to motivate teachers to think critically about critical thinking and to recognize the potential of using writing as a tool for promoting cognitive growth.

To help us develop a theoretical frame for our project and to serve as a "critical friend," Sheridan participated in our design process over multiple summers. The first phase of our endeavor generated what Sheridan would call "creative chaos." Ideas were voiced, pondered, debated, tabled, and reintroduced as we struggled to establish, define, and refine what we knew. We soon became aware of our differing learning styles. Some people had to hear an idea over and over again in order to grasp it, while others had to verbalize their thoughts, using the group as a sounding board. During these lofty and often recursive discussions, our more visual learners pleaded with us to translate abstract concepts into diagrams on the board; strips of colored butcher paper with lists, charts, and favorite quotations began to adorn the walls of our room. Meanwhile, those of us who explore what we think by writing it down were furiously scribbling in our notebooks. These understandings about ourselves as learners later translated into strategies to use with our students. As he watched us engage in this process, the seeds of ideas for Sheridan's own philosophy of teaching and learning continued to germinate. In the foreword to the book that resulted from our project, *Thinking/Writing: Fostering Critical Thinking Through Writing* (Olson, 1992), Sheridan wrote:

> As I revisited these teachers over the years, watching the continuing growth of their expertise and of their manuscript, my admiration and affection for them also continued to grow, as did my sense of wonder at their continuing commitment to each other and to their collaborative project. I was particularly struck by the remarkable synergy that their collaboration seemed to produce. As a group they energized and continually drew out the best from all their members and from anybody else who came into their circle. In the middle of one of my own presentations to these teachers, I found myself articulating ideas

> that constituted a real advance for me in my own thinking about the teaching of literature. I hastily made some notes on a scrap of cardboard, outlining my new thinking. These notes became crucial to me in much of the research, writing, and instructional development work I have been engaged in over the past several years. (p. XIV)

What Sheridan presented to us was a concept he initially called Humane Literacy. He posited that the goal of instruction is to cultivate humane literacy in students by fostering three domains of knowing: textual literacy (knowing how), cultural literacy (knowing about), and personal literacy (knowing how to know about). Drawing on the work of Robert Scholes (1985), Sheridan defined textual literacy as "*procedural knowledge* and experience in the kind of evidentiary reasoning that accounts for a reader's knowing how to construe the plain sense of a text, apprehend its evoked meaning, and evaluate or challenge its significance" (Blau, 2003, p. 204). Figure 2.1 illustrates how Sheridan translated Scholes's literary theory into practice in a professional development handout, making it more accessible to teachers:

Textual Activity	Problem	Kinds of Thinking/Writing	
		Bloom	Moffett
a. Reading (facts; text in the text)	What does it say? How do I feel about it? What is my experience of it?	Knowledge	Recording Reporting
b. Interpretation/Analysis (inferences; text on the text)	What does it mean? How does it mean?	Inference Analysis	Generalizing Explaining
c. Criticism (applications; text against the text)	What does it matter? What's its value? So what?	Evaluation Synthesis	Arguing Theorizing Speculating

FIGURE **2.1.** *Humane Literacy*

While textual literacy involves the procedural knowledge or knowing how, cultural literacy concerns informational knowledge or knowing about. This entails a range of prior knowledge of literary genres, social practices, history, religion, and specialized cultural knowledge that enables readers to immerse themselves "as deeply as possible into the lifeworld of the cultures they study"

(Blau, 2003, p. 208), etc. While Sheridan drew this term from E. D. Hirsch (1987), he later changed the term cultural literacy to intertextual literacy to avoid the controversies associated with Hirsch's work.

Personal literacy is enabling or performative knowledge, a dimension of literary competence that empowers students to become "autonomous, engaged readers of difficult literary texts at any level of education" (Blau, 2003, p. 10). These are habits of mind or cognitive processes that characterize more experienced, expert readers. Seven traits or dispositions are associated with personal or performative literacy:

1. Capacity for sustained focused attention.
2. Willingness to suspend closure: to entertain problems rather than avoid them.
3. Willingness to take risks: to predict and be wrong, to respond honestly, to offer variant readings.
4. Tolerance for failure: willingness to reread and reread again.
5. Tolerance for ambiguity, paradox, and uncertainty.
6. Intellectual generosity and ego-permeability: willingness to change one's mind, to appreciate alternative visions, and to engage in methodological believing as well as doubting.
7. Metacognitive awareness.

To my knowledge, most of the traits Sheridan identifies as comprising personal or performative literacy are not derived from other sources. They represent Sheridan's unique contribution to the field.

In the ensuing years, Sheridan changed the term *humane literacy*, which encompassed the entire humanistic view of the dimensions of literacy, to *disciplined literacy*. He did so in order to move beyond what was meant by the acclaimed literary critic George Steiner (1963), from whom he borrowed the term. Steiner referred to humane literacy as a tradition of literary knowledge among European intellectuals. Sheridan's concept of disciplined literacy was to advocate for and identify "a set of practices in reading that defined a discipline or way of operating that wasn't merely individual or the product of a critical theory but a genuine mental discipline among all highly literate readers" (Personal communication, August 17, 2022).

Sheridan's concept of humane literacy had a profound impact on the thinking of our Writing Project group. The traits he saw as integral to becoming an engaged, experienced reader seemed to us to be just as crucial to becoming an accomplished writer. In our own work, to reinforce textual literacy, we designed lesson scaffolds to help students move from reading to interpretation to criticism or from knowledge telling to knowledge transformation (Bereiter & Scardamalia, 1987). To cultivate cultural literacy, we selected texts that would serve as a mirror in which students from diverse backgrounds could see their cultures reflected or windows to enable them to align themselves with other cultures. These included "The War of the Wall" by Toni Cade Bambara, "Coming into Language" by Jimmy Baca, "The Medicine Bag" by Virginia Driving Hawk Sneve, and "Ribbons" by Laurence Yep. To foster personal literacy and promote agency, we engaged students in analyzing their own growth as learners and then writing metacognitive reflections about their progress. While we had been relying primarily on our knowledge of the work of writing researchers and scholars like Flower and Hayes (1981a), Bereiter and Scardamalia (1987), Applebee (1981), and others to develop our theoretical frame, Sheridan inspired us to turn not just to literary theory but to reading research to enhance our knowledge and expertise. One of our first discoveries was the work of Paris, Lipson, and Wixon (1983), whose description of declarative, procedural, and conditional knowledge (a concept that dovetails nicely with Sheridan's dimensions of literacy) introduced us to the power of cognitive strategy instruction.

Readers and writers engage in similar processes of meaning construction involving the drafting and redrafting of ideas.

Sheridan pointed out to us that "reading like writing is a process of meaning or text construction that is frequently accompanied by false starts and faulty visions, requiring frequent and messy reconstruction of revision" (Blau, 2003, p. 31). In other words, both readers and writers engage in the drafting and redrafting of ideas. This is the central point Tierney and Pearson make in their landmark article "Toward a Composing Process of Reading" (1983). They identify reading and writing as "essentially similar processes of meaning construction" (p. 568) involving the use of cognitive strategies as readers and writers engage in planning, drafting, aligning, revising, and monitoring in a continuous, recurring, and recursive fashion. Sheridan argues that reading and writing "aren't simply reciprocal processes but are virtually the same process" (Blau, 2017, p. 284). However, many scholars disagree with him. For example, Langer (1986) noticed that while students access the same cognitive strategies when they make meaning from or with texts, the degree to which they access certain strategies while composing differs. In investigating the patterns of cognitive behaviors of third, sixth, and ninth graders undertaking parallel reading and writing tasks, readers paid the most attention to formulating meaning, seeking validation for interpretations, citing evidence, and revising meaning. Perhaps this focus on meaning is necessitated by the fact that readers are co-constructing meaning from the text. That is, they must build their envisionment around a tangible text produced by an author. Writers face a different constraint. They must "fit what they know to the needs of another person, a reader, and to the constraints of formal prose" (Flower & Hayes, 1981b, p. 42). Because writers are simultaneously developing, translating, and shaping their envisionment for a reader rather than negotiating with the existing text of an author, Langer found more concern with goal setting on the part of writers. Further, although writers spend a substantial amount of time generating ideas and formulating meaning, they do so more recursively. This need to stop, reread bits of text, and monitor their own progress in order to move forward slows down the process. Perhaps because writing is so time consuming and the writer must attend not only to *what* to say but also *how* to say it, Langer found more concern with process on the part of writers—and more evidence that students had a better grasp of the strategies they used to get at meaning when they wrote as compared with when they read. To sum up, writing tasks called for significantly more attention to global concerns than did reading.

It is precisely because reading and writing access similar cognitive strategies but in differing degrees that reading and writing make such a powerful combination when taught in connection with each other. Using writing as a learning tool in reading instruction leads to better achievement, and using reading as a resource for elaborating on ideas or for understanding opposing views leads to better writing performance (Tierney & Shanahan, 1991). More importantly, reading and writing taught together engage students in a greater use and variety of cognitive strategies than do reading and writing taught separately (p. 272). This exposure to and practice in an array of cognitive strategies promotes and enhances critical thinking. This is why Recommendation 2 of the IES Practice Guide *Teaching Secondary Students to Write Effectively* (2016) is to integrate reading and writing instruction, to explicitly identify the connections between reading and writing, and to teach students to use cognitive strategies to "improve students' writing and encourage strategic thinking" (Graham et al., p. 7).

Early on, our Thinking/Writing group became intrigued with the reading/writing connection and explored the ways in which readers and writers select and implement appropriate strategies and monitor and regulate their use in order to construct and refine meaning. Borrowing an analogy from Flower and Hayes (1981a), who liken the use of strategies within the writing process to having "a writer's tool kit" (p. 376) that the writer can access, unconstrained by any fixed order, to solve the problem of constructing a text, we developed our own reader's and writer's tool kit of cognitive strategies that underlie the reading and writing process to make visible to teachers and students the acts of mind that are fundamental to the construction of meaning (Olson, 2003).

The teaching of literature should not be transmission but transaction; the locus of authority should be shifted from the teacher to the student.

Part of what prompted Sheridan's focus on the development of humane literacy in students was his own "pedagogical awakening" (Blau, 2003, p. 2) that in his early teaching career, he was working exceptionally hard to interpret the text *for* the students instead of enabling them to carry out the intellectual work necessary to arrive at thoughtful interpretations on their own. As Robert Scholes (1985) reminds us, "There is a bright little student inside most teachers who wants to set the class straight because he or she knows the 'right answer.' Still, the point of teaching interpretation is not to usurp the interpreter's role but to explain the rules of the interpretative game" (p. 30). Sheridan's epiphany was that he needed to find ways to switch roles with his students and provide opportunities for them to engage in transactions with texts (Rosenblatt, 1978) that honor "the individual responses of students over the authoritative readings that teachers once thought necessary to communicate to students as valid literary knowledge" (Blau, p. 4).

One of his workshops that influenced our Thinking/Writing group, and countless UCIWP fellows in our summer institute over the years, was the commentary project. Taking an inductive approach to instruction, Sheridan presented teachers with a high-interest text and asked them to write a page or so of commentary about it. He was often quite cagey about *not* providing much explanation about what a commentary should consist of, preferring to answer yes or no questions, and usually responding with "We'll see." Teachers in the summer institute then shared their commentaries in small groups and made lists of what they noticed about each other's commentaries, which included cognitive tasks such as asking questions, forming interpretations, presenting a thesis, resisting the text, or writing from a character's perspective. These discussions surfaced most of the acts of mind that experienced readers and writers engage in as they construct meaning without the need for explicit instruction. The commentaries on which the discussions were based could be used as prewriting for more formal analytical essays. While, in our project, we still see value in explicit instruction (see our later section, "Two Roads Diverge"), we nevertheless embrace the widely held notion, demonstrated by Sheridan's workshop, of being the guide on the side rather than the sage on the stage in order to enhance students competence and confidence as independent learners.

The process of meaning construction takes place within a rich social and contextual context of a community of learners.

The idea that writing is socially situated, that writers write to participate in social contexts, that writing takes place in the light of former texts, and that writers gain voice and identities through participation in a community is a widely held tenet of sociocultural theory. In his Writers-within-Community model, Graham (2018) has emphasized that writing development is the consequence of participation in writing communities as well as individual changes in writers' capabilities and that a writing community includes the "social, cultural, political, institutional, and historical influences that shape it" (p. 2). While the concept is not new, Sheridan's contribution to this area of study is his discussion of how participation in a National Writing Project Summer Institute, where teachers write and share on a daily basis, transforms teachers' professional lives. Dick Dodge, former director of the UCLA Writing Project, liked to say (partially in jest) that the Writing Project was one-third seminar, one-third group therapy, and one-third religious experience. He was getting at the spirit of community that is engendered when people share themselves through their writing. Sheridan put it another way:

> Teachers seem able to conceive of their classrooms as authentic learning communities only because they themselves have learned through their continuing involvement in Writing Project activities how to participate productively. . . . Writing in such learning communities—whether in Writing Projects or actual classrooms—is both actually and metaphorically the most indispensable activity. That is because for most learners writing is actually (literally) the most powerful available instrument for making meaning and constructing knowledge for oneself in the context of a community of readers. (Blau, 1993, pp. 17–19)

In our own Writing Project site, we have an ongoing monthly school-year study group called Writing Project 2 that has been continuous for over twenty years. The fifty or so teachers who participate each year range in age from 25 to 75 and from two years of teaching to thirty plus years, including retirees with even longer teaching histories and a desire to stay connected. The flame that ignites and forges that community begins with writing and sharing. Our project has welcomed Sheridan into our community, and we consider him to be an honorary member.

Learning is both affective and cognitive; revising meaning involves commitment and detachment.

Based on his presentations at our Thinking/Writing Project, Sheridan contributed an article to our UCIWP publication *Practical Ideas for Teaching Writing at the High School and College Levels* (Olson, 1997) entitled "Competence for Performance in Revision." In this article, Sheridan posited that there are two dimensions of competence in revision—the affective dimension, which involves commitment, and the cognitive dimension, which involves detachment. The first quality of mind that accounts for a writer's competence in revision is *commitment,* which, in turn, "requires two underlying acts of will—one finding value in the completion of the writing task and the other consisting of faith (despite feelings to the contrary) in one's capacity to meet the challenge of the writing task" (p. 156). The second enabling or prerequisite skill is *detachment.* Sheridan explains, "This entails distancing ourselves from our own writing in order to take the perspective of a reader. Such a perspective is especially necessary as writers move from retrospective structuring to projective—from getting their ideas straight for themselves to getting them straight for a reader, or in moving from writer-based to reader-based revising" (pp. 156–157).

Sheridan's thinking about the dimensions of revision had a significant impact on our group. We had been focusing on Bloom's Taxonomy of the Cognitive Domain (1956) in our thinking/writing framework. His discussion of the connection between affect and cognition led us to discover that, working with colleagues, Bloom had created a *Taxonomy of Educational Objectives: Affective Domain* (Krathwohl et al., 1964), of which we were unaware. These researchers liken the interdependence of the affective and cognitive domains to a man scaling a wall via two intertwining stepladders:

> The ladders are so constructed that the rungs of one ladder fall between the rungs of the other. The attainment of some complex goal is made possible by alternately climbing a rung on one ladder, which brings the rung of the next ladder within reach. Thus, alternating between the affective and the cognitive

> domains, one may use the attainment of a cognitive goal to raise interest (an affective goal). This permits the achievement of a higher cognitive goal, and so on. (p. 60)

Based on this idea that students not only need the skill but the will to invest themselves in learning to succeed as readers and writers, we began to design learning activities to cultivate socio-emotional literacy in students. In other words, we looked for ways to deepen their engagement, attract and hold their attention, foster their intention, and develop their stamina to follow through with challenging reading and writing tasks.

Students should engage in metacognitive processing, treating their own products and processes as objects of inquiry.

Sheridan believes that engaging students in metacognitive processing is an important step in shifting the locus of authority from the teacher to the student, positioning the student "in a pedagogical relationship that entails a shared or distributed expertise" (Blau, 2003, p.13). In the early years, he suggested that students keep writing process logs in which they record and reflect upon their composing processes. In later years, he created a more formal approach to prompt students to think about their own thinking through the Reading Process Research Report. In this assignment, students study themselves as readers of a difficult text by reporting on their own mental processes as they construct meaning, share these reflections with classmates, and are given an opportunity to revise or supplement them prior to final submission. Sheridan observes, "No characteristic seems to me to better differentiate the strongest readers from the weakest among students in late adolescence than this capacity for metacognition, for paying attention to the state of one's understanding while reading so one can catch problems and solve them as they arrive, and for being able to describe the state of one's understanding . . ." (p. 57).

According to Paris, Lipson, and Wixon (1983), "Thinking about one's thinking is the core of strategic behavior" (p. 295). However, in order to move from declarative to procedural to conditional knowledge, students must be able to monitor and regulate their own cognitive efforts, including goal setting, planning, evaluating their progress, remediating difficulties, and revising strategies for learning. While Sheridan primarily has students write about their meaning construction as readers, we have not only involved students in writing about their reading using cognitive strategies bookmarks as a point of departure but in metacognitively reflecting upon their writing and revising. To facilitate this process, we developed a two-part revision planner that engages students in assessing an initial draft, identifying strengths and areas for improvement, and setting goals for revision before revising (Part 1) and then in writing a reflection about what changes they made in their revised draft and why, what they are most proud of, and whether they felt they met the goals they set for themselves (Part 2). In a study we conducted, students who participated in this metacognitive process had higher writing outcomes than students in a comparison condition on a post-test writing assessment ($r = .57$; $p < .001$) and demonstrated improved self-efficacy in the writing subdomain of revision ($p < .05$) (Chung et al., 2021).

Teachers themselves must be models of humane literacy, willing to take risks, evolve, make mistakes, and grow.

Finally, by modeling humane literacy himself, Sheridan taught us this very important principle that we, as teachers, must make ourselves vulnerable and practice what we preach. When he presented his workshops at our summer institute, we loved to watch the wheels turn in his mind, as, shaping at the point of utterance—to use Britton's term (1978), he would take a risk and offer some insight that had just then occurred to him. Often, these insights were brilliant. But if one of our fellows advanced an opposing view, he would thoughtfully consider it and sometimes change his mind right on the spot. He often made a point of challenging us with difficult texts that he himself was encountering for the first time so that we could navigate them together. Drawing from Rosenblatt (1978), he made reading an experience in which we could participate affectively as well as cognitively, exhibited respect for multiple interpretations of a text for each of the Writing Project fellows sharing those interpretations, and emphasized his belief in the capacity of all students to become confident and competent contributors in a community of learners where the teacher serves as the senior member who encourages and enables students to engage in intellectual work on their own. We always left these sessions feeling energized and inspired, eager to apply his principles in our own classrooms.

Two Roads Diverge

While Sheridan has been a role model for our Thinking/Writing group, and we have learned many invaluable lessons from him about the *So What?* of literacy instruction, we have diverged from him in our enactment of some of his key principles and respectfully disagree with some of his stances—in particular, on the role of strategy instruction, whether or not to engage in explicit strategy instruction, and the value of teaching students the "traditional" literary analysis essay. These differences in perspective may be influenced, in part, by the teachers and students we have served. Sheridan brought to the South Coast Writing Project (SCWriP) his experience as a professor specializing in teaching Milton to undergraduates at UC Santa Barbara and advising doctoral students in the Gevirtz Graduate School of Education. At Teachers College, he continued to work with MAT and doctoral candidates. This is not to say that he was not involved with K–12 teachers through SCWriP, but the demographics of Santa Barbara County are not as diverse as some areas in greater Los Angeles and Orange County. As our Thinking/Writing Project evolved into the Pathway to Academic Success Project in the 1990s, we specifically focused our research and practice on how to help teachers in low SES schools with culturally diverse populations and high percentages of English learners (ELs) to empower their students to become stronger academic writers.

Researchers have noted a "growing inequality" in classroom instruction, in which students designated as "honors students" are exposed to rigorous academic work designed to promote higher literacy, whereas lower achievers, children of the poor, and second-language learners often receive instruction that places a premium on the "transmission of information, providing very little room for the exploration of ideas, which is necessary for the development of deeper understanding" (Applebee et al., 2003, p. 689). Our goal has been to address this growing inequality by making visible to teachers and their students the thinking tools, or cognitive strategies, that research indicates experienced readers and writers access in order to construct meaning from and with texts to help them become strategic readers and analytical writers. Both theoretically and practically, we have embraced strategy instruction, blended both explicit instruction in reading and writing strategies with more student-centered approaches, and directly taught students how to compose analytical essays. In these approaches, we have taken a different road from Sheridan.

Strategy Instruction

Based upon his published work, Sheridan has only recently articulated his skepticism of the use of strategy instruction in literacy instruction. This may be a response to the way secondary reading programs have taken up cognitive strategies, teaching them one at a time as "discrete skills," something Sheridan sees as a practice that "corrupts much traditional instruction" (Blau, 2023) and/or that strategy instruction is becoming increasingly emphasized in reading programs at the college level. Regardless, Sheridan sees teaching cognitive strategies as "superfluous" to literacy instruction. As a case in point, he critiques the widely taught strategy of visualizing, maintaining that any six-year-old is perfectly capable of visualizing if he or she can perform a chore like responding to a verbal request to find Mom's glasses on the nightstand, for example. Further, he maintains that any child who has been read to regularly would have no difficulty visualizing. However, responding to a verbal request is different from picturing words on the printed page, and not every child has been consistently read to by parents, grandparents, or older siblings. Tierney and Pearson (1983) have identified visualizing as a form of alignment that develops "comprehension maturity" and "is akin to achieving a foothold from which meaning can be negotiated" (p. 573). Jeff Wilhelm (2008) describes an interchange between two middle school boys, Jon and Ron, as they were charged with describing their experience in the "world" of a book. While Jon could offer "absolutely nothing" about what he read or "lived through," Ron was highly articulate about his reading process. Wilhelm writes,

> After Ron shared . . . with his reading partner Jon, Jon said, "I can't believe you do all that stuff when you read! Holy crap, I'm not doing . . . like nothing . . . compared to you!
>
> Ron responded that "I can't believe you don't do something. If you don't you're not reading man . . . It's gotta be like wrestling, or watching a movie or playing a video . . . you've got to . . . like *be* there." (p. 49)

Sheridan might be interested to learn than several community college instructors in the UCIWP have reported that they also have students who feel like they're "doing nothing" and struggle to *be* there as readers, to visualize.

Numerous reports from policy centers and blue-ribbon panels "implicate poor understandings of cognitive strategies as the primary reason why adolescents struggle with reading and writing" (Conley, 2008, p. 84). Further, research conducted over the past 15 years on the content of college courses and instructor expectations indicates that cognitive strategy use is the key to college and career readiness (Conley, 2013). Countless studies demonstrate the efficacy of cognitive strategy use in reading (National Reading Panel, 2000; Tierney & Pearson, 1983; Tierney & Shanahan, 1991). Similarly, Graham and Perin (2007) indicate that strategy instruction is the most effective of 11 key elements of writing instruction ($d = .82$) for all students and particularly for students who find writing challenging.

Increasingly, recent instructional frameworks and recommendations also support approaches that incorporate strategy instruction to advance ELs' development of English (Goldenberg, 2008; Schleppegrell, 2009). Short and Fitzsimmons (2007) hypothesize that strategy instruction is especially effective for ELs because it provides them with an explicit focus on language, increases their exposure to academic texts, makes the texts they read comprehensible, gives them multiple opportunities to affirm and to correct their understanding and use of language, assists them in retrieving new language features and in using these features for academic purposes, and provides them with the means of learning language on their own, outside of class.

Cognitive strategy instruction is the centerpiece of the Pathway to Academic Success Project (the successor to the Thinking/Writing Project). In the IES Practice Grade *Teaching Secondary Students to Write Effectively* (Graham et al., 2016) of the 3,400 research citations yielded from an exhaustive search of effective writing interventions, the 55 studies screened and sent for review, and the 15 studies that met What Works Clearinghouse Standards, eight of the studies focused on strategy instruction, four of which were Pathway studies (Kim et al., 2011; Olson & Land, 2008; Olson et al., 2012; Olson et al., 2016). Effect sizes in these studies favor the treatment group range from $d < .35$ to $d < .67$.

Should Reading and Writing Be Taught Explicitly?

Sheridan's answer to this question would most likely or perhaps even emphatically be "No." Our answer would be "Yes," but as a means to an end—the development of independent readers and writers. Sheridan has long been a proponent of a more inductive approach to teaching, believing that teachers who focus on "correct" interpretations of literature or ways to write do more harm than good "because they do not enable students to learn either how to acquire a valid and accurate experience of a literary text or how to produce such interpretations for themselves" (Blau, 2017, p. 270). He maintains that students are better off being placed in small discussion groups, where they can learn from other students who are perhaps "only a step or two ahead of themselves" (Blau, 2023). Sheridan is not alone in his criticism of explicit literacy instruction, which has long been a matter of debate.

In the area of reading strategies, one school of thought that is consistent with Sheridan's perspective holds that teachers should guide students through a sequence of activities that involve strategy use without intentionally and explicitly teaching what the strategies are or how to use them, assuming that students will become strategic learners over time by acquiring the tools to construct meaning through repeated practice. For example, Fountas and Pinnell (1996) remark,

> Just as strategies cannot be directly observed, neither can they be directly taught. We teach *for* strategies. Experience is a powerful influence on the construction of reading strategies. Anyone who has taught someone to swim knows that merely explaining the process does not work. Even modeling and showing is insufficient. The future swimmer must get in the water. (p.149)

Another perspective involves directly teaching the strategies. In the explicit teaching approach, the teacher does the following:

- Introduces the task to be undertaken (for example, reading a text)
- Makes an explicit statement about "what strategy [needs] to be learned (declarative knowledge), when it would be used in the upcoming selection (conditional knowledge), and the critical attribute one must attend to in order to do the strategy successfully (procedural knowledge)"
- Models the use of the strategy by "thinking out loud" about mental processing
- Provides scaffolded practice with "gradually diminishing amounts of coaching"
- Closes the lesson with explicit statements about the strategy, its use in other settings, and how to implement it. (Wilhelm, 2001, pp. 42–51)

In our Pathway to Academic Success Project, we have adopted the practice of explicitly introducing cognitive strategies, following the National Reading Panel's (2000) recommendation of a multiple strategies approach, in the context of reading high-interest, culturally diverse texts, to showcase that strategies (declarative knowledge) provide practice on *how* to use strategies while reading—from whole groups, small groups, or individual annotation (procedural knowledge), and then engaging students in writing reflections about their cognitive strategy use (*when*, *why*, and for what reasons) during independent reading for book clubs (conditional knowledge). One key component of explicit instruction is the "gradual release of responsibility" (Pearson & Gallagher, 1983) in which the teacher gradually gives the students more and more responsibility to perform tasks independently, apply them in new situations, and eventually internalize skills and/or strategies. Our experience has been that approaching the teaching of cognitive strategies to students in this manner gives them a language with which to talk about constructing meaning and contributes to their sense of agency.

In the area of writing, we have explicitly taught writing strategies and skills. Recommendation #1 of the IES Practice Guide *Teaching Secondary Students to Write Effectively* (Graham et al., 2016) is to explicitly teach writing strategies for planning, goal setting, drafting, evaluating, and revising and to monitor students' progress while teaching strategies and skills. We believe that all students can benefit from some explicit instruction but, given the many demands of academic writing and the few opportunities to practice, ELs, in particular, need access to high-quality curricula, explicit instruction, and ongoing support as they strive to become college and career ready. Current literature based on research and practice calls for contextualized, literacy-rich activities. These activities should be integrated into curricula that focus on developing the higher-level interpretive and analytical aspects of writing. For instance, Walqui and Bunch (2019) argue for the amplification of the curriculum rather than reduction and simplification, and they emphasize the importance of enacting "stimulating, demanding, well-supported lessons to transform what is currently offered to many English learners" (p. 21).

In a fine-grained analysis of the syntactic features of student writing in grades 6 through 12 involving the manual coding, sentence-by-sentence, of 340 Pathway pretest essays, 34 percent of all sentences in the sample were unconventional sentences with boundary issues and other structural problems, making up the most frequent pattern. Unconventional sentences include run-ons and comma splices (16.83 percent), faulty sentences that have semantic and structural problems (10.95 percent), and fragments or incomplete sentences (6.10 percent). While one might assume that the sentence boundary issues were primarily present in the essays of ELs, non-EL students' essays in the sample also contained errors. In fact, no significant differences among L1 groups (English only), Romance languages (Spanish and French), and all other languages (Arabic, Hmong, Somalian, Russian, Tagalog, etc.) were found in the following syntactic components: 1) unconventional sentences, 2) complex and compound sentences, and 3) mean length of clause. These findings suggest that all students in the sample of this study, regardless of their home and first-language backgrounds, had similar performance on clause-level syntactic features, including sentence boundaries and complexity (Maamuujav et al., 2021). Our conclusion is that all students can benefit from some explicit instruction on sentence boundaries through specific mini-lessons, which teachers can choose to deliver based on their assessment of their students' written work. We follow this with sentence variety exercises, explicitly teaching sentence-generation strategies called grammar brushstrokes (Noden, 2006) and then releasing students to practice on a project-created website (www.grammarbrushstrokes.com) where they can write sentences and receive feedback from their peers. In our most recent study of secondary students in the classrooms of 230 teachers affiliated with four California Writing Project sites (Olson et al., 2020), treatment students had higher scores on sentence fluency than students in the control condition *(d < .27)* as measured by the National Writing Project Analytic Writing Continuum for Literary Analysis.

The Value of Teaching Students the "Traditional" Literary Analysis Essay

Sheridan found that even when his university students produce well-organized literary analysis essays with evidence and commentary, they use a "species of discourse" that seems to him to be "pseudoliterate" or "counterliterate" (Blau, 2003, p. 101). He blames this, in part, on how students have been taught to write a model essay in secondary school that seems to him to be a "perverse version of an academic paper" (Blau, 2023). Again, many scholars have pointed out that school genres can be narrow in scope and lead to "formula" writing (Hillocks, 2002; Applebee & Langer, 2009).

Our project has endeavored to teach students the school genre of the literary analysis essay because we believe students must be exposed to form making before they engage intentionally in form breaking; that writing an essay with an introduction, main body, and conclusion is not necessarily formulaic; that the critical thinking that can be elicited from a serious prompt about a high-interest literary or nonfiction text can help move students from knowledge telling to knowledge transformation (Bereiter & Scardamalia, 1987); and that to fail to teach this school genre, particularly to students in low SES schools with high percentages of ELs, does them a disservice, as it denies them access to codes of power (Delpit, 1988).

In our Pathway intervention, we begin by administering a pretest on-demand writing prompt about a literary or nonfiction text to obtain a baseline of what students know and are able to do independently. We typically find that a large percentage of those essays are written as one long paragraph and are composed primarily of retelling. English learners, in particular, who have often been fed a steady diet of narrative reading and short-answer writing, have not been exposed to reading essays and many have not been taught how to write an essay. Being able to write essays in English language arts that "make claims about the worth or meaning of a literary work or works" is an expectation of the Common Core State Standards (National Governors Association Center for Best Practices & Council of Chief State School Officers, 2010, Appendix C, p. 23). The same is true for nonfiction texts. Therefore, we provide teachers with a wide array of strategies to help their students develop competence as academic essay writers. As they use these strategies to revise their pretest into a multiple draft process essay and apply what they have learned to other writing assignments, they become more adept, more confident, and more able to engage in analytical writing on their own.

We focus both on the structure and the content of these essays because, using confirmatory factor analysis, our research indicates that structure and ideas are not separate and independent constructs in writing assessment (Steiss et al., 2022). Rather, criteria used to measure structure and ideas are measuring the same underlying dimension (National Writing Project, 2005, 2010). Practically, text-based analytical writing needs to be well organized with a logical structure for ideas to be communicated effectively. For example, when attending to the quality of an introduction, a scorer thinks about how the introduction organizes key ideas, such as a claim that carries ideas throughout the essay. Figure 2.2 indicates gain scores on the post-tests of 57 ELs (Treatment versus Control) in a stratified random sample of 398 students (EO, IFEP, RFEP, and EL) pulled from extant Pathway data and analytically coded by trained coders for 15 dimensions of writing quality. All essays were written to prompts that asked students to present a theme statement about the author's message in either "Sometimes, the Earth Is Cruel" by journalist Leonard Pitts or "The Man in the Water" by journalist Roger Rosenblatt. Half of the students took one prompt at pretest and post-test and half took the other prompt to control for order effects.

Note the degree to which Treatment ELs outscored their peers in the Control condition on Structure (Organization, Introduction, and Conclusion) and Ideas Evidence, Commentary, and Balance of Summary, Evidence, and Commentary. These types of gains are exemplified by a pretest and post-test interpretive essay written by Marisela, a sixth-grade EL student who had just transitioned out of English language development and was participating in

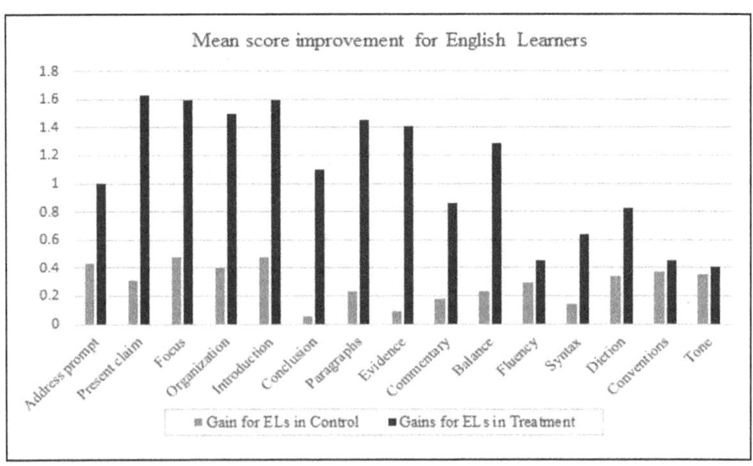

FIGURE 2.2. *Mean Score Improvement for English Learners*

her first mainstreamed ELA classroom in a large urban district where 98 percent of the students are Latinx and 88 percent are designated as ELs.

> In this story there was alot of people that sufferd. People died and sufferd from all the earthquakes. Also, littel boys and girls parents died. People had to reboit their houses when they Gought destroyed. Alot of people sufferd because every year there was an earthquake. It only happened to haiti that why people were tired of it. After the arthquack happened people were very bore. It was very bad alot people died over 100,000 people died this last earthquack. Sometimes when it raind it will not stop for days. Sometimes the earth was cruel, but they had no choice but to exept it. That is how much the sufferd. When people died the dig there selfes they weep and mourn we recover and memoriaize the dead. People also got very sick and neded medisen. People use to pray that begins, "There, but for the grace of good . . . ." People did everything they can. People use to write relief checks, donate blood, volunteer material and time and to fear. That what people did to help people that were very sick. Thats why we should be happy to be safe. This story is a good example. so people can see what will happen if that was us. Also, people can help and doneate stuff like close, shoes, meony, old stuff, to us. I think we should do that to help our people that are very sick. alot of people died of bing hongry because the earth quake distroyed there homes and there food. (Fitzgerald et al., 2014, p. 216)

While Marisela relied primarily on retelling in her essay, her teacher, Maria Goméz-Greenberg, was proud of her for taking the assessment so seriously, for trying her best to respond to the prompt, and for the genuine empathy she demonstrated for the plight of the Haitian people Pitts writes about. However, she did notice that Marisela had little understanding of how to structure a formal essay, and she pondered how to move Marisela beyond a pure summary of the events to actually analyze and comment on the theme of Leonard Pitts's article. These are areas of writing she decided to focus on as she led Marisela and her classmates through a sequence of Pathway activities designed to revise this pretest into a multiple draft essay.

Seven months after Marisela wrote her timed essay on "Sometimes, the Earth Is Cruel" and after revising that pretest into a multiple draft essay and then applying what she learned to other writing assignments, she wrote the following timed post-test essay analyzing "The Man in the Water" by Roger Rosenblatt:

> Are you willing to risk your life to save someone else? "The Man in the Water," by Roger Rosenblatt, is a nonfiction story about a man who died to save strangers. My theme is to try to save as many people as you can. On January 13, 1982, Air Florida Flight 90 crashed into a river. Then, the plane hit seven vehicles, killing four motorists and 74 passengers. Well there is good news 6 passengers got to survive in this airplane crash. Let me tell you readers there was one passenger from the plane that was very brave. He saved 6 people life. They didn't know his name but he had an extravagant mustache. A park police helicopter team lowered a rope, but the man let those 6 people to go before him. "In a mass casualty, you'll find people like him." I can't believe how brave this man was and that he was a stranger to other passengers.
>
> The author uses lots of good language to describe the accident. Like one of them he uses the simile "like famished gulls" describing how the planes swoop in the sky. And the Air Florida plane is like "a flying garden" that is destroyed by the icy water. Rosenblatt feels so proud of our hero because he saved as much people as he could. He gave a lifeline not just to the people but to us. This means that we have hope. The article taught me to always try to save as many people as you can. The message is that if a regular guy can do this for strangers then we could do it to. (Olson et al., 2015, p. 25)

While some issues linger, it is clear that Marisela's writing is much improved. She is well on her way to moving from knowledge telling to knowledge transformation.

Another frequent visitor to our UCI Writing Project Summer Institute was the late George Hillocks. Because of his dismay with the way high-stakes testing was dumbing down writing instruction (Hillocks, 2002), he used to particularly enjoy ranting about the five-paragraph essay. I once gave him a stack of Pathway student essays and asked him to explain what his issues were. After reading a few papers, he remarked that these were *not* five-paragraph themes but perfectly respectable interpretive essays. When asked for clarification, he explained that the essay prompts he objected to were of the "three reasons why students shouldn't have to wear school uniforms" sort that call for a three-part "thesis" followed by a paragraph for each reason and a repetition of the three reasons in the conclusion. We maintain that Marisela's post-test essay demonstrates her impressive progress toward becoming a thoughtful academic writer.

Two Roads, One Destination

Although we have sometimes taken a different road from Sheridan to support and empower students like Marisela, we are, ultimately, heading toward the same destination. When all is said and done, like Sheridan, we want to honor teachers and invite them into a professional learning community, to nurture and challenge each other's thinking and to, in turn, invite their students to participate as collaborators in communities of practice to socially construct meaning. We also want students to develop a sense of agency and to assume responsibility for their own learning as readers and writers. This is what we have thought long and hard about in the Thinking/Writing and Pathway Projects, and that is due in no small part to the lessons we have learned from Sheridan and from the example he set for us. We share his values of enhancing the features of disciplined literacy in students to develop competent, confident, and self-directed readers and writers, and we honor him for teaching us what *really* matters in literacy instruction.

Works Cited

Applebee, A. (1981). *Writing in the secondary school: English and the content areas.* National Council of Teachers of English.

Applebee, A. N., & Langer, J. A. (2009). What is happening in the teaching of writing? *English Journal, 98*(5), 18–28.

Applebee. A., Langer, J., Nystrand, M., & Gamoran, A. (2003). Discussion-based approaches to developing understanding: Classroom instruction and student performance in middle and high school English. *American Educational Research Journal, 40*(3), 685–730. http://dx.doi.org/10.3102/00028312040003685

Bereiter, C., & Scardamalia, M. (1987). *The psychology of written communication.* Lawrence Erlbaum.

Blau, S. (1993). Constructing knowledge in a professional community: The Writing Project as a model for classrooms. *The Quarterly of the National Writing Project, 15*(1), 16–17.

Blau, S. (1997). Competence for performance in revision. In C. B. Olson (Ed.), *Practical ideas for teaching writing as a process* (pp. 239–244). California Department of Education.

Blau, S. (2003). *The literature workshop: Teaching texts and their readers.* Heinemann.

Blau, S. (2017). How the teaching of literature in college writing classes might rescue reading as it never has before. In P. Sullivan, H. Tinberg, & S. Blau (Eds.), *Deep reading: Teaching reading in the writing classroom* (pp. 265–290). National Council of Teachers of English.

Blau, S. (2023). On not teaching college-level reading in order that students might learn it: Honoring our pedagogical legacy in the composition classroom. In P. Sullivan, H. Tinberg, & S. Blau (Eds.), *Deep reading, deep learning* (Vol. 2, pp. 299–314). Peter Lang.

Britton, J. (1978). The composing processes and functions of writing. In C. R. Cooper & L. Odell (Eds.), *Research on composing: Points of departure* (pp. 13–28). National Council of Teachers of English.

Chung, H., Chen, V., & Olson, C. B. (2021). The impact of self-assessment, planning and goal setting, and reflection before and after revision on student self-efficacy and writing performance. *Reading and Writing, 34*, 1885–1913.

Conley, D. T. (2013). *Getting ready for college, careers, and the Common Core: What every educator needs to know.* Jossey-Bass.

Conley, M. W. (2008). Cognitive strategy instruction for adolescents: What we know about the promise, what we don't know about the potential. *Harvard Educational Review, 78*(1), 84–106. http://dx.doi.org/10.17763/haer.78.1.j612282134673638

Delpit, L. (1988). The silenced dialogue: Power and pedagogy in educating other people's children. *Harvard Education Review, 58*(3), 280–298.

Fitzgerald, J., Olson, C. B., Garcia, S. G., & Scarcella, R. C. (2014). Assessing bilingual students' writing. In A. B. Clinton (Ed.), *Assessing bilingual children in context: An integrated approach* (pp. 215–240). American Psychological Association.

Flower, L., & Hayes, J. R. (1981a). A cognitive process theory of writing. *College Composition & Communication, 32*(4), 365–387.

Flower, L., & Hayes, J. R. (1981b). Plans that guide the composing process. In C. H. Frederiksen & J. F. Dominic (Eds.), *Writing: The nature, development, and teaching of written communication* (Vol. 2, pp. 39–58). Lawrence Erlbaum.

Fountas, I., & Pinnell, G. (1996). *Guided reading: Good first teaching for all children.* Heinemann.

Goldenberg, C. (2008). Teaching English language learners: What the research does—and does not—say. *American Educator, 32,* 8–44.

Graham, S. (2018). A revised writer(s)-within-community model of writing. *Educational Psychologist, 53*(4), 258–279.

Graham, S., Bruch, J., Fitzgerald, J., Friedrich, L., Furgeson, J., Greene, K., Kim, J., Lyskawa, J., Olson, C. B., & Smither Wulsin, C. (2016). *Teaching secondary students to write effectively* (NCEE 2017-4002). National Center for Education Evaluation and Regional Assistance (NCEE), Institute of Education Sciences, U.S. Department of Education. https://ies.ed.gov/ncee/wwc/Docs/PracticeGuide/508_WWCPG_SecondaryWriting_122719.pdf

Graham, S., & Perin, D. (2007). A meta-analysis of writing instruction for adolescent students. *Journal of Educational Psychology, 99*(3), 445–476. http://dx.doi.org/10.1037/0022-0663.99.3.445

Hillocks, G., Jr. (2002). *The testing trap: How state writing assessments control learning.* Teachers College Press.

Hirsch, E. D. (1987). *Cultural literacy: What every American needs to know.* Houghton Mifflin.

Kim, J., Olson, C., Scarcella, R., Kramer, J., Pearson, M., van Dyk, D., Collins, P., & Land, R. (2011). A randomized experiment of a cognitive strategies approach to text-based analytical writing for mainstreamed Latino English language learners in grades 6–12. *Journal of Research on Educational Effectiveness, 4*(3), 231–263.

Krathwohl, D. R., Bloom, B. S., & Masia, B. B. (1999). *Taxonomy of educational objectives: Book 2. Affective domain.* Longman.

Langer, J. A. (1986). Reading, writing, and understanding: An analysis of the construction of meaning. *Written Communication, 3*(2), 219–267.

Maamuujav, U., Olson, C. B., & Chung, H. (2021). Syntactic and lexical features of adolescent L2 students' academic writing. *Journal of Second Language Writing, 53*, Article 100822.

National Reading Panel. (2000). *Teaching children to read: An evidence-based assessment of the scientific research literature on reading and its implications for reading instruction.* National Institute of Child Health and Human Development.

National Writing Project. (2010). *The Analytic Writing Continuum: A comprehensive writing assessment system.*

Noden, H. (1999). *Image grammar: Using grammatical structures to teach writing.* Heinemann.

Ogle, D. (1986). K-W-L: A teaching model that develops active reading of expository text. *The Reading Teacher, 39*(6), 564–570.

Olson, C. B. (Ed.) (1992). *Thinking/writing: Fostering critical thinking through writing.* HarperCollins.

Olson, C. B. (Ed.) (1997). *Practical ideas for teaching writing at the high school and college levels.* California Department of Education.

Olson, C. B. (2011). *The reading/writing connection: Strategies for teaching and learning in the secondary classroom.* Pearson Education.

Olson, C. B., & Land, R. (2008). Taking a reading/writing intervention for secondary English language learners on the road: Lessons learned from the Pathway Project. *Research in the Teaching of English, 42*(3), 259–269.

Olson, C. B., Kim, J. S., Scarcella, R., Kramer, J., Pearson, M., van Dyk, D., Collins, P., & Land, R. (2012). Enhancing the interpretative reading and analytical writing of mainstreamed English learners in secondary school: Results from a randomized field trial using a cognitive strategies approach. *American Educational Research Journal, 49*(2), 323–355.

Olson, C. B., Maamuujav, U., Steiss, J., & Chung, H. Q. (2023). Examining the impact of a cognitive strategies approach on the argument writing of mainstreamed English learners in secondary school. *Written Communication, 40*(2), 373–416. https://doi.org/10.1177/07410883221148724

Olson, C. B., Matuchniak, T., Chung, H. Q., Stumpf, R., & Farkas, G. (2017). Reducing achievement gaps in academic writing for Latinos and English learners in grades 7–12. *Journal of Educational Psychology, 109*(1), 1–21. http://dx.doi.org/10.1037/edu0000095

Olson, C. B., Scarcella, R., & Matuchniak, T. (2015). *Helping English learners to write: Meeting Common Core standards, grades 6–12.* Teachers College Press.

Olson, C. B., Woodworth, K., Arshan, N., Black, R., Chung, H. Q., D'Aoust, C., Dewar, T., Freidrich, L., Godfrey, L., Land, R., Matuchniak, T., Scarcella, R., & Stowell, L. (2020). The pathway to academic success: Scalping up a text-based analytical writing intervention for Latinos and English learners in secondary school. *Journal of Educational Psychology, 112*(4), 701–717.

Paris, S. G., Lipson, M. Y., & Wixon, K. K. (1983). Becoming a strategic reader. *Contemporary Educational Psychology, 8*(3), 293–316.

Pearson, P. D., & Gallagher, M. C. (1983). The instruction of reading comprehension. *Contemporary Educational Psychology, 8*(3), 317–344.

Rosenblatt, L. (1978). *The reader, the text, the poem: The transactional theory of the literary work.* Southern Illinois University Press.

Schleppegrell, M. J. (2009, October). *Language in academic subject areas and classroom instruction: What is academic language and how can we teach it?* [Paper presentation]. The National Academy of Sciences, Menlo Park, CA. http://www7.nationalacademies.org/cfe/Paper_Mary_Schleppegrell.pdf

Scholes, R. (1985). *Textual power: Literary theory and the teaching of English.* Yale University Press.

Short, D., & Fitzsimmons, S. (2007). *Double the work: Challenges and solutions to acquiring language and academic literacy for adolescent English language learners.* Alliance for Excellent Education.

Steiner, G. (1963). *Language and silence: Essays on language, literature, and the inhuman.* Open Road Media.

Steiss, J., Krishnan, J., Kim, Y. G., & Olson, C. B. (2022). Dimensions of text-based analytical writing of secondary students. *Assessing Writing, 51*, Article 100600.

Tierney, R. J., & Pearson, P. D. (1983). Toward a composing model of reading. *Language Arts, 60*(5), 568–580.

Tierney, R. J., & Shanahan, T. (1991). Research on the reading-writing relationship: Interactions, transactions, and outcomes. In R. Barr, M. Kamil, P. Mosenthal, & P. D. Pearson (Eds.), *Handbook of reading research* (Vol. 2, pp. 246–280). Lawrence Erlbaum.

Walqui, A., & Bunch, G. C. (2019). What is quality learning for English learners? In A. Walqui & G. C. Bunch (Eds.), *Amplifying the curriculum: Designing quality learning opportunities for English learners* (21–41). Teachers College Press.

Wilhelm, J. D. (2001). *Improving comprehension with think-aloud strategies.* Scholastic.

Wilhelm, J. D. (2007). *You gotta be the book: Teaching engaged and reflective reading with adolescents* (2nd ed.). Teachers College Press.

Chapter Three

Learning to See Learning: A Retrospective of Sheridan Blau's Influence on the Development of a New Writing Project Site

Ralph A. Córdova and Jeff Hudson

> *Though I do not believe that a plant will spring up where no seed has been, I have great faith in a seed . . . Convince me that you have a seed there, and I am prepared to expect wonders.*
>
> —Thoreau, p. 1236

Introduction: The Roots and Routes of Ideas, Practice, and Innovation

It was the summer of 2008, nearly one week into our first Invitational Summer Institute as a newly founded writing project site. The group had gone to lunch, but a fellow stayed behind to chat. Patti had been acting as our ethnographer of the day, a role of participating in and observing the day-to-day life of our writing project. She wanted to know how we chose the members of that summer's cohort. Two things occur to us as we reflect upon Patti's question. First, she and other fellows recognized a difference between our newly forming writing project culture and what had counted for them as professional development in their careers. Second, because the summer institute experience is different, they wanted to know what we saw in them to invite them to join. It matters, we realize, that she asked this question. Her role as ethnographer poised her to notice the emerging culture and to interrogate how she both shaped and was shaped by what she noticed.

This chapter and the work we have engaged in since that first summer institute have been attempts to answer Patti's question. In her question, we see her reaching for affirmation and substance. Sheridan Blau would push us to understand Patti's question by asking, "So what?" From our earliest beginnings as fellows in our respective summer institutes to later founding a writing project site, the So What, or why, behind our decision making and practices has been the focus of our professional work.

Blau's perspective on writing project culture helps us understand Patti's question and offers answers that transcend our summer institute. While the uninitiated might mistake Blau's two points as prescriptive dogmatic nouns, we view them as dynamic and ever-changing verbs or actions that evolve in response to each writing project site's local teaching and learning cultures. In 2006, at the annual NWP convocation, Blau posited:

> Writing is the best and most reliable instrumentality for learning and therefore for ensuring change of many kinds, including the changes that transpire dramatically and regularly for teachers in and through the writing project. (Blau, 2006)

We argue that the ethnographic perspective we drew on in our summer institute was a kind of writing instrumentality for learning. From this perspective, we ask the following question: How does the instrumentality of writing manifest itself in the form of an ethnographic perspective to conceptualize our NWP Summer Institute as a culture in the making?

Blau goes on to argue that the fidelity to foundational features makes space for innovation and transformation:

> The theme of change is about the paradoxical character of the writing project itself: how the writing project is a powerful agent for deep and transforming change in persons, in professional development, and in the nature of schooling in part because we have so scrupulously resisted any change in our fundamental principles and practices, insistently monitoring and assisting all NWP sites to ensure that they demonstrate fidelity to the foundational features of a model that originated in the Bay Area Writing Project in 1974—one of whose distinctive features is that for 33 years it hasn't changed. (Blau, 2006)

A foundational feature of all writing project summer institutes is a sharing and modeling of practice often referred to as a demonstration. What does it look like and sound like to navigate the paradox of remaining faithful to foundational features of the writing project model and facilitating deep and transformational change in personal and professional development? We address this question by examining the consequences for professional growth by transforming the teaching demonstration into an inquiry into practice and the ways in which an ethnographic perspective can assist fellows to make visible the sometimes invisible "why," or epistemological reasoning behind fellows' pedagogical approaches to writers and writing.

Theoretical and Methodological Perspectives

We conceptualize classrooms and writing projects as cultures in the making (Kelly & Green, 2019); therefore, a theoretical language is needed in order to account for the complexity of situated human activity in the moment and over time.

Our theoretical orientation is grounded in an interactional ethnographic perspective (Santa Barbara Classroom Discourse Group, 1992a), described in Telling Case 1. We take up an ethnographic perspective (Green & Bloome, 1997) in order to understand everyday life inside a community (Yeager & Córdova, 2010), in this case what comes to count as a writing project (Green et al., 2003), as well as learning, to members of the community in a given moment and over time. An ethnographic perspective enables teacher-researchers to understand how disciplinary knowledge and practices are the result of actions taken by people and how they can "take up" the actions associated with particular disciplines (Yeager et al., 1998, p. 16), as well as see relationships across disciplines.

We complement our interactional ethnographic perspective by drawing on approaches from the field of anthropology in order to account for the ways a community constructs a language as a meaning-making system (Gumperz & Cook-Gumperz, 1986), with patterned production and interpretations (Spradley, 1980), how language patterns become discourses which members inhabit

(Frake, 1977), and referential systems (Bloome et al., 2004) its members use to interpret everyday life (Bloome & Theodorou, 1988). Further, we draw on literary theory (Bakhtin, 1986) in order to conceptualize and understand the significance of spoken and written discourses as particular kinds of texts. Finally, we draw upon critical discourse analysis (Fairclough, 1992; Ivanic, 1994) to understand how these texts come to count as knowledge to the group and the ways in which individual and collective members draw upon this language and knowledge to become ethnographers of their dynamically unfolding writing project as a culture in the making.

Overview of Telling Cases

Telling cases, proposed by Mitchell (1984), serve to make visible something previously not available to be known. We present two telling cases: 1) the role that an interactional ethnographic perspective played in the intentional co-construction of our writing project; and, 2) the evolution of the presentation or demonstration of practice into an inquiry into practice. Our goal is to make visible in the analyses of these two telling cases the origins or seeds of ideas; innovations of practice; and the implications for practitioners in classroom and writing project-based settings.

Telling Case 1: Interactional Ethnography as Epistemology for a Culture in the Making

In order to examine the tenet of the instrumentality of writing, we focus our analysis on the role that an interactional ethnographic perspective played in the co-construction of our writing project culture. Distinct from classical ethnography in which the researcher is removed from the culture being studied, interactional ethnography positions both the researcher and the members of the culture being observed as coparticipants, and coresearchers. This matters because what comes to count as the described, moment-to-moment and over-time life of a group, is *co*-examined, *co*-analyzed and *co*-written. From this perspective, the culture studied is not objectified or othered. We learn with and from rather than about the emerging writing project and what counts as literacy within that group. This co-participatory approach, therefore, allows for making visible the ways in which the individual shapes the collective, and thus the collective shapes the individual.

SCWriP: In the early 1990s, the Santa Barbara Classroom Discourse Group, led by Drs. Judith Green and Carol Dixon, profoundly impacted the South Coast Writing Project by introducing it to an interactional ethnographic perspective. Green and Dixon co-directed SCWriP with Sheridan Blau (director), Jack Phraener (co-director and high school teacher), and Drs. Hsiu Zu Ho and Judith Green (co-directors and UCSB professors). Castanheira et al (2000) posit interactional ethnography as:

> What counts as literacy can be examined across a wide range of social and cultural contexts. From this perspective, the interactional ethnographer examines what members count as literacy, literate processes, literate actions, literate practices, and literate artifacts. The ethnographer also considers how these processes, practices, and artifacts contribute to situated definitions of and principles for defining what counts as literacy within and across times and events in the classroom (and other institutional settings). (Castanheira et al., 2000)

Building on the wide range of social and cultural contexts in which what counts as literacy can be examined, Castanheira, Crawford, Dixon, and Green (2000) draw our attention to the temporal and unfolding nature, in which literate practices are socially constructed:

> The interactional ethnographer, therefore, must look at what is constructed in and through the moment-by-moment interactions among members of a social group; how members negotiate events through these interactions; and the ways in which knowledge and texts generated in one event become linked to, and thus a resource for, members' actions in subsequent events. In this way, the ethnographer examines how literacy is talked, acted, and written into being, and how, through their actions, members make visible to each other what counts as appropriate discursive and literate practices. (p. 357)

Blau, Green, and Dixon introduced an interactional ethnographic perspective as a method and epistemology for SCWriP members to interact with and learn from the writing project culture they co-constructed in the summers. This allowed for the development of an empirical base for SCWriP. In retrospect, we can now see the interacting, interdisciplinary nature of SCWriP directors' expertise, the teaching of writing (Sheridan), interactional ethnography (Green), and literacy development (Dixon) in order to co-construct a conceptual framework for a SCWriP.

In 1995, when the first author became a SCWriP fellow, Louise Jennings, a graduate student of Judith Green, played the role of the resident ethnographer for the summer institute. The ethnographer's role involved gathering data records (video footage, written artifacts, and interviews) produced by members of the summer institute each year. The summer ethnographers were graduate students guided by Judith Green and Carol Dixon. This research was conducted in order to develop an empirical conceptual base for what constituted a summer institute in and through the actions and interactions of participants. In other words, it sought to make visible the epistemological underpinnings, or *the why,* of the transformational nature of writing project culture. In the role, the ethnographer set up the video camera and began recording first thing in the morning, concluding with the wrap-up at each day's end. Her video footage also included capturing each fellow's demonstration of practice, book club discussions, and writing response group activities. Each day of the summer institute, a different participating teacher fellow would 'shadow' Jenning's ethnographer activities, as a coparticipant ethnographer, by co-documenting the day's events. The following day, Jennings and the previous day's participant ethnographer would share with the entire group their observations and questions about participants' activities during that previous day. The ethnographic perspective was interactional in that it positioned both the university researcher and the teacher co-ethnographer as participant-observers who interacted with and learned from the teacher-leaders as they co-constructed what came to count as being literate of SCWriP tenets and practices as a culture in the making. In doing so, interactional ethnography and the production of daily written ethnographic records served as an epistemology meaning-making perspective by producing a shared written text of what constituted daily life for summer institute participants.

Further, we argue that the ethnography both as written by the ethnographers and as recorded by the video camera became literate practices for what counted as members of the writing project. Participants produced cultural resources that participants could review and draw upon in order to make visible the nature of the co-construction of professional learning. The practice of recording activities and presenting them to the collective assisted participants in making visible the moment-to-moment and over-time nature of SCWriP as a culture in the making. Rather than professional development being "delivered" to passive learners and each activity and day's events viewed discretely from each other, an interactional ethnographic perspective enabled participants to conceptualize the dynamic and over-time nature of teacher leadership development repositioning professional development as *professionals developing professionals*. The collaborative writing of the daily ethnographies further nuances the definition of writing as something much more than a transaction and instead a creative source of new knowledge.

Innovations

In 2008, the authors of this chapter founded the Piasa Bluffs Writing Project (PBWP) in Southern Illinois. Given the first author's initiation to an interactional ethnographic perspective from Sheridan Blau and Judith Green that was first formulated (Vygotsky, 1978) at the South Coast Writing Project, the practice became an important one to later reformulate and implement in the fledgling writing project site that the two authors were directing. Bakhtin's (1986) perspective helps us understand how the written ethnography genre from its genesis in one site and later transplanted to another site evolves:

> Sooner or later what is heard and actively understood will find its response in the subsequent speech or behavior of the listener. In most cases, genres of complex cultural communication are intended precisely for this kind of actively responsive understanding with delayed action. Everything that we have

> said here also pertains to written and read speech, with the appropriate adjustments and additions. (p. 60)

PBWP did not have one sole ethnographer of the day, but instead each day a different PBWP fellow took on the role. Individually, and then collectively, members produced what came to be known as the ethnography of that summer institute. One innovation was that the prior day's ethnographer of the day mentored the subsequent ethnographer in the taking of notes, running the camera, and downloading and archiving video footage. As in SCWriP, each ethnographer of the day led the opening of the summer institute day by presenting observations of the previous day's experiences and compelling questions that the fellows would write about and share.

The cultural practice of producing individual ethnographies of each day, and collectively producing a meta-ethnography of the summer institute, involved the formulation of referential texts (Bloome & Theodorou, 1988). The summer institute became a text to be read and written, producing a shared referential meaning-making system (Bloome & Egan-Robertson, 1993) that allowed participants to account for the moment-to-moment and over-time activities and transformations of the group.

The interactional ethnographic perspective, as we will see in the next telling case, became an epistemological, meaning-making process, one that fellows would draw upon to participate in, observe, document, and examine each fellow's teaching demonstration, what PBWP leadership would later redefine as an Inquiry into My Practice (IMP).

Telling Case 2: Transforming the Teaching Demonstration as Inquiry into My Practice

The Piasa Bluffs Writing Project rose from the ashes of the Mississippi Valley Writing Project at SIUE. As new directors, we enacted, along with twenty-four new fellows, our first summer institute in June of 2008. We put in place that summer a traditional NWP architecture: writing groups, book clubs, and the demonstration of teaching practice.

These demonstrations were sprawling, theatrical, inspirational, wobbly, all of it. The potential lives of these demonstrations abruptly ended after they were enacted. Absent was a way to honor and examine them in order to appropriate them and integrate them in new contexts and spaces that the participants inhabited. Once a demonstration ended, participant observers offered handwritten letters of feedback. These letters, broadly speaking, were gentle, sincere pearls of praise.

As directors, we realized we wanted something more from the experience, both for the lead teacher and for the participants. We were dubious of the polish and confidence of the lessons. Or, if they were polished and objectively good, how did they come to be? If they were to become available to us to learn from, to appropriate for our own contexts and purposes, we'd have to slow down the process—change the direction of momentum. Rather than a show, suggesting momentum outward, we wondered how we might reverse that direction, move this fundamental tenet of writing culture from that of presentation to one of inquiry, momentum inward rather than out.

In our endeavor to make the sharing of practice an inquiry, we reformulated the teaching demonstration as an Inquiry into My Practice (IMP). Coaching became a fish-bowl conversation known as the pre-brief in which the lead teacher and her thinking partner engaged in a professional conversation about practice and in which the lead teacher shared some pedagogical question she was wrestling with. While the conversation was structured and intentionally guided by three framing questions, it was not scripted. The framing questions were: (1) What do you think you are exploring with this lesson, both in terms of content and pedagogy? (2) How do you envision the lesson unfolding—beginning, middle, and end? (3) Once enacted, what do you hope participants take away?

Skilled thinking partners (coaches) paraphrased responses and asked clarifying follow-up questions. Thinking partners built empathy with and for the lead teacher, as well as with and for the participant observers. The lesson would be enacted in a traditional manner, actual teaching in the moment with and for colleagues. The letter of feedback became a much more intentional debrief with rounds of noticing, analyzing, sharing, and reflecting.

One way to look at the implications of this innovation—moving from a demonstration of practice to the IMP—is to look at the language of teachers in the 3×2 debrief protocol or feedback form of the IMPs over time. The shared cultural practice of interactional ethnography and participant observation lived in multiple iterations. The practices and utility of the ethnographies of the day, discussed in our first telling case, expanded into how we understood the potential that the teaching demonstration had for both lead teachers and participants. The interactional ethnographic perspective became an epistemological approach for how we conceived of, interacted with, and made sense of the teaching demonstration as lived inquiry into practice. The 3×2 feedback protocol became, itself, an ethnographic record of the learning that took place across the life of a summer institute.

Figure 3.1 is an actual 3×2 debrief response to an IMP. In it, we examine the process by which participants developed the ability to notice the pedagogical significance of the lead teacher's IMP.

"I noticed people enjoyed my clock," the observer recorded. While this may be so, the observation is more of an assessment or an evaluation. What evidence supports the claim that people enjoyed the clock? Continued practice in descriptive observations of the IMP over time resulted in the following observation from the same teacher:

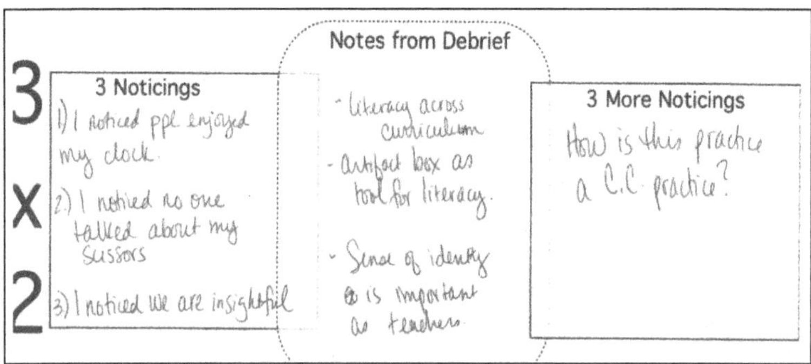

FIGURE 3.1. *IMP Debrief Protocol*

What did the teacher say/do?

Invited the students to contribute throughout the lesson via Twitter. Asked us ~~the~~ to find a quote that resonated with us + respond to it.

What did the students say/do?

Accessed Twitter accounts while multi-tasking. Identified quote + wrote why we ~~choose~~ chose that particular quote.

Midway through class:

What did teacher say/do

Gave us instruction for "The Last Word." ~~A~~ Provided structure to fascilitate discussion/analyzation of the text. The teacher also stayed out of our 'way' + did not try to direct or dominate the discussions.

What did students say/do?

Read their quotes + ~~reactions~~. Then we took turns reacting/responding to each quote with the "owner" of the quote reading their reaction last. We discussed the text without realizing it really!

Closing the lesson:

FIGURE 3.2. *IMP Debrief Implications for One's Own Practice*

In Figure 3.2, the teacher is noticing actual words and actions from the lesson: evidence. She wrote, "Invited the students to contribute to the lesson via Twitter. Asked us to find a quote that resonated with us and respond to it." In this later debrief, we see the shift from evaluative language to descriptive and evidentiary language. This shift in ability did not spontaneously emerge. Rather, the cultural context and practice of inquiry, over time, enabled this participant to demonstrate interactional ethnographic language use. Castenheira et al. (2000) state, "From this perspective, the interactional ethnographer examines what members count as literacy, literate processes, literate actions, literate practices, and literate artifacts" (p. 355). In this shift from evaluative to descriptive, the teacher demonstrated a principle from international ethnography, which is acting in literate ways and both engaging in and creating literate artifacts about the IMP.

In the earlier example, "people liked my clock," the observation did not lead to any pedagogical insight or understanding, whereas the second observation gives this teacher and participants more access to formulate compelling and potentially transformational pedagogical questions about practice.

In Figure 3.3 (an excerpt from Figure 3.2), the observing teacher wrote, *1) What were the literary practices the students did before today's lesson?*

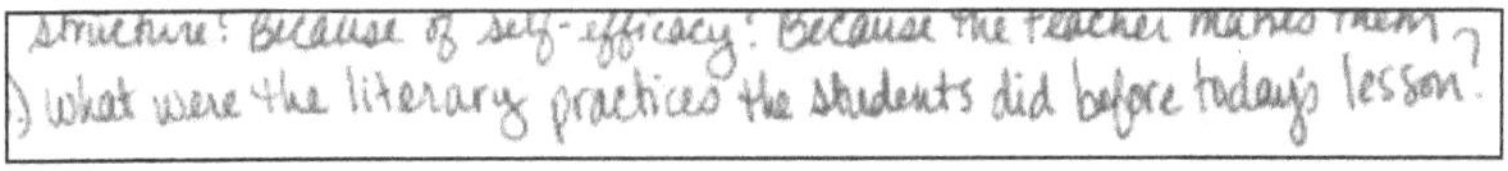

structure? Because of self-efficacy? Because the teacher makes them?
) what were the literary practices the students did before today's lesson?

FIGURE 3.3. *A Closer Look*

Her question positions the phenomena observed as contextualized (Bloome & Theodorou, 1988) within a history of what came before, of literate practices. This teacher is now thinking pedagogically and of consequential progressions of teaching and learning. How, this teacher is wondering, did these learners come to be, and where do we take them next?

So What?

We conclude by circling back to Sheridan Blau's eternal question, *So What?* He pushed us to dig into what matters in the teaching of writing, positioning educators as both participants and theorizers of the instrumentality and transformative nature of writing to learn. In the 2006 keynote at the annual National Writing Project meeting, Blau reminded us of the difference between knowledge consumed versus knowledge earned:

> The problem with knowledge consumed rather than earned is twofold. First, if you consume knowledge rather than make it, you don't know how it was ever made and don't know how you might revise or refine it and you will be very reluctant to give it up for the insecurity of having to learn. Second, if you value yourself pridefully for what you know, you will feel devalued by any challenge to your knowledge and fearful of all questions that might call for the revision or suspension of your knowledge. (Blau, 2006)

In the first telling case, we examined the phenomenon of the use of an interactional ethnographic perspective as an epistemology for learning to see learning. Without that perspective, a summer institute runs the risk of being no more than an intensive course in which knowledge is consumed. An interactional ethnographic perspective as a literate practice, in the context of a summer institute, enables participants to ask how teachers make knowledge, both for self and for others. Moreover, when teachers understand that knowledge construction is a dynamic act of making, they are positioned as owners of their knowledge, thus enabling them to honor, interrogate, and potentially further refine it. An interactional ethnographic perspective protects teachers from becoming prideful once having arrived at a state of grace or as a purveyor of curriculum. Rather, it positions teachers as creators and revisors of knowledge in a community of practice.

In the second telling case, we examined the consequences of reformulating the teaching demonstration into an inquiry into practice. A demonstration implies certainty of the presenter's knowledge. This certainty as Blau suggests is problematic and false, shielding the presenter from alternative interpretations for why something works, whereas an inquiry stance invites participants to conceive of knowledge of practice as evolving and sometimes uncertain. This uncertainty, when experienced in the summer institute, can become a generative space. Sheridan taught us to embrace the ambiguity of not knowing, a desired and essential space for learning and professional growth.

The act of writing this chapter was not just demonstrating or telling a story with certainty. It became an opportunity for shared inquiries into our practices, leading to new understandings of Blau's intellectual influence on who we are today as educators, leaders, and human beings.

Works Cited

Bakhtin, M. M. (1986). The problem of speech genres. In M. M. Bakhtin, *Speech genres and other late essays* (C. Emerson & M. Holmquist, Eds., V. W. McGee, Trans., pp. 60–102). University of Texas Press.

Bateson, M. C. (1994). *Peripheral visions: Learning along the way.* HarperCollins.

Blau, S. (2006, November 17). *The National Writing Project's unchanging principles and practices for change.* National Writing Project. https://lead.nwp.org/knowledgebase/unchanging-principles-and-practices-for-change

Bloome, D., Carter, S. P., Christian, B. M., Otto, S., & Shuart-Faris, N. (2004). *Discourse analysis and the study of classroom language and literacy events: A microethnographic perspective*. Routledge.

Bloome, D., & Egan-Robertson, A. (1993). The social construction of intertextuality in classroom reading and writing lessons. *Reading Research Quarterly*, *28*(4), 304–333.

Bloome, D., & Theodorou, E. (1988). Analyzing teacher-student and student-student discourse. In J. Green & J. Harker (Eds.), *Multiple perspective analyses of classroom discourse* (Vol. 28, pp. 217–248). Ablex.

Castanheira, M. L., Crawford, T., Dixon, C. N., & Green, J. L. (2000). Interactional ethnography: An approach to studying the social construction of literate practices. *Linguistics and Education*, *11*(4), 353–400.

Frake, C. O. (1977). Plying frames can be dangerous: Some reflections on methodology in cognitive anthropology. *Quarterly Newsletter of the Institute for Comparative Human Development*, *1*(3), 1–7.

Green, J., & Bloome, D. (1997). Ethnography and ethnographers of and in education: A situated perspective. In J. Flood, S. B. Heath, & D. Lapp (Eds.), *Handbook of research on teaching literacy through the communicative and visual arts* (pp. 181–202). Macmillan.

Gumperz, J. J., & Cook-Gumperz, J. (1986). Interactional sociolinguistics in the study of schooling. In J. Cook-Gumperz (Ed.), *The social construction of literacy* (pp. 45–68). Cambridge University Press.

Kelly, G. J., & Green, J. L. (2019). Framing issues of theory and methods for the study of science and engineering education. In G. J. Kelly & J. L. Green (Eds.), *Theory and methods for sociocultural research in science and engineering education* (pp. 1–28). Routledge.

Mitchell, C. J. (1984). Typicality and the case study. In R. F. Ellen (Ed.), *Ethnographic research: A guide to general conduct* (pp. 238–241). Academic.

Santa Barbara Classroom Discourse Group. (1992). Constructing literacy in classrooms: Literate action as social accomplishment. In H. H. Marshall (Ed.), *Redefining student learning: Roots of educational change* (pp. 119–150). Ablex.

Spradley, J. (1980). Participant observation. Harcourt Brace.

Thoreau, H. D. (2013). *Complete works of Henry David Thoreau*. Delphi Classics.

Yeager, E., & Córdova, R. (2010). How knowledge counts: Talking family knowledge and lived experience into being as resource for academic action. In M. L. Dantas & P. C. Manyak (Eds.), *Home-school connections in a multicultural society: Learning from and with culturally and linguistically diverse families* (pp. 218–236). Routledge.

CHAPTER FOUR

Becoming Blau: Learning ([Not] to Teach) through Academic Apprenticeship

NOAH HARRIS GORDON

> *Teachers who become researchers, writers, authors—persons who are engaged in the construction of knowledge—will understand experientially what it means to construct knowledge in a community of learners and will devote themselves to figuring out how to turn their own classrooms into such communities for their students.*
>
> —SHERIDAN BLAU

I didn't grow up knowing that I wanted to be a teacher. I often felt alienated from school, and my stance as a student was subversive. Most of my energy was spent trying to evade or combat my teachers' aims and interests. I share this embarrassing fact only to provide contrast to the person I became in graduate school. When I entered Teachers College, I made the conscious decision to change, to reorient myself as a student in good faith. I set aside skepticism and embraced receptivity. I became more openhearted, curious, humbled, dedicated, and teachable—not docile but willing to be schooled. It's difficult to convey, then, how complex being this kind of student became when I entered Sheridan's class because what I learned first about him was that he believed that teaching was anathema to learning. My experience was deeply confusing, and yet, even as a preservice teacher, this confusion seemed rich and important. What does one learn about teaching from a teacher who advocates for its abolition?

Academic Apprenticeship: Constructing Knowledge in a Community of Learners

My initial confusion contained within it many questions, particularly given that Sheridan's classes, which he refers to as an "academic apprenticeship" (Blau, 2023, p. 303), are meant to help people with little or no experience teaching develop their pedagogical practices and principles.

What should one do as a student in this academic apprenticeship? In more traditional classes, the expectation might be to take notes on what the teacher says, but, in this class, a great deal of the talk was storytelling, discussion, and debate. And the professor wasn't the only one speaking—everyone was talking and writing and looking back to the assigned readings. It seemed impossible to look on from outside the community to write things down; there was no periphery from which to passively watch.

Who should one be in academic apprenticeship? I couldn't act as my professor's parrot, repeating the ideas that I was being taught; nor did I feel that I could authentically be myself, someone who had no experience teaching and who rarely had meaningful experiences in school. I saw in Sheridan the teacher that I wanted to become, but imitating him seemed to be the epitome of false knowledge.

What is learned in an academic apprenticeship? In traditional craft apprenticeships, the answer seems clear: a novice tailor learns to make a suit, a novice potter learns to throw a pot. One might expect to learn a craft and to become a version of the master, someone who can take their wares to market. Traditional academic spaces, too, seem straightforward: presumably a student learns what the teacher teaches and passively recites or reproduces what has been taught. Students' performances of knowledge-telling tasks are evaluated and translated into grades and credits, which are added to the student's transcript. Traditional models of school and conventional theories of learning—in which ideas can be decontextualized and transferred from one person to another—are simplistic, reductive. While it's true that a learner may accumulate the trappings of learning as credentials, this misses the meaning, the experience, the activity, the community.

In Sheridan's academic apprenticeship, I wasn't reproducing content or demonstrating a skill but contributing to an emerging community in pursuit of what Sheridan—the teacher who seemingly ceaselessly refuses to teach—calls "true knowledge" (Blau, 2011b, p. 5). Sheridan argues that even true knowledge isn't fixedly true. Held too tightly, true knowledge can become an obstacle to learning. When knowledge (even knowledge gained through experience) is professed to be complete, codified as transferable content or delineated into discrete skills, its truth becomes suspect.

My work as Sheridan's student has been powered by questions and confusion and fraught with paradoxes and problems. As much as I love him and hope to honor him, I almost always find myself making trouble for him. Perhaps I haven't outgrown my contrarian self. But gone is my desire to evade my teacher or to coolly shrug off a class's challenge. The trouble that I'm intending to make is honest. And Sheridan is a self-described fallibilist. Drawing from pragmatist philosophers like Ann Berthoff, Sheridan defines fallibilism as a learner's "willingness to surrender the security of their knowledge and to launch . . . into the abyss of uncertainty" (Blau, 2003b, p. 46). He seemingly wants to make more trouble than I do. I know I have much to learn from him.

Sheridan's ability to uncover problems far surpasses mine. He looks for trouble everywhere: in his students' commentaries, in the canonical writings of authoritative readers, even in his own most assured ideas. His doubt is methodological! Sheridan credits Peter Elbow with offering "the technique of methodological believing and doubting . . . a method of encouraging more collaborative rather than competitive discourse between persons who take opposing views on any subject" (Blau, 1993, p. 10). He makes space for what might be historically considered misreadings or fallacies with the understanding that a student's personal engagement with a text—even an encounter that seems peripheral or contrarian—might represent some autonomous literary theory, some future school of criticism, some novel way to contribute. This means that any problem raised in good faith might be a contribution that could transform the field, the room, or the conversation. To this problem, Sheridan leaves the door open.

And, crucially, Sheridan's pedagogy isn't only powered by doubt. His classes aren't merely exercises in exposing weaknesses or finding what's wrong or problematic. I'm still struck by Sheridan's note accompanying his first assignment in studying Milton:

> Skepticism is intellectually fashionable, but it is also easier than understanding ideas and concepts that may be new and difficult. Skepticism in the face of wisdom beyond our own will help us learn only if it is combined with a strong sense of our own fallibilism, our recognition that our resistance to an idea may represent our own limitation. And that may suggest that we should also experiment with believing. This isn't blind faith at all. It's an exercise in reason. (Blau, 2011a, p. 1)

Sheridan's classes are founded on belief in Reason and evidentiary reasoning, belief in aesthetic experience, belief in dialogue. And, perhaps most paradoxically for a fallibilist, he believes in "true knowledge" and in his students' ability to discover it.

I write this chapter to trace an intellectual history of Sheridan's academic apprenticeship and to look for possible sources for the ideas that I hold so dear. I've learned these lessons directly from Sheridan—through conversations and classes and projects and, most transformatively, through engaging in his workshops, which now serve as the foundation for my own pedagogy. I share my confusion, my doubts, and my questions in his same spirit, with the hope that exploring these initial states might lead to larger and more capacious understandings; I argue wholeheartedly with students as a sign of my greatest respect for them and their ideas; and I remain open, always, to my own fallibility and to the possibility of learning. Perhaps most importantly, Sheridan's belief in a learner's potential contribution to an emerging discourse community—that is, his faith in me as a contributor—has become my belief: for my students and for myself. Which is all to say that I have become a teacher as Sheridan's student. It is my hope that by tracing Sheridan's history as a learner, I might see him more clearly as my teacher.

An Induction into Academic Apprenticeship

I first met Sheridan when I enrolled in "Literature and Teaching" in the summer of 2010. I was a preservice teacher who'd never led a class of my own. Sheridan's course began with the commentary workshop (see pages 31–48 in Blau [2010] for a dramatization).

My first experience was humbling: my response to George Bogin's poem "Nineteen" detailed a similar imagined romance, and I was embarrassed to learn that my ideas were common, immature, and sexist. I learned this from listening to Sheridan's commentary, a version of which he published in "Academic Writing as Participation": Bogin's poem is "a cheap, sentimental cliché of a poem, indulging in a fundamentally adolescent fantasy about true love and happiness and destiny—a fantasy that is as dangerous as it is stupid" (Blau, 2010, p. 44). Sheridan's commentary made me doubt my experience as a reader, but listening to him and my colleagues talk, I saw how productive my doubt might be. My confusion, I learned, was essential; it was a generative force; it was an advanced state of understanding (Blau, 2003b, pp. 21–22). I could always be more thoughtful, look more carefully, attune myself more sensitively to my experience.

The "Literature and Teaching" course required participants to read literary texts and pedagogical articles and to talk about the difficulty we found in making meaning of them. I was intimidated because I was poorly read and lacked confidence, but Sheridan's workshop model authorizes participants to speak from their lived experience. I was curious, openhearted, willing to fail publicly and repeatedly, and determined to take part in what I could to contribute the best of what I knew. I worked to create a new experiential context—what Sheridan describes as "the way a writer experiences himself in his own active engagement in the process of composing" (Blau, 1987, p. 6)—and reimagined my earlier resistance to school and my "deferent stance" (Smith, 2012, p. 64) as valuable sources of experience.

In July 2010, I participated in the commentary workshop for a second time. Sheridan was a plenary speaker at Student Press Initiative's Summer Institute, and he presented the same script that I had experienced from "Literature and Teaching." I was familiar with Bogin's poem, and I was determined to write something smarter that I could share with the community.

When participants were invited to read their work to the room, I listened to the people who volunteered themselves or members of their group. Participating in the commentary workshop inducted me into a community of teachers. Our ongoing conversations have made me feel personally responsible for developing commentary-based communities in my own classroom. As I have increasingly identified as a contributor to ongoing research, my facilitation of the commentary workshop has become more sensitive and more nuanced, which has led to deeper conversations with students and teachers who have helped me to further refine my understanding of the workshop's value, principles, and limitations. This practice of inviting others into the commentary project has transformed and informed my identity as a learner, teacher, and researcher.

It's not surprising that taking part in workshops would have this effect on me. Sheridan's workshops were constructed to change the culture of instruction common in secondary schools, colleges, and universities and to create in its place communities devoted to learning from literature and from participants' conversations with each other about their meaning-making processes. This pedagogical practice and the principles that underlie it—what Sheridan now refers to as academic apprenticeship—grew out of his experiences of learning to teach.

As a relative newcomer, I've often wanted to know more about the person I was imitating. Where did these beliefs about teachers and classrooms and schools come from? How did Sheridan become the teacher he is? These questions are particularly striking when I think about how fundamentally different the classes I've taken with Sheridan are from his teaching at the University of Michigan in the academic year of '68–'69. Students in his first Milton class would have been an audience for his lectures. That is, they would have heard his prepared remarks on background information and specialized knowledge and a survey of his ideas and interpretations. By the time I became his student, Sheridan had fully reframed the central activity of his classes as inquiry.

When I've asked Sheridan to explain this change in his pedagogy, he can't say exactly, though he often recounts moments that were transformative both professionally and personally.

It's tempting to attribute his instructional practice to a seminal experience of an influential teacher, but I want to keep the mystery intact. That is, while sharing some of these stories, I hope to avoid what Bloom (1997) calls the "the wearisome industry of source hunting, of allusion counting" (pp. 30–31) in tracing Poetic Influence. Mehta and Fine (2019) are similarly tentative: "The reality is that some combination of personal preferences and earlier teaching experiences probably helps shape one's teaching stance, which in turn shapes practices" (p. 433). I offer the following educational biography because I believe that it may be instructive for future teachers and researchers.

Sheridan Blau: An Educational Biography

Throughout his early life, Sheridan felt an internal push and pull as a learner. He grew up in a striving Jewish family in Trenton, New Jersey, in a house near a park and a couple of blocks from a school, surrounded by tree-lined streets, semi-detached houses, good students, and bright role models. He was restless, filled with nervous energy, and bored to death by school. His curiosity often put him at odds with his teachers and with his mother. As a student in elementary and middle school, he generally received poor grades, always with some variation of the same comment: "Sheridan is a bright boy but he has to learn self-control" (S. Blau, personal communication, August 10, 2020). He was constantly in trouble in school, especially in junior high, which was caused by his desire to make sense of the poems and stories that his teachers gave him. Sheridan tells me that he got into trouble not because he wasn't interested in school, but because he was. That is, he would carefully reread the text as the teacher and class moved on.

He remembers being treated badly by his teachers and seeing himself as bad in school, but he also remembers being a devoted Boy Scout (S. Blau, personal communication, June 30, 2023). At roughly the same time that he was telling the older, tough boys at Trenton Junior High School No. 3 that he would drop out like they would, he had the ambition to be the youngest Eagle Scout ever. He earned badges quickly and was initiated into the Scouts' Honor Society. After one summer at Scout Camp when he was 11 or 12 years old, Sheridan was invited to write a report for a local newspaper about his experience. He remembers going to the Scouts' Council Headquarters in an office at the Trenton War Memorial and being treated like a real writer: an adult carefully read what he wrote and asked questions that prompted him to make thoughtful revisions. The piece was published in the paper along with his picture. This is one of Sheridan's first memories of being celebrated as a writer.

When he was 13, Sheridan inherited a box of books from his older cousin, Wayne, who was leaving for the University of Pennsylvania. Five years older than Sheridan, Wayne was his hero and role model: he was a respected athlete, a card player, a tough kid. Wayne was traditionally masculine, but he was also an intellectual, an academic. Sheridan found the books he received from Wayne powerful, especially the philosophical conversations in Norman Mailer's *The Naked and the Dead*. He realized that meaning was the heart of intellectual discourse, not the formality of the words or how they were phrased. Mailer's profanity inspired him to see value in his own spoken language and to realize that a person could use casual or even coarse language to talk about serious intellectual matters. Mailer's language shifted Sheridan's identity: he realized that he "could write and talk about things that were important . . . [but he] didn't have to give in to the culture of the school, which [he] found really alien" (Blau, 2009).

Sheridan had a dear friend at the time whose sister was dating a senior in high school. When he would visit their house, a group of older boys—high school seniors and college freshmen—would often sit in the sunroom and talk. Sheridan describes listening to their discussions:

> I would go sit in the sunroom with these kids . . . and never say anything. I would just sit there and listen. I loved being with them. . . . They too were role models for me, but I didn't know that they were role models. It's just that I knew that I loved that kind of talk. I loved hearing it; I loved the way they were thinking. I think that that was my experience of real intellectual discourse. (S. Blau, personal communication, August 10, 2020)

At the same time, Sheridan had a literature teacher whom he liked and who encouraged him to write. He memorized poems in her class and wrote pieces that were published in the school paper. Sheridan was both stimulated as a writer and recognized for being a writer, which helped him to see himself more "as a guy who could write pretty well, and who could read literature and understand and care about it" (S. Blau, personal communication, August 10, 2020).

The following year, Sheridan entered high school. He remembers noticing that the highest-achieving students were part of an extracurricular activity called the Forum Club. He was struck by how they dressed compared to himself and to the tougher kids he identified with—Sheridan wore cleated shoes and combed his hair into a ducktail. He vividly remembers making the conscious decision to change: "I want to be one of *those* kids. I joined the Forum Club and . . . I started changing how I think. . . . I became a good student" (S. Blau, personal communication, August 10, 2020). After deciding to change his identity, Sheridan started to receive good grades and to be recognized for academic achievement. He became a prize student in physics and his tenth-grade biology teacher told him he was someone who was bright and could succeed in all academic spaces. By senior year, Sheridan was identified as a gifted student and admitted into an independent reading course, which he describes as the one high school course in which he learned a lot (S. Blau, personal communication, June 21, 2023).

After high school, Sheridan left to earn his undergraduate degree at Rutgers University. The transformative experiences he had during adolescence—experiences that fed his natural curiosity for learning and intellectual discourse, his changing participation in school and positive relationships with his teachers, and his active decision to become a good student—helped him feel at home in college in a way that many of his friends from high school didn't. He joined a Jewish fraternity at Rutgers, which surrounded Sheridan with highly motivated Jews who had come to Rutgers hungry for knowledge. He received good grades but quickly became bored and rarely went to his classes after the first semester.

Although he didn't want to be an English major when he first arrived, he studied with two influential teachers in Rutgers's English department: John Ciardi and Paul Fussell. Sheridan liked them and wanted to be like them; they represented identities he could try on for himself. He especially loved classes with Ciardi, which focused on interpreting poetic techniques and were steeped in New Critical approaches. Listening to Ciardi's interpretations gave Sheridan the thrilling feeling that he was learning literary secrets, and being Ciardi's student helped Sheridan see himself as a poet and as someone who could analyze and interpret poems. Later in his career, Sheridan largely rejected Ciardi's ideas and approaches. In *Building Bridges Between Literary Theory and the Teaching of Literature*, Sheridan counters Ciardi's claim that "we talk about the meaning of a poem only when we don't know what else to say about it" (Blau, 1993, p. 3) with his own pedagogy centered on making meaning, honoring aesthetic experiences, and fostering students' identities as confident and competent readers and writers.

Sheridan wrote his senior honors thesis on contemporary American Jewish literature, but this work was a departure from the literary criticism that he saw his professors doing. In fact, Sheridan felt uniquely qualified as a reader of American Jewish culture. He knew the language and understood the themes running through the novels better than his teachers did. But, he says, "I had to teach myself what to say by doing it" (S. Blau, personal communication, June 30, 2023). He graduated from Rutgers in 1960.

Sheridan taught high school English for two years before pursuing a master's degree and doctorate in English and American literature at Brandeis University. At Brandeis, he studied under two professors who were deeply influential to him: J. V. Cunningham and Allen Grossman. Sheridan tells me, laughing: "they were the two best teachers I ever had . . . [but] by every standard that I now advocate, [they] were the worst teachers" (S. Blau, personal communication, June 21, 2023).

J. V. Cunningham was a poet, a close textual reader, and a great scholar of Renaissance culture. From Cunningham, Sheridan learned to read texts as culturally and historically situated; many poems of the Renaissance are written "less by a man than by a tradition" (Blau, 2003b, p. 70). He also adopted Cunningham's attitude toward language—Cunningham was epigrammatic as a poet, and he taught Sheridan to write in a style that was fastidious and precise. Cunningham used to say, "Don't volunteer. Don't say more than you need to." Sheridan remembers wanting to be like Cunningham as a scholar; he experienced his classes as though he was learning to play a game. But he also remembers that Cunningham was a terrible teacher because he was mean to his students, catching them in their inexactitude and humiliating them, often making them cry.

Allen Grossman was brilliant as a professor and bardic as a poet. His lectures focused intensely on what poems said, but, ironically, they were often so far beyond Sheridan that he didn't understand what Grossman was saying. From Grossman, Sheridan learned to take seriously what poets say—to believe them and to attend to each line with devoted seriousness—and his stance shifted from the New Critics' focus on technique to the sacredness of poetic meaning. As with Cunningham, Sheridan learned to see himself differently under Grossman; he adopted his attitude and tried on an identity. But Sheridan tells me he didn't want to be like Grossman because he couldn't imagine himself in that role. Grossman was doing serious work.

Sheridan's dissertation on the devotional poetry of George Herbert represents the fruit of their combined influence along with Sheridan's own budding scholarship. His preface acknowledges his teachers' influence:

> My interest in George Herbert and in devotional poetry was first generated and has since been sustained by the contagious enthusiasm and moral example of Professor Allen Grossman, whose discourse I echo throughout these pages. My interest in the larger field of Renaissance studies was first stimulated by Professor J. V. Cunningham, whose own criticism and scholarship I try to emulate in all my work. (Blau, 1967, v)

Shortly after defending his dissertation, Sheridan joined the faculty at the University of Michigan, the site of his first lectures on Milton's *Paradise Lost*. He carried his teachers with him—their enthusiasm, their moral example, their scholarship—and yet, dissatisfied with their pedagogy and with his own practice, he entered the field, learning for himself how to teach.

Apprenticing into the Love of Learning and the Conundrum of Loving the Master

What I've discovered in researching Sheridan's educational biography brings me back to my own transformation as his student and to George Bogin's poem "Nineteen." That is, to love. Lovely last chance, first love; love without relationship; love founded on no experience.

Sheridan argues in his commentary that Bogin's poem isn't about love at all. But, I wonder, maybe it touches a place where love might begin: noticing a space of emptiness, a recognition of possible fulfillment, a desire, a hope, the search for a beloved led by faith in who someone might be. Aren't these feelings at the heart of a conscious decision to change? That is, isn't it something like love that made Sheridan want to be one of the kids in the sun room, in the Forum Club, in on Ciardi's New Critical literary secrets? Isn't it love that makes a student want to echo or emulate their teacher? At the very least, love must account for some part of the feeling that is the thought. Falling in love with the idea of intelligence, with masculine toughness, with intellectual generosity are close in kind to Bogin's attraction to cuteness. Maybe because Sheridan's experience was literary or because it was in pursuit of deeper meaning, his love is somehow more serious. But Bogin made his love into a poem; what could be more serious than that? Is a love of ideas wiser than Bogin's adolescent infatuation? I'm not so sure. Wisdom, it seems to me, comes after the shock of inchoate feelings; and "true" love—like "true" knowledge—is this feeling transformed through relationship and time and openhearted commitment, through one's return to oneself and to the beloved and to uncertainty.

Bogin's poem makes me reconsider the feelings that I had entering Sheridan's class. On the first day of "Literature and Teaching," I was already middle aged, but I was hoping—perhaps sentimentally, perhaps naively—to become the learner I hadn't yet been in school. The workshop opens with an invitation to enter a complex drama: participants imagine themselves as high schoolers who ask questions about what a commentary is or might be. But the workshop also invites us to imagine and to enact possible future-teaching selves and best-student selves, and, through serious scholarship, through writing and discussing and playing at different ways of contributing, these selves become realer, truer. Somewhere near the center of this apprenticeship was Sheridan, who, somehow, impossibly, seemed to experience every commentary as a new opportunity to learn. Even after he had likely heard the same questions asked countless times from countless students in previous years, he heard my questions, honored my confusion, and drew me in closer to the community. He wasn't merely modeling; that is, as far as I could tell, he wasn't performing some perverse school drama but was actively taking part in an open, ongoing, and still-emerging conversation about George Bogin's "Nineteen" and what it might mean to contribute to a discussion about literature.

As much as this poetic return delights me, I'm troubled by the possibility that, in academic apprenticeship, one must fall in love with one's teacher. Academic apprenticeship encourages newcomers to identify with masterful practitioners and to take part in the problems, questions, dispositions, attitudes, languaging practices, and motives of the learning community. When teachers act as craft masters of their discipline, they become a kind of content that students learn to become through imitation, through appropriation. Appropriation creates tension; caught between acting as the teacher or acting as one's self, a student experiences dialectical pulls and double binds of competing motives and activity systems (Russell, 1997, pp. 516–519). This tension exists in all learning environments, but academic apprenticeship likely exacerbates it, particularly for students who don't see themselves in their teacher. Centripetal participation may seemingly be more demanding for a community's most peripheral students, which means that academic apprenticeship may deepen and reinforce inequity. This is a deep and pernicious problem for academic apprenticeship as an instructional model, especially if its overriding aim is, as Sheridan claims, "identity work"—that is, "the work of assisting students in the process of coming to see themselves as contributing members of a genuine community of learners" (Blau, 2023, pp. 305–306).

Teachers might reduce this tension by helping students see that the role of contributing members isn't restricted to or defined by a particular identity or practice. Lave and Wenger (1991) argue emphatically that a community of practice has no single core or center (pp. 36–37). It is part of the teacher's work to do justice to the diversity of relations in varying forms of membership. To act as a craft master in this way is to contribute while staying open to the endless diversity of possible approaches, unwilling to accept anything as more than provisionally true. To be central is to be an imitable public, perpetual learner.

And yet many students identify as contributors by seeing themselves in the teacher, the teacher in themselves. I did. Sheridan enacted my values and fulfilled them in ways that I wasn't yet ready to. Like Sheridan's childhood experience of sitting in the sun room and listening to the older kids talk, I remember sitting in "Literature and Teaching" thinking, "I want to talk like that." Or, following Lave's (2019) wisdom that "'What you know' may be better thought of as doing rather than having something," (p. 95) what I was feeling, though I didn't know it then, was "I want to know like that."

Sheridan's teaching against teaching lent authority to my feelings, gave me language to voice them, and affirmed my identity in our shared role. This leads me to wonder if I fell in love with Sheridan's teaching because I saw so much of myself in him: white, Jewish, male, alienated by school, subversive, contrarian. Was it our affinity that made my experience so powerful? I'm troubled by this thought and by the possible irresolvability of this problem. And I'm troubled by the idea that I've been merely mimicking him. And yet through mimicry, I've become more knowledgeable about who I am and what I feel. Sheridan helped me discover myself as a student in good faith, he helped me find my voice as a teacher, and he helped me recover my curiosity. I know that the impassioned speeches I make in my own classes—polemics cast in the same pitch and same phrasing that I heard in Sheridan's classes—are impossibly both testament to and refutation of his experiential and transformative pedagogy.

Sheridan started experimenting with the commentary project as a way to teach Milton. His syllabus from 2003 introduces the genre: a commentary may be "an explication or analysis of a complicated idea, an exploration or inquiry into a problematic passage or concept, a meditation on a narrated event or theological doctrine, or a reflection on some lines or scene of interest" (Blau,

2003a, p. 1). Through years of continued practice, he learned about *Paradise Lost*, about the repertoire of writerly and readerly moves that students often make as they invent an academic genre, about the principles that underlie academic apprenticeship. By 2007, Sheridan had reframed the commentary project as a workshop to teach teachers, though in his presentations, like in an unpublished paper shared in 2008 at Writing Research Across Borders, Sheridan is clear that his findings are provisional and that he is engaged in an open study—the paper concludes with a postscript: "Every pedagogical method and experiment, no matter how efficacious, creates new problems and invites questions to trouble its findings" (Blau, 2008, p. 14). "Academic Writing as Participation" ends with a similar call for continued experimentation with commentaries "to improve and perfect our practice in the face of any problems that might arise" (Blau, 2010, p. 54).

But as Sheridan has refined the practice into a workshop for teachers, what was an open study has settled into a script—so much so that it is almost indistinguishable from 2010 to 2023: same poem, same questions, same commentary. This isn't to suggest that the project has lost any of its transformative power—it worked on me on the first day of "Literature and Teaching," and I've seen something similar happen for newcomers in Sheridan's and in my own classes ever since. The commentary project is, without doubt, an artifact of masterful teaching, and its results, as I have continued to experience them, are almost magical. But the more it has become a transferable, transmittable, performable workshop that anyone can try for themselves, the more its words have become an incantation, the more its facilitator, seemingly spellbound, has shifted in his role from learner to teacher. The workshop script has troublesomely become a *teaching*.

I'd be wise, then, to reject Sheridan's scripts as false knowledge and imitate instead his insatiable love of learning. Sheridan's project isn't finished, complete. No, we—my students and I—must tarry; wrestle; question; enact; test it using different texts; trace its principles; disrupt its center; thaw its language and flex it; create new and more useful approaches; expand its pathways for new participants, new possibilities. I know that nothing in Sheridan's teaching is ultimately true. And I know that he knows this, too.

"The test of true knowledge," he writes, "lies not in its possession but in the capacity of its holder to relinquish it in the interest of learning" (Blau, 2006, False Knowledge and True Knowledge section, para. 8). This is the mentor whom I know and love; this is the craft master who is always interested in learning, whose questions have become my questions—our questions. In this voice, I hear, too, the mentors that he learned to echo and emulate, the transformative experiences that gave his teaching its color and pitch and substance. I've internalized my teacher's voice as completely as I can, so much so that I can't be sure who it is who says, "Teaching is often the enemy of learning rather than its instrument." Have I been taught to say these words? Have I learned them for myself?

I can hear Sheridan's voice clearly, still resonant, as I remember visiting him in his office just after I graduated with my master's. I was a newcomer entering the profession, about to begin my first year. What advice did he have for me? What did he say that has stayed with me and remained at the heart of my practice?

"You can't always teach," he told me, "but you can always learn."

Works Cited

Blau, S. (1967). *Texts and contexts: Studies toward a reading of George Herbert* (Publication No. 6716537) [Doctoral dissertation, Brandeis University]. ProQuest Dissertations & Theses.

Blau, S. (1987). Contexts for competence in composition. *The Quarterly of the National Writing Project*, 9(4), 4–7, 27.

Blau, S. (1993). *Building bridges between literary theory and the teaching of literature* (Report Series 5.6). National Research Center on Literature Teaching and Learning.

Blau, S. (2003a). *English 162, Milton* [Syllabus]. Santa Barbara, California: University of California.

Blau, S. (2003b). *The literature workshop: Teaching texts and their readers*. Heinemann.

Blau, S. (2006). *Unchanging principles and practices for change* [Speech]. National Writing Project Annual Meeting, Nashville, TN. https://

lead.nwp.org/knowledgebase/unchanging-principles-and-practices-for-change/

Blau, S. (2008). *Toward the experimental confirmation of North American genre theory: A study of student online forum writing in undergraduate literature classes* [Conference session]. Writing Research Across Borders 2008 Conference, University of California, Santa Barbara, CA, United States.

Blau, S. (2009, March 13). *Discovering my intellectual identity in reading Norman Mailer* [Video]. Digital Archive of Literacy Narratives. www.thedaln.org/#/detail/4a38893e-3545-4b49-a97c-56f299d8e272

Blau, S. (2010). Academic writing as participation: Writing your way in. In P. Sullivan, H. Tinberg, & S. Blau (Eds.), *What is "college-level" writing? Vol. 2. Assignments, readings, and student writing samples* (pp. 29–56). National Council of Teachers of English.

Blau, S. (2011a). *Assignment for the first week with a note on reading Milton* [Class handout]. Columbia University, A&HE 5514.

Blau, S. (2011b). Fostering authentic learning in the literature classroom. In J. Milner & C. Pope (Eds.), *Engaging American novels: Lessons from the classroom* (pp. 3–17). National Council of Teachers of English.

Blau, S. (2023). On not teaching college-level reading in order that students might learn it: Honoring our pedagogical legacy in the composition classroom. In P. Sullivan, H. Tinberg, & S. Blau (Eds.), *Deep reading, deep learning* (Vol 2., pp. 299–314). Peter Lang.

Bloom, H. (1997). *The anxiety of influence: A theory of poetry*. Oxford University Press.

Lave, J. (2019). *Learning and everyday life: Access, participation, and changing practice*. Cambridge University Press.

Lave, J., & Wenger, E. (1991). *Situated learning: Legitimate peripheral participation*. Cambridge University Press.

Mehta, J., & Fine, S. (2019). *In search of deeper learning: The quest to remake the American high school*. Harvard University Press.

Russell, D. (1997). Rethinking genre in school and society: An activity theory analysis. *Written Communication*, *14*(4), 504–554. https://doi.org/10.1177/0741088397014004004

Smith, C. H. (2012). Interrogating texts: From deferent to efferent and aesthetic reading practices. *Journal of Basic Writing*, *31*(1), 59–79.

II

"Milton said you can never have a church of more than one member, because as religious as he was, he knew that as soon as you have more than one member, you have somebody telling somebody else how to think and how to pray."

—Blau interview, 2021

Chapter Five

What We Talk about When We Talk about Theory: Sheridan Blau, Contemporary Theory, and the Teaching of Literature

Deborah Appleman

> *As long as teachers are teaching, students are not going to learn, because the kind of experience teachers have that enables them to learn what they have to teach is the experience that students need to have, if they are to be the ones who learn.*
>
> —Sheridan Blau

When it comes to literary interpretation, Sheridan Blau is a bundle of contradictions. Although he is a masterful teacher of literature, he often minimizes the role of teaching in the interpretive process. This is a precarious position to hold for a teacher of hundreds of literature teachers. When pressed, he worries that teachers get in the way of the interpretive process, which he describes as natural, almost mystical. One might think that the frame of reader response, focusing on the transactional nature of reading, would help explain Sheridan's emphasis on valorizing the response of the reader. Yet he somehow overlooks the pedagogical implications of creating a classroom that enables that kind of response.

Sheridan is also both well versed in, yet skeptical of, contemporary literary theory, including Reader-Response Theory, Deconstruction, Gender Theory, Marxist Theory, Postcolonial Theory. Yet despite or perhaps because of his familiarity with them, Sheridan remains skeptical of the role of these theories in the contemporary language arts classroom. Rather than seeing these theoretical frames as guiding and enriching a reader's response, Sheridan often eschews their role to the individual reader as useless at best, intrusive at worst. He worries that the frames of literary theory will preempt the natural and authentic responses of the reader. This skepticism is guided by Sheridan's reverence for the natural brilliance of individual readers and his wariness of the ways in which our teaching can sometimes, ironically, get in the way of student learning.

This chapter explores the complexities of literary interpretation from, if you will, a Blauian perspective. We will explore the nuances of what it actually means to teach literature from Sheridan's perspective, since he seems to both humbly and fiercely minimize the effect of teaching on literary response. Similarly, using Sheridan's own ambivalence to contemporary theory, we will appraise its usefulness in the literature classroom as well as its place in the evolution of the field of English education. As preparation for this chapter and to be sure I accurately presented Sheridan's perspective on literary theory, I asked him to describe his current thinking about it. With his permission, I have integrated excerpts from his correspondence with me.

Sheridan and the Teaching of Literature

Although he is well known for contributing to many aspects of English language arts—the National Writing Project, English language arts teacher education, and governance and policy matters through NCTE, to name a few—Sheridan is also considered to be a kind of guru for the teaching of literature. He has given countless national and international presentations about the teaching of literature to hundreds of thousands adoring teachers. Perhaps more significantly, he has trained thousands of literature teachers and English teacher educators. For example, in his award-winning book *The Literature Workshop*, Sheridan recreates some of his renowned teacher workshops to accomplish the following:

- help students read more difficult texts than they think they can read
- explore where interpretations come from
- consider problematic background knowledge in teaching texts
- navigate competing and contradictory interpretations
- explore what's worth saying about a literary text
- balance respect for readers with respect for texts and intellectual authority
- ensure that literary discussions are lively and productive (Blau, 2003)

This list of goals reveals some significant aspects of Sheridan's philosophy of teaching literature. He has high expectations for students' ability to read difficult and canonical texts; he respects both readers and authors and thinks common ground can be forged between their respective and sometimes competing authority; and he finds intrusive and cumbersome apparatuses such as background knowledge about authors as well as background information on literary theory. It is the conversations about literature among and between readers that are as important to Sheridan as the act of reading itself. This latter point may have a great deal to do with Sheridan's relentlessly social self. Reading literature for Sheridan is not a solitary activity. It is a social one, where understanding texts and affinity for the act of reading happens in social contexts. If it is scholarship, it is scholarship in community with others. If it is teaching, it is teaching that activates a group discussion that extends well beyond teacher talk or even teacher-student discourse.

When I consider Sheridan's perspectives on teaching literature, I often think about his original training as a Milton scholar. His embrace of a wide variety of texts to teach, both canonical and contemporary, might have served as a kind of literary corrective to a predictable, steady diet of classic literature. His fervent belief in the interpretive powers of young people as well as the advantage of creating confusion rather than clarity seems universes away from a scholarly New Critical recitation in a seminar room at the University of Michigan. Perhaps his embrace of ambiguity and his distaste for approaches to the teaching of literature that seem overly intellectual can be traced back to a sense he had that the teaching and learning of literature needs to be more inclusive, more spontaneous, more affectively derived. This feeling might well have influenced his pedagogical practice, which I will now attempt to briefly describe.

Sheridan in Action

I'll never forget the first time I saw Sheridan teach literature. It was nearly three decades ago, in a crowded meeting room at the old Bismarck Hotel in Chicago for NCTE's Assembly of Research Annual Meeting. Sheridan was teaching a short-short story, in the genre of sudden fiction, called "Any Minute Mom Should Come Blasting through the Door" by David Ordan. The story is dramatic, astonishing, and unusual—a boy's mother drops dead while she is making him a sandwich.

Sheridan's pedagogical approach was as follows:

He read the very short text aloud to great effect. Then he asked each person to underline or highlight a line or a phrase that "stood out to them, that struck them in a particularly evocative way." Sheridan then did what he called a "rendering," in which he reread the text very slowly and instructed the group to read along when he got to the line they had underlined. Some lines were read just by Sheridan, some by only one or two other readers, and others by a whole chorus, for example the line, "That's when you've got your whole life to live, and all it's going to be is one excuse after another, for why you didn't save her." Another line that nearly everyone in the room chimed in on was "I should have known better." With the participation of the group, Sheridan created a kind of verbal underlining where the readers actually underscored the most significant passages of the text, first individually and then collectively, a classic Blauian move. Sheridan then asked the group to write individually about their response to both the short story and the rendering. Then he asked the participants from groups of three or four to share their responses.

Those responses were subsequently shared with the entire group, evoking a "terrific" or "interesting" or a sigh of either surprise or delight from Sheridan. He refrained from commenting directly on the text itself or on the ways in which each response did or didn't contribute to our collective understanding of the story. The responses were left uncategorized or evaluated, though appreciated, and somewhat left to quiver in their raw emotion. That was it—no explicit reader-response query of what this might have transactionally evoked, no feminist theory about the role of women and mothers and why she was making a sandwich, no psychological theory on what effect the sudden death would have on the narrator, no formalist discussion of style or voice. We read it and responded. Sheridan was the conductor, but he didn't sing along.

This approach is consonant with Sheridan's belief about the main purpose of teaching literature. He writes:

> The responsibility of every teacher of literature must first be that of providing students with ample opportunities to experience what it means to engage authentically with texts that move and delight their readers, and to discover their own capacity to reflect on their experience, and express dimensions of that experience (including confusion and indifference) in a community of readers who are engaged in sharing and interrogating and celebrating their individual and collective experience. (Blau, 2022)

This sentiment is very much in line with Robert Scholes's notion of the "crafty reader." Scholes believes interpreting literature can be learned and practiced and demystified but that the act of reading and interpretation cannot be separated from the lived experiences of readers. "We must open the way between the literary and the verbal text and the social text in which we live" (24). The notion of "authentic engagement" is also very much in line with Louise Rosenblatt's formulation of the transactional nature of reader response. But reader response is also a theory that Sheridan gently yet firmly repudiates.

Wasn't That Reader Response?

To some astute observers of literature pedagogy, the foregoing description of Sheridan teaching the short story might seem grounded in the theory of reader response, in which individual readers are encouraged to transact directly with the text, and the "meaning" or significance of the text is derived from that transaction. Decades ago, in response to the New Criticism when it was actually "new," Louise Rosenblatt located the meaning of a text not in the autonomous text but within the transaction between the reader and the text: "the reading of any work of literature is, of necessity, an individual and unique occurrence involving the mind and emotions of some particular reader and a particular text at a particular time under particular circumstances" (*Literature as Exploration,* 132).

Readers bring their experiences both textual and otherwise. What an adolescent reader brings to the transaction with a text is *reader* knowledge (Rosenblatt, *The Reader).* It is precisely the importance of reader knowledge that middle and high school teachers have counted on to help create robust and meaningful interactions with literature.

The decontextualized, New Critical view of literature, as autonomous artifact, the one that Sheridan as a Milton scholar was most likely encouraged to practice, is what brought many literature teachers to view reader response as a kind of humane corrective. What counts as literary knowing then, what constitutes literary knowledge, exists *both* inside *and* outside the text rather than drawing some kind of interpretive red line between the text and the reader.

To be sure, Sheridan's approach valorizes the reader's response, although he is in reality fonder of reader-response theory as a pedagogical practice rather than as a theory. This is an important element of Sheridan's stance on theory. He sees literary theories as separate and potentially intrusive frameworks that can distort or artificially influence a reader's natural engagement with literature. In fact, as with other literary theories, Sheridan refuses reader response. He writes:

> My account of how students develop as persons who can write and talk about literature, both to clarify their own thinking and feelings about what they have read and to contribute to a discussion of texts in a community of readers does not suggest any subscription on my part to what many teachers mistakenly refer to as "reader-response theory." I am not talking about

> how an individual reader interrogates a text. If there is a theory informing my account of classroom discourse about literature, it is situated learning theory, not literary theory. (Personal communication, June 1, 2022)

In some ways here, Sheridan may be making a distinction without a difference. Reader response is often used as a kind of learning theory, an explanation for what happens when students read texts that can inform how teachers should teach them. What makes Sheridan such a remarkable teacher is his unfailing attention to the characteristics of the readers in his classroom as well as his willingness to amplify and honor the readings and interpretations of his students. These predispositions seem to me to be the hallmark of the educational implications of reader-response theory, whether or not Sheridan wants to acknowledge it as such.

Sheridan's Objections to Literary Theory

What is at the core of Sheridan's objection to the inclusion of literary theory in the secondary curriculum? As a teacher and practitioner, Sheridan is an incurable romantic and a kind of experiential purist. He firmly believes that literary response is both personal and spontaneous. Anything that interferes with that natural process should be eschewed. For Sheridan, most literary theory exists as an unwelcome presence, a third wheel, a stranger interrupting the intimacy between reader and text. He writes:

> What I want to avoid is the usurpation of the literary experience by an imposed critical lens, before the student has begun to construct his or her own reading and response to the text, which might be a highly ethical response that emerges unprompted. And this brings me to my principal objection to the teaching of critical theory as a mode or lens for an initial reading of a text. That objection begins with the anti-literary or hyper-literate reading of a literary work as an object for critique and analysis from a superior stance—a stance that Wayne Booth has referred to as "overstanding the text." The first responsibility of a reader of literature or of any work of art (most especially works curated by literate friends or possibly responsible and respected teachers) is to submit oneself to the experience of the work by reading it in good faith and with an open heart, or what

> is sometimes referred to as "the immersive experience," and what virtually every respected literary theorist from Aristotle to Sir Philip Sidney, to Northrop Frye has insisted is the first and primary responsibility of the auditor or reader. (Blau, 2022)

It is not that Sheridan is completely opposed to theory; he just doesn't want theories to be introduced to students prematurely, before they are able to engage naturally using their own responses. While I like to think of literary theories as critical lenses, Sheridan believes that those lenses don't help students see more clearly; rather, they distort what they are viewing. He doesn't want prior knowledge of the lenses to preemptively influence a reader's response. This is a fair point. In order to prevent theory-influenced responses or interpretations to become automatic and inauthentic, I suggest we consider the power of multiple perspectives. In other words, if students are presented with multiple possibilities for interpretation, one cannot accuse the resulting interpretation as being "canned."

Sheridan also differentiates and evaluates the theories based on where they originated. He rejects theories that originated in a field of study other than literary studies. While this issue is particularly salient for critical race theory, it's a charge of origin that could be leveled against other theories as well. Here's Sheridan's perspective on the matter:

> But finally, it's not that I am against teaching students some of the basic ideas of current critical theories. It's that I am against privileging the fashionable theories imported from philosophy and the social sciences for formulaic use in the classroom over the culturally acquired theories that students carry around with them for use in conversations with friends and in their interpretation of ordinary life and popular texts. Students must first learn to respect and employ those personally authoritative theories in their discourse about their genuine experience of literature, before they are provided with formulas dictated to them for use in their academic reading lives. (Blau, 2022)

This point of Sheridan's is important indeed. Sheridan raises the question of the degree to which the frames provided by literary theory are natural and organic or whether they are frames artificially imposed. Sheridan also feels that much of what is taught as literary theory is not literary theory at all, a legitimate point that has made me hesitate about the application of critical race theory to literary study, given its origin in legal studies. Here, Sheridan's objection to studying literary theory is both disciplinary and educational. As a well-trained literary scholar, he resists the conflation of literary study with other disciplines. From an educational perhaps almost Deweyan perspective, he wanted to be certain that students' encounters with literature are authentically grounded in their own experiences. On the other hand, I think it's unclear what he means by "the culturally acquired theories that students carry around with them for use in conversations with friends and in their interpretation of ordinary life and popular texts." One might argue that all those culturally derived theories are not neutral but are inflected by those very cultural forces, such as issues of power and privilege that shape the theories themselves.

The Changing Role of Literary Theory in Secondary Classrooms

During the decades of Sheridan's career as a literary scholar and teacher of literature, the teaching of literature has undergone significant changes. At the prompting of literary scholars, classroom practitioners, and, perhaps most importantly, an increased acknowledgment of the diversity of our students and our schools, English language arts (ELA) educators have reconsidered the texts, contexts, and pedagogical approaches that comprise the teaching of literature (Appleman, 2015; Beach et al., 2021; Gillespie, 2010). Until recently, literary theory had not been regularly integrated into preservice teacher education, although its inclusion in ELA methods courses has become more widespread (Appleman, 2015; Beach et al., 2021).

It is not only Sheridan who has articulated ambivalence about contemporary literary theory. Literary theory and ELA education have had a complicated relationship. In the 1960s, the field of English language arts moved from a strict allegiance to a New Critical approach (Richards, 1956) to a reader- (and student-) focused emphasis on reader-response theory (Beach, 1993;

Rosenblatt, 1976). This theoretical approach figured strongly in literature instruction for several decades, although the tenets of reader-response theory were often not explicitly taught (Beach et al., 2006). More recently, the presence of literary theory in ELA classrooms has evolved to include multiple theoretical perspectives (Appleman, 2015; Gillespie, 2010; Shade-Eckert, 2006; Soter et al., 2008). This approach challenges the mono-theoretical approach by offering a variety of theoretical perspectives, including such theories as feminist or gender criticism, postcolonial, new historical, structuralism deconstruction, and, most recently and controversially, critical race theory.

Although it is still not universally reflected in the practice of secondary teachers, the notion that literary theory can be useful has gained a greater voice in the field of ELA education. Critics such as Robert Scholes (1985) have forcefully argued that contemporary literary theory opens the barriers between the literary text and the social text in which we live. It is at this intersection of text and social context that the explicit study of contemporary literary theory can help adolescent readers make meaning of literary texts, as well as the ideologies of power and privilege that are inscribed therein. In other words, in the Freirean tradition, literary theory helps students read both words and worlds (Freire & Macedo, 1987).

A Counter-Argument: Why Teach Literary Theory

The purpose of teaching literary theory at the secondary level is not to turn adolescents into critical theorists; rather, it is to encourage adolescents to inhabit theories comfortably enough to construct their own readings and to learn to appreciate the power of multiple perspectives. Literary theory can help secondary literature classrooms become sites of constructive and transactive activity, where students approach texts with curiosity, authority, and initiative. Several English educators have written books specifically designed to help secondary teachers navigate the often-unfamiliar area of theory and integrate considerations of theory into their pedagogy (Appleman, 2015; Gillespie, 2010; Shade-Eckert, 2006). Others, such as Lois Tyson (2015), offer extended models of teaching literary theory that can be used at both the secondary and college levels. These texts have made the incorporation of literary theory into literature instruction both more possible and more prevalent. For example, teaching literary theory is now frequently included in preservice literature methods classes (Appleman, 2015; Beach et al, 2015; Webb, 2001, 2015) as well as in inservice training. Several recent books on literature teaching include literary theory (Appleman, 2015; Beach, et al, 2016; Gillespie, 2010; Shade-Eckert, 2006) and conferences such as NCTE, IRA, and LRA include teacher-led sessions that offer specific lessons and rationales for teaching literary theory.

In addition to the work of college teachers and English educators (Appleman, 2015; Gillespie, 2010; Shade-Eckert, 2006; Soter et al., 2008), there is a proliferation of material generated by secondary ELA teachers promoting and facilitating the use of literary theory in the secondary language arts classroom. Teacher websites and blogs are filled with tips, text selections, and the rationales for teaching with theory. For example, Cody Miller (2016) in a recent NCTE blog writes, "We know that knowledge is not objective; what is considered 'right' and 'common sense' are often manifestations of dominant cultural values and norms. Using literary theory with fiction and nonfiction alike helps students articulate and confront their own belief system in analyzing the world around them.". When literary theory is taught to students as a framework for understanding the broader sociocultural realities students experience, then theory is not a form of academic esoterica. Rather, literary theory becomes a vehicle for students to adopt and implement new perspectives on a similar topic.

Other teacher voices laud the importance of teaching literary theory. The Moore English website (2018) offers several lessons and teacher-generated material on teaching critical lenses and offers these primary reasons to use critical lenses in the secondary literature classroom:

1. **Improve critical thinking.** First, applying a critical lens to a text requires students to make inferences, analyze text, and synthesize the text with the critical lens. Further, all of these skills improve students' ability to think critically about a text.

2. **Close reading.** In order to successfully apply a critical lens, students have to read a text at depth, paying attention to details. This includes figurative language, symbolism, and diction. Such focus improves students' understanding of a text.
3. **Perspective taking.** Because literary lenses have a variety of motives, applying various lenses requires students to "try on" different perspectives. By "trying on" an alternative perspective, students have the chance to understand a different way of life.
4. **Encouraging empathy.** As students try on multiple lenses and perspectives, they begin to empathize with different causes, beliefs, and value systems. And any practice that encourages students to practice empathy is an essential part of preparing them for life as future leaders.

When taught explicitly, literary theory can provide a repertoire of critical lenses through which to view literary texts as well as the ideologies of power and privilege that are often unexamined in literature. This ability to interrogate texts is important, as many classical and canonical texts come under fire because a contemporary reappraisal has revealed problematic content due to offensive language, situations, or stereotypical portrayals. Teachers are often confronted with the dilemma of either teaching difficult texts uncritically or choosing not to teach them at all. For example, it may no longer be advisable to teach *Adventures of Huckleberry Finn* or *To Kill a Mockingbird* without regard for the problems engendered by the use of offensive language and demeaning portrayals of characters representing historically marginalized people. That decision privileges the arbitrary literary value of a canonical text over the significance and relevance of a changing student demographic. However, banning or removing these books from the literature curriculum also removes the opportunity for students to engage in critical analysis. By reading texts with theory rather than banishing them altogether from the secondary classroom, students can learn to disrupt, resist, and analyze the texts by using interpretive tools that literary theory provides. Rather than have the teacher make curricular decisions on the basis of power and privilege, students can do that interpretive work themselves. The students become an important part of the conversations about curriculum content and text inclusion rather than cancellation (Appleman, 2022).

On the other hand, educators should not simply offer a single theory to their students, for that truly is dogmatic/propagandistic teaching. Even a reader-response lens is limiting if it is the only possible theoretical frame in which one can produce a reading (Appleman, 2015; Beach et al., 2021). These multiple ways of seeing have become vital skills in increasingly diverse classrooms as educators explore the differences between and among us, what separates us and what binds us together.

Changing Goals of Literature Instruction

Teaching literary theory is not a repudiation of the goal of teaching adolescents to become better readers. It is, in fact, a way of doing just that. Lisa Shade-Eckert (2006) points out, "Teaching students to use literary theory as a strategy to construct meaning is teaching reading. Learning theory gives them a purpose in approaching a reading task, helps them make and test predictions as they read, and provides a framework for student response and awareness of their stance in approaching a text" (p. 8).

While incorporating literary theory into the high school literature curriculum can serve both text-oriented and student-oriented goals, for those of us who engage with adolescents through literature, our charge is not simply to help students read and write; it is to help them use the skills of writing and reading to understand the world around them.

As Lois Tyson explains,

> theory can help us learn to see ourselves in our world in valuable new ways, ways that can influence how we educate our children, parents and teachers; how we view television, from the nightly news to situation comedies; how we behave as voters and consumers; how we react to others with whom we do not agree on social, religious, and political issues; and how we recognize and deal with our own motives, fears, and desires. And if we believe that human productions—not just literature but also, for example, film, music, art, science, technology, and architecture—are outgrowths of human experience and therefore reflect human desire, conflict, and potential, then we can learn to interpret those productions in order to learn so something important about ourselves as a species. Critical theory . . . provides excellent tools for that endeavor, tools

> that not only show us our world and ourselves through new and valuable lenses but also can strengthen our ability to think logically, creatively, and with a good deal of insight. (2015, p. 2)

We want our students to learn to reflect on themselves and the world around them with insight and perspective. We want our students to become, in the words of bell hooks, "enlightened witnesses" (1997, p. 8), critically vigilant about the world in which we live. In order to become enlightened witnesses, young people must understand the workings of ideology as we teach them literature. These ideologies include prevailing social attitudes about race, gender, religion, and ethnicity—ideologies that are inscribed in the texts students read, in the structure of their schools, in the beliefs of their families and communities, in the political systems at play. Inviting students to acquire the tools they need to read these ideologies may often be fraught with conflict and resistance, but it is one of the primary reasons for reading literature in the first place.

Ideology and Literary Study

Teaching literary theory in the secondary school helps young people learn to read the often-unarticulated assumptions or ideologies that are present both in and out of school. From the perspective of literature teaching, literary theory provides students with the tools to uncover the often-invisible workings of literary texts. As Bonnycastle explains:

> The main reason for studying theory at the same time as literature is that it forces you to deal consciously with the problem of ideologies. . . . There are many truths and the one you will find depends partly on the ideology you start with. [Studying theory] means you can take your own part in the struggles for power between different ideologies. It helps you to discover elements of your own ideology, and understand why you hold certain values unconsciously. It means no authority can impose a truth on you in a dogmatic way—and if some authority does try, you can challenge that truth in a powerful way, by asking what ideology it is based on. . . . Theory is subversive because it puts authority in question. (1996, p. 34)

A literature or language arts class at the secondary level is an ideal place to help students learn to read and, if necessary, resist the ideology that surrounds them. In our literature classes, we teach texts that are full of ideology. As Fairclough suggests:

> Ideology is most effective when its workings are least visible. . . . Invisibility is achieved when ideologies are brought to discourse not as explicit elements of the text, but as the background assumptions, which, on the one hand, lead the text producer to textualize the world in a particular way, and on the other hand, lead the interpreter to interpret the text in a particular way. Texts do not spout ideology. They so position the interpreter through their cues so that she brings ideologies to the interpretation of texts—and reproduces them in the process! (1989, p. 85)

For example, when we read Frost's "The Road Not Taken," one of the most commonly taught and anthologized poems in Applebee's study, we tend to assert that "taking the road less traveled by" makes all the difference. From Fairclough's perspective, the text "positions" us to embrace the ideologies of American individualism and nonconformity. In Twain's *Adventures of Huckleberry Finn*, a text that is both currently widely taught and banned from classrooms, the racialized portraits of Huck and Jim as well as the use of the "n" word normalize a particular kind of America, one whose ideology of inequality was unquestioned for too long. Our responsibility as literature teachers may well be to help make the ideologies inherent in those texts visible to our students. The best way to uncover and explore these ideologies is through the explicit teaching of contemporary literary theory.

For Sheridan, this notion of reading and resisting ideology is perhaps the most compelling and acceptable reason for teaching with theory. He believes it is imperative to help young people recognize the multiple systems of power and injustice that are at play in our society. He wrote in personal correspondence with me:

> From you, Deborah, I have gotten at least one much more robust and compelling answer about the value of teaching theory to kids. But that answer was only tangentially related

> to the study of literature. Rather, your focus on theory is persuasively based (at least in part) on your admirable desire to help students recognize and critique the multiple systems of injustice that operate to privilege some students and marginalize others in schools and in classrooms and in the administration of rewards and punishments in school systems and in the political communities that control them. Theory here is needed because students (and teachers) are generally unable to recognize the injustices they experience as unjust, but have been conditioned culturally to see as "natural" and inevitable and historically determined (Blau, 2022).

Thus, the argument of using theory to read and resist ideology especially with regard to what Sheridan calls "injustice" is, for him, a powerful one. However, Sheridan's trust in the power of literature itself to teach those lessons of injustice diminishes his sense that teaching with theory can be valuable in this way.

So why wouldn't the same argument hold for seeing the injustices that are represented in novels or stories or poems? They could very well be useful for such purposes after the students have read and discussed a text, but the use of theory would be intellectually and emotionally dishonest if the students were taught texts through a political lens and thereby experienced the text itself through that lens before they had the more direct and immersive experience of the text itself. In most cases, moreover, the experience of a good novel—a novel by Steinbeck or Dickens, or Faulkner, for example—is more powerfully instructive about the nature and sources of injustice in the world and the world of the novel, than any analysis made available through a critical theory (Blau, 2022).

In other words, we need to have the texts do that work; however, the texts themselves might also need to be read through an ideological lens.

Limitations of Teaching with Theory

To be sure, there are limits to this approach to teaching literature. The emphasis on multiplicity can lead to a broad and superficial familiarity with a variety of literary theories rather than a vertical in-depth study of one or two. Teachers need to be mindful to spend enough time with each theory in multiple contexts to help students gain a rich understanding of the theory. Students can also experience the approach as a kind of cookie-cutter one and might thoughtlessly apply theories because they are expected to, not because they have produced authentic readings. This last point is a key element of Sheridan's objections. He writes:

> So, let me finally get directly to my primary reasons for being concerned, if not entirely opposed to the teaching of literary theory to adolescent readers. First, I am concerned about the implications of the very argument that my English dept colleagues typically give in favor of teaching theory. Now that they teach some theories, they assert, their students finally seem to have something to say about the assigned literary works, whereas students previously seemed to have nothing or almost nothing to say. That argument is problematic for a number of reasons, aside from its uncritical preference for copiousness. What it implicitly asserts, however, is that students don't have anything to say about a literary text they have read, unless they are fed an already-prepared formula for talking about a text, which is to say a formula that represents somebody else's thinking or, worse, a prescribed set of questions or focal concerns to be addressed by the theory and not by the student as a reader.
>
> The student reader in this case becomes merely the ventriloquist for the theory, in the same manner that the student who learns and observes the 5-paragraph essay method for composing is not really composing but merely filling in the blank spaces in a pre-composed essay form. Hence teachers resort to giving students something to say, thereby artificially solving the false problem of filling up a page, rather than the real problem represented by the fact that their students seem to have read literary works that have reputedly moved and deeply engaged generations of previous readers, yet seemingly had no expressible impact on their current students. Such an approach to teaching literature is equivalent to the practice of a physician who would treat adolescent anorexia by stuffing the pockets of his patients with coins before having them step on a scale to be weighed. In other words, the resort to theory is frequently evidence of the pedagogical cluelessness of a teacher of literature. (Blau, 2022)

While I admire Sheridan's unwavering faith in the value of "unschooled" and natural student response to a literary text, I firmly reject the accusation that reading with theory causes the student to be a ventriloquist. This is largely because rather than "pushing" a single theoretical perspective to be parroted back, I argue for the importance of multiplicity.

As I have written elsewhere:

> It is very important that we don't offer only a single theory to our students, for that truly is dogmatic or propagandistic teaching. It is the monotheoretical approaches of most secondary English classrooms that drew me to the notion of multiple perspectives as an antidote. Even a reader–response lens is limiting if it is the only possible theoretical frame in which one can produce a reading. Offering students several ways to look at texts does more than help them learn to interpret literature from multiple perspectives; it also helps them develop a more complex way of thinking as they move from the dualism of early adolescence to the relativism of adult thinkers (Perry, 1970). These multiple ways of seeing have become vital skills in our increasingly diverse classrooms as we explore the differences between and among us, what separates us and what binds us together. (Appleman, 2015, p. 30)

Conclusion

The approach of adolescents to read through multiple theoretical perspectives is not solely about how to help students create multiple readings of a literary text, though that is clearly important. The most significant intellectual advantage of using multiple theoretical perspectives as an interpretive tool for literature is to learn to read and resist ideology (Bonnycastle), whether it's the ideology inscribed in a text, in the context in which the book was written, in the canonical context in which the text does or doesn't reside, or in the sociocultural context of school, community, and classroom. It can also help us read the ideology of mandated standards for reading.

By teaching literature with theory, teachers help students decipher the world inscribed within the texts, as well as read the world around them. The teaching of literary theory in secondary English classes will better prepare adolescent readers to respond reflectively and analytically to literary texts, both canonical and multicultural. Contemporary literary theory provides a useful way for all students to read and interpret not only literary texts but also their lives—both in and out of school.

Teaching literary theory in the secondary school also requires a kind of epistemological shift of our goals. No longer are we transmitting cultural heritage in an untroubled way; we are considering that heritage and what it might say about us and our humanity in different ways. Neither are we shifting all the meaning making to the personal experience of the reader. Instead, we offer a kaleidoscope of possible ways of seeing, of possible kinds of learning, of different kinds of knowledge.

This kind of teaching changes our conception of what we teach and why. We are no longer merely transmitting knowledge, offering literature as content, as an aesthetic experience or as neutral artifacts of our collective cultural heritage. Instead, we are offering our students the chance to view the world through a variety of lenses, each offering a unique perspective sure to transform how adolescents read both words and worlds. Even Sheridan grudgingly agrees to the fact that contemporary literary theory does have some value in our literature classrooms. The following is both his endorsement and his qualification:

> In a classroom where literature and literary reading are responsibly taught, the discourse of contemporary critical theories can make a legitimate contribution without becoming the only mode of reading or the only theories that can serve as interpretive lenses. For all readers and speakers and participants in conversations where stories get told or in classrooms where literature is read, every interpretive response is informed by a theory (theories of how families work, or what behaviors are expected or acceptable in given situations, or what friendship entails, or what love requires and so on), and that every student employs a repertoire of theoretical lenses to understand the events and experiences of everyday life. One of the functions of literary study is to expand (largely by exposing and sharing) the repertoire of critical lenses that students can employ in reading texts and reading their worlds; and that process needs to begin by discovering and honoring the interpretive lenses students bring with them to the classroom and that (with the proper invitation) they are fully capable of employing in their

> reading of literature, before they are introduced to the currently fashionable and largely political lenses of contemporary critical theories—theories, by the way, that are based on prior texts and philosophical orientations that students know almost nothing about and are in no position to critique. (Blau, 2022)

As Sheridan acknowledges, literary study can be meaningfully expanded through literary theory to help readers learn to interrogate both texts and worlds. By reading with literary theory, our students can become the enlightened witnesses that bell hooks (1994) calls for, noting how power and privilege are inscribed all around us and learning to read both texts and worlds with a critical eye. We are no longer transmitting knowledge, offering literature as content, as an aesthetic experience, or as neutral artifacts of our collective cultural heritage.

We teachers and our students live in a particularly turbulent time, one fraught with increasing divisiveness and an awareness of the myriad ways in which power and privilege shape the educational experiences of students, especially with regard to inclusion and equity. It is critical for our students to learn to read literary texts *and* to read and resist the instantiation of power and privilege that are inscribed in those texts. These patterns of power and privilege can be best revealed and resisted by considering the ideologies that undergird texts. Literary theory provides students with the tools to uncover the often-invisible workings of the text. Our students can become, with our help, truly educated in the way James Baldwin (1985) envisions, able to critique their own society intelligently and without fear. Sheridan admits that this is a powerful reason for teaching with theory.

In the end, our positions on the role of contemporary theory and the teaching of literature may not be so far apart. As the title of this chapter suggests, perhaps it all depends on what we mean by theory. Sheridan's final point about the teaching of literacy theory is as generous, student-centered, and conciliatory as he is.

Works Cited

Applebee, A. (1993). *Literature in the secondary school: Studies of curriculum and instruction in the United States.* National Council of Teachers of English.

Appleman, D. (2015a). *Critical encounters in secondary English: Teaching literary theory to adolescents.* Teachers College Press.

Appleman, D. (2015b). Critical literary theory in a literature methods class. In J. Brass & A. Webb (Eds.), *Reclaiming English language arts methods courses: Critical issues and challenges for teacher educators in top-down times* (pp. 177–189). Routledge.

Appleman, D. (2022, September 23). "I've become a reluctant warrior against cancel culture." *Newsweek.* www.newsweek.com/cancel-culture-reluctant-warrior-schools-books-teaching-1743395

Baldwin, J. (1985). *The price of the ticket: Collected non-fiction 1948–1985.* St. Martin's Press.

Beach, R. (1993). *A teacher's introduction to reader-response theories.* National Council of Teachers of English.

Beach, R., Appleman, D., Fecho, B., & Simon, R. (2021). *Teaching literature to adolescents* (4th ed.). Routledge.

Beach, R., Appleman, D., Hynds, S., & Wilhelm, J. (2006). *Teaching literature to adolescents.* Lawrence Erlbaum.

Blau, S. (2003). *The literature workshop: Teaching texts and their readers.* Heinemann.

Bonnycastle, S. (2007). *In search of authority: An introductory guide to literary theory* (3rd ed.). Broadview Press.

Carey-Webb, A. (2001). *Literature & lives: A response-based, cultural studies approach to teaching English.* National Council of Teachers of English.

Fairclough, N. (1989). *Language and power.* Longman.

Fitzgerald, F. S. (1964). *The crack-up.* New Directions.

Freire, P., & Macedo, D. P. (1987). *Literacy: Reading the word and the world.* Praeger

Frost, R. (2011). *Robert Frost: Selected poems.* Fall River Press.

Gillespie, T. (2010). *Doing literary criticism: Helping students engage with challenging texts.* Stenhouse.

hooks, b. (1994). *Teaching to transgress: Education as the practice of freedom.* Routledge.

hooks, b. (1997). https://www.mediaed.org/transcripts/Bell-Hooks-Transcript.pdf

Lee, H. (1999). *To kill a mockingbird* (40th anniversary ed.). HarperCollins.

Miller, C. (2016, September 20). Literary theory's potential in secondary ELA classrooms. *National Council of Teachers of English.* https://ncte.org/blog/2016/09/literary-theorys-potential-secondary-ela-classrooms/

Moore, E. (2018). *Introducing literary criticism.* Moore English. https://moore-english.com/introducing-literary-criticism/

Ordan, D. (2013). Any minute Mom should come blasting through the door. In R. Shapard & J. Thomas (Eds.), *Sudden fiction: American short-short stories* (pp. 196–197). Gibbs Smith.

Perry, W. G., Jr. (1970). *Forms of intellectual and ethical development in the college years: A scheme.* Holt, Rinehart & Winston.

Richards, I. A. (2004). *Practical criticism: A study of literary judgment.* Routledge.

Rosenblatt, L. (1994). *The reader, the text, the poem: The transactional theory of the literary work.* Southern Illinois University Press.

Rosenblatt, L. (1995). *Literature as exploration.* Modern Language Association.

Schade-Eckert, L. (2006). *How does it mean? Engaging reluctant readers through literary theory.* Heinemann.

Scholes, R. (1985). *Textual power: Literary theory and the teaching of English.* Yale University Press.

Scholes, R. (2001). *The crafty reader.* Yale University Press.

Soter, A. O., Faust, M., & Rogers, T. (Eds.). (2008). *Interpretive play: Using critical perspectives to teach young adult literature.* Christopher Gordon.

Staton, S. F. (Ed.). (1987). *Literary theories in praxis.* University of Pennsylvania Press.

Twain, M. (2003). *The adventures of Huckleberry Finn.* Bantam. Original work published 1884.

Tyson, L. (2015). *Critical theory today: A user-friendly guide* (3rd ed.). Routledge.

Webb, A. (2015). A cultural studies approach to literature methods. In J. Brass & A. Webb (Eds.), *Reclaiming English language arts methods courses: Critical issues and challenges for teacher educators in top-down times* (pp. 190–202). Routledge.

Chapter Six

Teachers Enacting Norms for Languaging Classroom Relations

Richard Beach and Faythe Beauchemin

At the 2019 NCTE Convention in Baltimore, Richard attended Deborah Appleman and Sheridan Blau's session, a conversation about how to help students think critically about what they read. The norm at most conference sessions involves presenters talking about their ideas without exploring other points of view on the same topic unless a discussant brings up a different viewpoint, or the session is called "a debate." This session was different. The two presenters deviated from these status-quo norms by deliberately not only voicing their competing perspectives on methods for teaching literature but also by openly critiquing each other's stances. Deborah posited the value of students adopting different critical perspectives, the focus of her 2015 book. Sheridan disagreed with her position, remarking that asking students to take critical viewpoints gets in the way of the "natural way a reader reads" and makes it hard for them to talk about how they really feel. He also argued that fostering the adoption of these perspectives intrudes on students' authentic response experience. Deborah countered by stating students always respond from a theoretical or critical point of view. Her remark invited the audience to see the ways student responses to literature are informed not only by theory but also by teachers' influence.

Michael Smith (Appleman, personal communication, 2022) served as discussant at the session. He reports being able to tell the difference between the Appleman and Blau points of view based on their questions. Deborah's question: "To what extent do they believe that which must be learned needs to be taught?" reflects her stance; Sheridan's question does the same: "To what extent do they believe that we learn how to read a text by the text itself, and to what extent is it our job as teachers to celebrate where students are instead of moving them to where they could be?"

Richard described the session as a memorable event. Because of his lifelong relationships with Deborah, Sheridan, and Michael, he had certain expectations and knew that both Deborah and Sheridan valued adopting competing, contrarian stances. However, given the typical norms for NCTE conference sessions that reify shared, compatible perspectives, he was surprised to experience how Deborah and Sheridan were openly willing to challenge each other's positions. What constituted Richard's experience was an engaging tension between assumed norms and Deborah and Sheridan's unique enactment of alternative norms within their session. Richard's response suggests disrupting norms may yield norms as more tentative and flexible (Blommaert, 2018).

In this chapter, we posit that rather than continually adhering to status-quo norms in order to shape classroom interactions, teachers and students might benefit from being open to enacting alternative, unfamiliar classroom norms in ways that invite engaging, novel interactions. We might find it productive to engage classroom interactions that challenge norms.

Teachers and Students Adhering to School and Classroom Norms

Teachers and students acquire norms from previous experiences in related school or classroom contexts (Hinchion, 2020). Based on their experiences in these contexts, students learn to adhere to norms based on noting specific, consistent actions. For example, students may learn a norm when a teacher asks the same follow-up questions in interacting with students (Agha, 2007). Students may reflect on these consistent actions to formulate a model for perceiving follow-up questions as typical for that teacher's interactions. And they may think that enforcing norms is meant to set standards for the right way to do things, like when teachers tell students to be on time for class and punish them for not doing so (Agha, 2007). Just as Richard drew on the norms for presentations and interactions in NCTE conference sessions for responding to Deborah's and Sheridan's interactions, teachers and students draw on norms of classroom presentations or interactions for their own behaviors. For example, while a teacher may explicitly state that they are giving a lecture, it is more likely that they will simply enact the actions of giving a lecture through their embodied actions. They may stand in front of the classroom and talk over an extended period with the students assuming a passive stance based on their acceptance of the norm of teachers giving lectures.

Teachers and students also enact specific identities or roles based on classroom norms. For example, students may adopt identities as readers based on norms operating in a classroom or a school constituting what it means to be a "good" or "poor" reader (Hall, 2012). They may also adhere to norms constituting identities or roles based on certain cultural practices associated with identification with social and racial groups. For instance, hip-hop pedagogy programs create classrooms as spaces that support and draw on experiences of non-dominant racial groups (Alim & Paris, 2017, p. 8).

The particular norms, roles, beliefs, and purposes constituting participation in classrooms is knowledge both teachers and students acquire from schooling systems. These systems employ what they perceive to be relevant, appropriate practices consistent with norms, roles, beliefs, and purposes. For example, teachers and students acquire norms for engaging in discussions that often reify the role of the teacher as central to directing and moderating discussions. A teacher may facilitate a discussion based on having students infer what the teacher perceives as a novel's theme in a manner consistent with the teacher's inference of that theme. However, teachers and students may also deviate from these traditional classroom norms by enacting alternative practices in ways that serve to enhance students' sense of agency. Doing so involves teachers enacting alternative, innovative practices and inviting students to adopt alternative practices and roles that deviate from classroom norms.

Enacting different classroom norms and inviting students to do the same can be controversial. And it requires trust. Teachers are now subject to extensive scrutiny from conservative groups and parents regarding the topics and books they teach. One important norm related to instruction is the idea of freedom to teach, a notion based on trusting educators to determine what and how to teach (Young, 2022). As the "Freedom to Teach: Statement Against Banning Books" states:

> Teachers need our support; they need our trust; they need to have the freedom to exercise their professional judgment. . . . In short, teachers need the freedom to prepare students to become future members of a democratic society who can engage in making responsible and informed contributions and decisions about our world. (National Council for the Social Studies, National Council of Teachers of Mathematics, National Council of Teachers of English, National Science Teaching Association, and the National Coalition Against Censorship, 2022)

One teacher who enacts the norm of the freedom to teach is LaMar Timmons-Long, an English teacher at Brooklyn's A-Tech High School (Young, 2022). Timmons-Long's approach to teaching acknowledges oppressive systems and looks to bring justice-oriented pedagogy into the classroom. Of his approach, he notes: "People may not agree that teachers should have this freedom to teach—I think they're very wrong because when we're creating curriculum, when we're creating lessons, when we're creating experiences with students and for students, my children come first. I think about my kids before I think about anything else" (Young, 2022, p. 23).

Creating experiences "with and for students," as Timmons-Long does, involves collaboration. An understanding of how teachers and students collaboratively enact norms is important, given how students continually attempt to determine the norms or criteria by which their literacy practices are being perceived and evaluated. Teachers may explicitly state norms or criteria for assessing students' writing, yet they are also enacting norms through their actions, such as in their response to and feedback on students' writing. And these norms are not the same as those in online spaces. Blommaert (2018) notes:

> A Facebook update, for instance, demands attendance to the (highly dynamic) norms of literacy and linguistic codes, the genre and register norms of an "update" (not too long,

> preferably multimodal, etc.), the tacit norms of one's community of "friends" regarding certain topics and ways to discuss them (think of prevalent political orientations in one's Facebook community), the Facebook rules of conduct (proscribing certain forms of obscenity, for instance), and the rules of the algorithmic system behind Facebook that render certain updates more visible than others. (p. 50)

Thus, in online contexts, students must understand how to adopt certain practices. Therefore, students continually contextualize their actions by attending to others' reactions to infer evolving norms in certain contexts.

Contextualizing Events Based on Injunctive Versus Descriptive Norms

In contextualizing events based on certain norms, people sense the difference between how injunctive and descriptive norms shape practices (Eyink et al., 2020). Injunctive norms serve to dictate or prescribe what people should or should not do in a specific context in order to achieve positive approval from others. For example, a teacher may tell students that they need to include specific actions to receive a positive evaluation of their essays. Students may then adhere to injunctive norms based on concerns about whether their teacher will approve of their actions (Busch et al., 2019). Highlighting injunctive norms reifies a status-quo focus on achieving performance goals in the classroom related to achieving prescribed extrinsic behavioral outcomes, such as pleasing the teacher by submitting work according to deadlines.

In contrast, descriptive norms are enacted based on what people are doing in a context related to what actions may be most effective in that particular context (Eyink et al., 2020). As a classroom event unfolds unpredictably, teachers and students adhere to descriptive norms based on sensing how they enact innovative, alternative actions—for example, a student raising a provocative question about a new, unrelated topic, resulting in the need to shift norms shaping a discussion. Elizabeth Erdmann, an English teacher, noted that when students sense they are not limited to having to adhere to certain norms, "they don't go in the direction that you would expect and sometimes you're trying to spin it back around and sometimes you're not like, hey, I didn't expect this, let's talk about this. Why did we have this outcome?" (Beach & Beauchemin, 2019, p. 82).

Enacting descriptive norms may shift the focus on achieving learning goals based on injunctive norms to fostering students' desires or curiosity to acquire particular novel, innovative practices. For example, to enact certain unique descriptive norms, teachers can have students generate community agreements based on identifying certain shared norms in a classroom context (O'Connor, 2021). Doing so then allows "students to build a set of expectations for themselves. The students are there every day and hold each other accountable for those expectations as they get to know each other better" (p. 3).

Given these deviations in classroom practices, teachers or students may determine which norms are most salient, and this may inform the adoption of alternatives. Teachers may learn to recognize the value and need to evoke descriptive norms for addressing perceptions of these competing norms to match these norms based on students' contributions and needs (Eyink et al., 2020). For example, teachers may recognize the need to deviate from predetermined lesson plans or structured time schedules to be open to students' enactment of spontaneous deviations from scripted instruction.

Enacting Norms Through Languaging Relations

How, then, do teachers and students enact norms? They enact norms through languaging related to how they use language to enact certain kinds of relations (Beach & Bloome, 2019; Linell, 2009). For example, people may use polite language rather than profanity in interactions with others to enact supportive versus combative relations consistent with norms related to perceptions of the polite versus the profane. People sometimes resist norms and establish new ones in interactions to create engagement.

Languaging Norms Based on "In-Between" Relational Meanings

A languaging perspective posits that rather than acting as individuals, participants act jointly based on their collaborative languaging actions for constructing "in-between" meanings (Bertau, 2014). This means that when someone acts, their activity cannot be accounted as wholly their own—for a person's acts are inevitably "shaped" in part by the acts of the surrounding others and also in part by their reactions to their overall surroundings (both social and physical)—and this is where all the strangeness of the dialogical begins (Shotter, p. 142).

In thinking back to the debate between Sheridan and Deborah Appleman at the NCTE session, the meaning of their interaction derived from the "in-between" language interaction itself to enact a contentious relationship. That they disagreed with each other meant they were languaging an alternative space to enact that relation in ways that deviated from the norms constituting NCTE sessions where each presenter gives their separate presentation.

Teachers Enacting Norms for Classroom Interactions

Teachers *enact* these norms through languaging interactions with students that imply these criteria. For example, teachers may employ and celebrate using informal or alternative dialects/registers related to translanguaging that invite students to employ similar languaging in their writing. An illustration of this approach is the work of Mrs. Hutchins, a first-grade teacher, who wanted to create read-alouds in her classroom that were engaging for her students to develop their listening comprehension in playful ways (Beauchemin, 2019). To accomplish this, she broke the norm that teachers rarely talk about topics central to childhood culture that could be perceived as too "childish" for the serious act of learning in school. Instead, she featured texts that drew upon students' childhood cultures to enact a new norm in her classroom during read-aloud time that centered on humor within childhood culture (Beauchemin, 2019).

In one read-aloud, the teacher asked students to identify something funny in the story, a question asking students to retell what happened in the story in an engaging way. Students offered moments from the text, such as when the dog came out in Mom's underwear. In an exaggerated tone, the teacher said, "Oh my gosh, that is so funny, yes!" to these humorous moments in the story signaling that this was something they could all laugh about together. In response, the students loudly laughed and smiled together while also initially looking around at one another to see if it was okay to laugh at such a moment in reading instruction. Mrs. Hutchins's languaging of the event also signaled to students that in the read-aloud space, a new kind of norm was being enacted for classroom relations, one that felt funny and somewhat transgressive during instructional school spaces.

Teachers may also enact norms based on discourses of race, class, or gender constituting languaging. For example, teachers may privilege the use of standard English in ways that marginalize alternative dialects or registers based on norms of white privilege. They may frame Black English as slang or informal language as inconsistent and impeding academic success (Baker-Bell, 2020; McClain et al., 2021). This suggests the importance of adopting an ethnographic, open-ended perspective on the meaning of languaging actions based on norms constituting unique chronotopes (Bloome et al., 2019). Implementing these practices signals the formation of new norms. Students learn to detect how their teachers' talk implies the adoption of certain norms regarding the use of language interactions in a classroom (Boyd & Markarian, 2015, p. 278). Teachers may employ and celebrate using informal or alternative dialects/registers related to translanguaging that invite students to employ similar languaging in their writing.

Learning to Engage in Languaging in Specific Contexts

A languaging perspective also involves people learning how their language operates in specific contexts. This is required in order for them to enact relations and adopt certain expectations for interacting in these contexts. Knowing how to interact in a sales transaction (Møller, 2016) is one example. Students learn to attend to specific cues signaling adherence to certain norms constituting their languaging actions in a context. For example, in their interaction with peers, they may note that their peers enjoy using "insider language" (Madsen et al., 2013), the meanings of which are unique to their group as a marker of group membership. In one study, a student noted how members of her peer group employed playful languaging actions associated with "'really sarcastic joking ways. We're very forward about what we want with each other and stuff like that, but at the same time it's also a lot of joking around'" (Beach & Aukerman, 2019, p. 63). She was initially "'skeptical to trust them because [she] was like, "I don't know if they're like this with everybody." Then I realized that they do it out of love.'"

In reflecting on adopting certain practices in roleplaying activities, one student identified three norms constituting his use of languaging with others related to attending to certain cues:

1. "You have to acknowledge that this person is not the person you're used to talking to. So, you can't assume things about them."
2. "'The other person is not me.' So, the first thing you always want to do, unless you have a reason for a character not doing this, is to assume that the other person is not going to react the same way that I would. So, it gives you a certain level of caution when interacting with someone or something that's really unusual."
3. "You have to acknowledge that, regardless of the actions they take, this does not reflect back upon the person. So, I could be playing a pyromaniac, and I could start burning down every house I see, and acknowledge that, no, in reality, I'm playing the character as a psychopath, instead of actually being a psychopath." (Beach & Beauchemin, 2019, p. 152)

Students also perceive differences between their adherence to norms from other contexts and norms operating in classrooms—for example, the difference between norms involved in playing digital games versus norms for engaging in formal classroom interactions (Hung et al., 2012). Students may be more engaged in contexts where they have a clear sense of norms—for example, norms constituting collaborative "team play" in basketball versus norms for learning in mathematics classrooms (Nasir & Hand, 2008).

In classroom interactions, teachers and students respond to each other's languaging based on the unfolding, spontaneous meanings for enacting relations in social contexts related to past and anticipated meanings evoked in others (Bakhtin, 1986). As these collaborative events unfold, teachers and students engage in "withness-thinking—the relationally-responsive kind of thinking and speaking we do spontaneously in our everyday conversations, in contrast to the kind of aboutness-thinking we do in referential-representational thought when talking philosophically or theoretically" (Shotter, 2016, p. 39).

Teachers and students engage in learning through and with each other by attending to or adopting novel perspectives and ways of thinking, leading to collaborative exploration of these novel ways of perceiving or thinking (Cunliffe, 2018) and have an ethical obligation to be responsive to each other by considering and benefitting from the other's novel perspectives (Sabey, 2022). Enacting relations also involves making

> ourselves addressable in certain ways. Interlocutors' relational becoming is a function of how they render themselves addressable and how they address (or not) that which each other makes addressable. Both prior to and in the process of making oneself addressable and/or by being addressed in certain ways, interlocutors become present to each other in certain ways . . . (p. A6).

Learning to engage languaging thus involves people making or attempting to make themselves available to one another.

Enacting Personhood through Languaging

Teachers as well as students also enact languaging norms by adopting personhood constituted through languaging certain kinds of persons with particular attributes, beliefs, and attitudes (Bloome et al., 2019). In the NCTE session, given that Richard knew both Sheridan and Deborah over many decades, he was not at all surprised by the fact that each was using languaging stances that challenged the other. This example demonstrates the ways Sheridan's influence goes beyond his writing; it includes being a certain kind of person and educator who, through his interactions with others, influenced his colleagues, students, and friends.

Teachers, therefore, assume an important role in modeling for their students, as they will emulate their teachers' languaging for adopting their own personhood consistent with the notion of teachers serving as "role models" for students. For example, as a high school English teacher, Elizabeth Erdmann moved beyond traditional linguistic norms in schooling for both spoken and written language to develop deeper learning and relations with students (Beach & Beauchemin, 2019). In addition to explicitly articulating those norms, she *enacted* them by sharing personal experiences in employing transgressive languaging and encouraged students' writing that more accurately reflected how people negotiated relations with each other by writing how "people really talk," rather than a more sanitized version that would enact a sense of procedural display of "doing school." As a result, students thought deeply about their lives and wrote about their languaging interactions with one another in ways that enhanced their sense of personhood.

But this freedom of self-expression is not at work in every classroom. An analysis of elementary Turkish students in a Danish school explores the ways students were wondering about whether or not they could employ a "'bad word'" in addressing each other as "stupid idiot." This demonstrates the need to determine whether there is a standard for languaging that may result in sanctions (Møller, 2016). These kinds of concerns about potential consequences for disrupting languaging norms in classroom settings seem to be something students outgrow. When comparing students' reflections on their languaging from elementary school to adulthood, students were increasingly able to reflect on and identify the applicability of certain norms operating in contexts that involved the possibility of competing norms in those contexts (Smith, 2020).

Over time, students therefore learn how to transfer their experiences of writing in a certain rhetorical context to another similar context. For example, students see how formulating an argument on the need for gun control based on the norms for providing relevant supporting evidence transfers to formulating an argument for challenges or attempts to censor books in the school library. This suggests the value of assessing students' writing across time using portfolio assessment to provide feedback on growth in their ability to transfer their languaging in their writing from one rhetorical context to another (Prior & Smith, 2020).

Teachers prescribe norms related to variation in languaging associated with assumptions about uniformity based on standardization of dialects/registers—for example, the need to employ "proper English" in a classroom (Wolfram, 2019). These prescriptions reflect racial or class hierarchies; for example, the use of African-American Vernacular English (AAVE) may be devalued and assumed inconsistent with the use of "proper English" (Metz, 2019). Yet this norm can be questioned. By listening to audio clips of movie characters speaking, students can think about rules regarding how language changes. Then, they can then identify the characters' race, class, and/or gender and think about how they use stereotypes to decide how to interpret certain norms (Metz, 2019).

Examples of Teachers Enacting Norms

The value of creating these supportive events suggests the further need to understand how teachers enact classroom norms. Teachers' actions can create supportive classroom contexts that foster engaging relations with students. Focusing on teachers' enacting norms shifts the focus from an explicit formulation of norms and rules for creating classroom spaces to teachers' use of their personhood as a way of being or knowing for interacting with students. This approach can foster certain literacy practices constituting supportive relations.

At the beginning of her classes, Cait O'Connor (2021) works with her students to define norms based on community agreements. These agreements "allow students to build a set of expectations for themselves, the students who are there every day, and hold each other accountable for those expectations as they get to know each other better" (p. 3). Students then determine how to support their peers based on these agreements by "using kind words, giving everyone's opinions space, prioritizing impact over intention, not interrupting, and not embarrassing people if they make mistakes" (p. 6).

In a first-grade classroom, Mrs. Taylor engages students in literacy learning while also making it fun and funny by transgressing traditional norms of speaking during read-alouds in the early childhood classroom (Beauchemin, 2021). She intentionally selects a series of "funny" texts to read to her students for providing playful learning opportunities. These texts also draw upon topics that are humorous in childhood culture but that are typically not appropriate for school. She then asks questions to enact a moment of joyful learning. For example, when reviewing the previous day's read-aloud, "Froggy Has a Doggy," she asks the students, as did Mrs. Hutchins, to identify a humorous event in the story: "'What's something funny that happened in the story?'" (Beauchemin, 2021, p. 432). A student answers about when he had to pick up all the dog's poop. Mrs. Taylor leverages the moment and shouts out, "Pooper Scooper!" while all the children laugh at the moment with their teacher about the funny event in the story. When a student cited the instance of the froggy wearing underwear, she agreed that this was a friendly relational key (Beauchemin, 2019, 2021) while all the children laugh at the moment with their teacher. By transgressing the norms of what is considered "appropriate" in the teacher-directed classroom spaces, Mrs. Taylor uses childhood culture and the logic of humor that it includes to engage students in literacy learning (Beauchemin, 2021).

Teachers Enacting "Emotional Rules"

Teachers also enact certain "emotional rules" as norms (Zembylas, 2002) related to whether and how they can employ or express certain emotions in the classroom (Benesch, 2018). For example, an English teacher, Rebecca Oberg, describes her supporting students taking risks related to "'getting weird'" in her classrooms based on "'what it means to be and belong together to learn alongside each other in the classroom'" (Beach & Beauchemin, 2019, pp. 49–50). She also believes in the importance of creating classroom events in which students assume some active roles that may deviate from norms constituting their usual, prototypical student roles or identities related to the display of competence. For example, she created a "Farm and Field Day" to have students give presentations about farming and food. She believed that this event would appeal to "'students who maybe don't necessarily always feel engaged at school or engaged in English class'" so that students experienced a sense of competence and ownership as themselves serving as teachers (Beach & Beauchemin, 2019, p. 75).

Enacting Norms Through Embodied Actions

Teachers may also enact norms constituting classrooms through embodied actions related to physical movements or voices for demonstrating how those actions reflect certain discourses (Jones, 2017). Teachers' physical interactions with students enact norms constituting students' own embodied actions. Teachers can also engage students in activities involving roleplay or standing in different places on a continuum to express their beliefs on topics or issues. In activities such as these, students can reflect on how their embodied actions adhere to or deviate from certain norms. For example, in one activity (Jones, 2017), students walked around their classroom as if they were male and female. They then reflected on norms based on certain stereotypical gender assumptions about whether their embodied actions were inborn or learned (Jones, 2017).

Teachers Attending to Alternative Norms in a Classroom

In any classroom event or context, multiple alternative norms operate simultaneously in those events or contexts, requiring that teachers assess which of these alternative norms they need to attend to in order to engage in certain actions. Teachers may also enhance students' engagement through attending to their use of specific "backstage" (Goffman, 1971) or "underlife" (Brooke, 1987) practices perceived as deviating from certain classroom norms (Lytra, 2007). Doing so requires teachers to attend to and be open to students engaging in practices deviating from their established classroom norms. For example, while a teacher may be lecturing, a group of students in the back of the classroom may be engaged in "underlife," transgressive activity of passing notes to each other based on enacting a counter set of norms (Brooke, 1987). Rather than admonish students engaged in "underlife" activity based on injunctive norms, a teacher may then reassess enacting their lecturing to shift to adopt alternative actions. A teacher may evoke descriptive norms supporting the value of students contributing to their ideas related to the lecture by engaging these students in a discussion. This is a kind of pedagogical shift in the moment. Deviating from predetermined norms involves what Rebecca Oberg described as "slowing down, and it's taking time to be thoughtful and not just rushing through an assignment. . . . So often teachers forget that it takes time sometimes to get them hooked into an assignment" (Beach & Beauchemin, 2019, p. 82).

Deviating from traditional classroom norms also entails being open to letting students set the agenda, being open to when students, as Elizabeth Erdmann noted, "don't go in the direction that you would expect . . . [so that] I didn't expect this, let's talk about this" (Beach & Beauchemin, 2019, p. 82). As an example of languaging as embodied actions, when students in Elizabeth Erdmann's class were performing a play, "I almost got fired the other day because I had them up on my teacher's desk pretending it was a balcony, and they proceeded because I said it was okay" (Beach, 2022, p. 53). The same teacher enacted an alternative norm when a student asked her to give her a hug. She noted that "I didn't used to hug kids. There was a senior boy who looked like he'd been crying and I was like, 'Man, do you need a hug?' And he was like, 'Yeah, actually, I could really use a hug right now.' So, I hugged him, and the other kids were like, 'Aww!' And they then started laughing and were like, 'Here's a hug for you bro'" (p. 53).

However, teachers are often conflicted about adhering to these alternative norms given the extent to which they can honor certain deviant "underlife" student practices as inconsistent with complying with school- or districtwide-mandates. For example, a case study analysis of a bilingual teacher identified how she voiced several competing, contradictory discourses constituting school-mandated norms. On the one hand, she perceived the need to build on students' different languages while, on the other hand, she adopted deficit discourses about these students' academic abilities related to their scores on standardized tests (Handsfield et al., 2010). At the same time, adopting these different discourses constituting norms was tactical in that rather than simply making do—implementing temporary measures to get through a day or week of instruction—she recontextualizes discourses across space-times to redesign the curriculum and forge multiple simultaneous possibilities (p. 428).

Teachers and students also acquire and apply certain "assumptions of normality" related to expectations making up schooling practices based on their previous school experiences and novel practices associated with experiences in teacher education or professional development (Vagle et al., 2017). For example, teachers often enact unmarked norms of monolingual ideologies in schooling by not questioning how teacher-directed instruction happens exclusively in English. However, some teacher education programs are challenging these norms and providing preservice teachers with experiences in reading translingual texts containing multiple languages on the same side-by-side pages of the text for their students. By challenging the unmarked monolingual norms of schooling, these read-alouds provide bilingual students with opportunities to be linguistic experts while teachers transition into the role of a learner. With such practices, students may experience the adoption of alternative norms in the classroom that deviate from or adhere to larger schoolwide institutional norms related to enforcing certain student behaviors or achieving standardized test outcomes. A case study analysis of a teacher engaged in a critical literacy forum with her colleagues noted that she perceived literacy learning as based on "how students identify themselves and how they understand the world around them and how they view their place within the world around them" (Riley, 2015, p. 420). The teacher also actively resisted norms operating in the school. For example, when school administrators observed students talking in the computer lab as problematic or dictated using "I" in academic essays, she voiced the need for alternative norms supporting her students. Teachers could then determine whether to adhere to problematic school norms in order to enact alternative norms in their classrooms that may be less punitive than these schoolwide norms.

Sheridan's Critique of Norms Shaping Literature Instruction

Throughout his long career as a literacy educator, Sheridan consistently fostered challenges of status-quo norms constituting students' enactment of meanings for responding to literature. As evident in his interactions with Appleman in the NCTE session, he was never shy about adopting alternative, even contrarian perspectives as a practice that was central to his identity as someone who actually enjoyed participating in contentious spaces. Given that people are often unwilling to voice alternative perspectives, his willingness to always challenge the status quo, however valid that status quo, served as a valuable pedagogical contribution for others' learning in the worlds he inhabited over time. For example, Sheridan consistently challenged norms based on traditional literature curriculum perpetuating instruction based on complex canonical texts (Blau, 2003; 2017). He posited that "students will remain unable to read these texts with sufficient confidence and sense of progress to begin to surrender their minds and senses to the imaginative experience that is the essence of the literary work of art" (Blau, 2014, p. 45).

Sheridan is also critical of norms associated with the imposition of impersonal literary critical analysis that can be "meaningless and alienating, because it will offer them the fruits of somebody else's experience and grant them no knowledge except a fraudulent knowledge that can be expressed in regurgitated formulations and possessed as mere information about a literary text rather than any genuinely experienced understanding of that text" (p. 45). His alternative approach has been to promote the use of collaborative small/large group discussions based on norms valuing students' sharing their unique problems and difficulties they encounter in their reading. For Sheridan, students are likely to discover the power of their questions and confusions in contributing to an emerging understanding of a difficult text. Moreover, by focusing on their questions and problems, they will also be acquiring the crucial habit of metacognition—of thinking about their own thinking and monitoring the state of their emerging understanding at the same time that they are discovering and practicing discursive strategies for addressing refractory and frustrating problems in constructing meanings. Adhering to these alternative social norms supporting shared problem solving is consistent with our previous focus on enacting norms constituting supportive, caring relations as central to students' collaborative learning (Beauchemin, 2019). This requires that teachers continually attend to their students' enactment of social and cultural norms operating in their classrooms and to honor and support those norms as central to fostering student learning.

Students Responding to Deviations from Norms in Literary Texts

Students draw on their knowledge of norms to respond to literary characters' deviations from norms constituting the "eventness" of their actions, deviations enhancing the "tellability" of those texts—what makes them worth telling, given the significance of those deviations (Labov & Fanshel, 1977). Students gain an awareness of "tellability" based on sharing deviations from norms by sharing narratives about their daily lives. For example, if a student reported to her peers that "I walked to school today," her peers may react with a "so what?" response to a report about a routine, mundane event that lacks "tellability." In contrast, she may report that "I was walking down this quiet street to school, where there was nobody around, when all of a sudden, this guy jumps out at me" (Beach & Beauchemin, 2019, p. 111). In doing so, she is dramatizing deviations from norms using words such as "all of a sudden" to enhance "eventness" contributing to "tellability."

Students Drawing on Knowledge of Norms for Responding to Literature

Students then draw on these experiences with personal narratives to respond to deviations from norms portrayed in literary texts based on applying their knowledge of norms to those texts. For example, in responding to the relationship between Othello and Desdemona in *Othello*, students draw on their knowledge of norms constituting supportive love relationships to infer how Othello's relationship with Desdemona deviates from those norms associated with love relationships (Beach et al., 2017). In a small-group discussion responding to the play, one student noted, "'I am not sure if Othello really ever loved Desdemona or if she ever really loved or accepted him past his race'" (p. 208). Another student posited that their relationship deviated from supportive relations given that "'Othello's fatal flaw was jealousy . . . and that is what is going to kill his love and trust to Desdemona" (p. 208). For responding to these deviations from norms constituting "eventness," teachers can have students draw on their prior knowledge of norms related to particular events in a text—for example, their knowledge of norms constituting supportive love relationships for responding to a text such as *Othello*.

The fact that students draw on their knowledge of norms for responding to literature suggests the value of employing literacy texts consistent with students' experiences and interests, something that Sheridan (2003, 2014, 2017) promoted in his publications on the need to value students' experiences and interests constituting certain norms. For example, a Black preservice teacher, Paula, planned and reflected on engaging students in a read-aloud of a children's picture book about a young Black girl's experiences of racism, despite Paula's white mentor teacher's reservations about using the book (Beauchemin et al., 2021). Paula struggled with being positioned as an outsider by her cooperating teacher, who opposed using this book based on discourses of whiteness. The need to challenge status-quo discourses of whiteness in teacher education will demonstrate that preservice teachers of color are valued for the cultural competencies they bring to their placements and the "inappropriateness" of race talk are dispelled.

In a roleplaying activity, students responded to the novel *Each Kindness* (Woodson, 2012), in which a female student of a lower-class status, Maya, experiences exclusion from her peers. In the roleplaying, their teacher assumed the role of Maya walking in the school playground and the students discriminated against their teacher—for example, whispering to each other behind her back about her wearing secondhand clothes (Edmiston, 2016).

Students may also engage in roleplaying related to enacting norms based on the use of alternative languages/dialects. For responding to the text, *My Diary from Here to There: Mi diario de aqui hasta alla* (Pérez, 2013), students wrote dialogue in Spanish or English in their journals based on dialogue in the text to engage in dramatic dialogues in roleplaying with each other using both languages (Medina & Campano, 2006).

Challenging Institutional Norms Constituted by Systems

In addition to enacting and challenging classroom/school norms, teachers and students also challenge institutional/societal norms constituting practices shaped by larger systems—economic, schooling, energy, agriculture, transportation, political—shaping their lives (Beach et al., 2017). For example, in a capitalist economic system, people follow the rules and spend money, which helps the economy grow, even if it hurts the environment. Challenging the norms making up these systems involves using "systems thinking" to critique norms driving status-quo systems. This may lead to adopting alternative norms to transform status-quo systems. For example, students may recognize that an agriculture system based on meat consumption requires deforestation to create grazing lands for cows and how cows produce methane emissions. Teachers and students participating in school environmental clubs employ systems thinking to engage in projects related to identifying the limitations of status-quo systems with negative climate change effects may lead to taking action to engage in alternative practices. For example, given the limitations of an agriculture system based on meat consumption, they perceive a need to shift in order to promote an increase in the use of plant-based foods in the school cafeteria.

Given their critique of the adverse effects of the management of food, plastics, and paper waste, students in the Earth Corps environment club at Jefferson High School, Bloomington, Minnesota (http://t.ly/ouMp), recognized the limitations of status-quo recycling practices in their cafeteria related to knowing how and where to recycle paper, plastics, or food. As a result, they created a video portraying specific practices for recycling different content for showing to their peers within the school to promote more effective recycling practices.

Reflecting on Adhering to Norms

Teachers and students could openly share how they reflect on identifying and adhering to certain norms given participation in specific contexts or events. They may also reflect on certain norms constituting practices related to school success based on standardized test scores as inconsistent with their successes in their coursework. Teachers may also model their reflections or provide students with frameworks or categories for sharing their reflections. For example, in her teacher education course, Faythe led students in transgressing norms of typical elementary reading instruction as commonly dominated by monolingual ideologies. Preservice teachers videotaped themselves engaging in reading instruction and then reflected on their teaching of literacy through digital annotations of their videos. The video annotations served as starting points for preservice teachers to think deeply about their practice through retrospective analysis. These preservice teachers noticed ways in which students engaged in sense making about texts that centered their cultural epistemologies and community knowledge. Teachers also marked ways students engaged in culturally sustaining teaching practices or missed opportunities to do so. By analyzing their teaching moment by moment, teachers were able to pause moments of instruction to recognize the strengths of their interactions and/or imagine discursive alternatives to what happened in their teaching practice as well as in the practices of others.

Conclusion

In conclusion, we have drawn on Sheridan's consistent focus on challenging status-quo norms for teaching literature to influence others to posit the need for teachers and students to enact alternative norms as well as challenge status-quo norms based on race, class, and gender norms. In doing so, students learn the importance of contextualizing events in everyday life and responding to characters' actions in literary texts.

Works Cited

Agha, A. (2007). *Language and social relations.* Cambridge University Press.

Alim, H. S., & Paris, D. (2017). What is culturally sustaining pedagogy and why does it matter? In D. Paris & H. S. Alim (Eds.), *Culturally sustaining pedagogies: Teaching and learning for justice in a changing world* (pp. 1–21). Teachers College Press.

Appleman, D. (2015). *Critical encounters in secondary English: Teaching literary theory to adolescents* (3rd ed.). Teachers College Press.

Baker-Bell, A. (2020). *Linguistic justice: Black language, literacy, identity, and pedagogy.* Routledge.

Beach, R., with Caraballo, L. (2022). *Drawing on students' worlds in the ELA classroom: Toward critical engagement and deep learning.* Routledge.

Beach, R., & Beauchemin, F. (2019). *Teaching language as action in the ELA classroom.* Routledge.

Beach, R., & Bloome, D. (Eds.). (2019). *Languaging relations for transforming the literacy and language arts classroom.* Routledge.

Beach, R., Falter, M. M., & Whitley, J. (2017). Making sense of events in literature and life through collaboration. English Teaching: Practice *& Critique, 16*(2), 207–221.

Beach, R., Share, J., & Webb, A. (2017). *Teaching climate change to adolescents: Reading, writing, and making a difference.* Routledge.

Beauchemin, F. (2019). Reconceptualizing classroom life as relational-key. In R. Beach & D. Bloome (Eds.), *Languaging relations for transforming the literacy and language arts classroom* (pp. 23–48). Routledge.

Beauchemin. F. (2021). Literacy practices as social: Relational-keys in literacy events. *English Teaching: Practice & Critique, 20*(3), 328–340.

Beauchemin, F., Hill, H., & Wilson, M. (2021). *Naturalized patterns of silence and disconnection: A critical discourse analysis of a Black female preservice teacher's counternarrative on the experience of teaching literacy* [Presentation]. Literacy Research Association Annual Conference, Atlanta, GA.

Benesch, S. (2018). Emotions as agency: Feeling rules, emotion labor, and English language teachers' decision-making. *System, 79*, 60–69. https://doi.org/10.1016/j.system.2018.03.015

Bertau, M.-C. (2014). Introduction: The self within the space-time of language performance. *Theory & Psychology, 24*(4), 433–441.

Blau, S. (2003). *The literature workshop: Teaching texts and their readers*. Heinemann.

Blau, S. (2014). Literary competence and the experience of literature. *Style, 48*(1), 42–47.

Blau, S. (2017). How the teaching of literature in college writing classes might rescue reading as it never has before. In P. Sullivan, H. Tinberg, & S. Blau (Eds.), *Deep reading: Teaching reading in the writing classroom* (pp. 265–290). National Council of Teachers of English.

Blommaert, J. (2018). *Durkheim and the internet: On sociolinguistics and the sociological imagination*. Bloomsbury.

Bloome, D., Brown, A. F., Kim, M.Y., & Tang, R. J. (2019). Languaging personhood in classroom conversation. In R. Beach & D. Bloome (Eds.), *Languaging relations for transforming the literacy and language arts classroom* (pp. 235–254). Routledge.

Boyd, M. P., & Markarian, W. C. (2015). Dialogic teaching and dialogic stance: Moving beyond interactional form. *Research in the Teaching of English, 49*(3), 272–296.

Brooke, R. (1987). Underlife and writing instruction. *College Composition & Communication, 38*(2), 141–153.

Cunliffe, A. (2018). Learning, reflexivity and knowing from within: Being inspired by John Shotter or why isn't he wearing socks?! *Teoria e Prática em Administração, 8*(2), 1–9. http://dx.doi.org/10.21714/2238-104X2018v8i2S-40871

Edmiston, B. (2016). Promoting teachers' ideological becoming: Using dramatic inquiry in teacher education. *Literacy Research: Theory, Method, and Practice, 65*(1), 332–347.

Eyink, J. R., Motz, B. A., Heltzel, G., & Liddell, T. M. (2020). Self-regulated studying behavior, and the social norms that influence it. *Journal of Applied Social Psychology, 50*(1), 10–21.

Goffman, E. (1971). *The presentation of self in everyday life*. Penguin.

Hall, L. A. (2012). Rewriting identities: Creating spaces for students and teachers to challenge the norms of what it means to be a reader in school. *Journal of Adolescent & Adult Literacy, 55*(5), 368–373.

Handsfield, L. J., Crumpler, T. P., & Dean. T. R. (2010). Tactical negotiations and creative adaptations: The discursive production of literacy curriculum and teacher identities across space-times. *Reading Research Quarterly, 45*(4), 405–431. https://doi.org/10.1598/RRQ.45.4.3

Hung, C.-M., Huang, I., & Hwang, G.-J. (2014). Effects of digital game-based learning on students' self-efficacy, motivation, anxiety, and achievements in learning mathematics. *Journal of Computers in Education, 1*(2–3),151–166. https://doi.org/10.1007/s40692-014-0008-8

Jones, C. E. (2017). Transforming classroom norms as social change: Pairing embodied exercises with collaborative participation in the WGS classroom (with syllabus). *Radical Teacher, 107*, 14–31. https://doi.org/10.5195/rt.2017.322

Labov, W., & Fanshel, F. (1977). *Therapeutic discourse: Psychotherapy as conversation*. Academic Press.

Linell, P. (2009). *Rethinking language, mind, and world dialogically*. Information Age.

Lytra, V. (2007). *Play frames and social identities: Contact encounters in a Greek primary school*. John Benjamins.

McClain, J. B., Harmon, M., & Galloway, E. P. (2021). Eliminating prerequisites for personhood: A framework for enacting antiracist language instruction. *Language Arts, 99*(1), 25–36.

Medina, C., & Campano, G. (2006). Performing identities through drama and teatro practices in multilingual classrooms. *Language Arts, 83*(4), 332–341.

Metz, M. (2019). Principles to navigate the challenges of teaching English language variation: A guide for nonlinguists. In M. D. Devereaux & C. C. Palmer (Eds.), *Teaching language variation in the classroom: Strategies and models from teachers and linguists* (pp. 69–75). Routledge.

Møller, J. S. (2016). Learning to live with "languages." *Applied Linguistics Review*, 7(3), 279–303.

Nasir, N.S., & Hand, V. H. (2008). From the court to the classroom: Opportunities for engagement, learning, and identity in basketball and classroom mathematics. *Journal of the Learning Sciences, 17*(2), 143–179. https://doi.org/10.1080/10508400801986108

National Council for the Social Studies, National Council of Teachers of Mathematics, National Council of Teachers of English, National Science Teaching Association, & National Coalition Against Censorship. (2022). *Freedom to teach: Statement against banning books*. National Council of Teachers of English. https://ncte.org/freedom-teach-banning-books

O'Connor, C. (2021, August 24). *Using community agreements to start the year strong. Edutopia.* www.edutopia.org/article/using-community-agreements-start-year-strong

Pérez, A. I. (2013). *My diary from here to there: Mi diario de aqui hasta alla* (M. C. Gonzalez, Illus.). Children's Book Press.

Prior, P., & Smith, A. (2020). Writing across: Tracing transliteracies as becoming across time, space, and settings. *Learning, Culture and Social Interaction, 24*, Article 100246. https://doi.org/10.1016/j.lcsi.2018.07.002

Riley, K. (2015). Enacting critical literacy in English classrooms: How a teacher learning community supported critical inquiry. *Journal of Adolescent & Adult Literacy, 58*(5), 417–425. https://doi.org/10.1002/jaal.371

Sabey, D. (2022). Relational becoming: Considering classroom dialogue in ethico-ontological terms. *Dialogic Pedagogy: An International Online Journal, 10*, A1–A29. https://doi.org/10.5195/dpj.2022.459

Shotter, J. (2013). Agentive spaces, the "background", and other not well articulated influences in shaping our lives. *Journal for the Theory of Social Behaviour, 43*(2), 133–154.

Shotter, J. (2016). *Speaking, actually: Towards a new "fluid" common-sense understanding of relational becomings*. Everything is Connected Press.

Smith, A. (2020). Across, through, and with: Ontological orientations for lifespan writing research. In R. Dippre & T. Phillips (Ed.), *Approaches to lifespan writing research: Generating an actionable coherence* (pp. 15–26). The WAC Clearinghouse; University Press of Colorado. https://wac.colostate.edu/docs/books/lifespan/chapter1.pdf

Vagle, M. D., Monette, R., Thiel, J. J., & Wester-Neal, K. (2017). Enacting post-reflexive teacher education. *Pedagogies: An International Journal, 12*(3), 295–312. https://doi.org/10.1080/1554480X.2017.1344555

Wolfram, W. (2019). Language awareness in education: A linguist's response to teachers. In M. D. Devereaux & C. C. Palmer (Eds.), *Teaching language variation in the classroom* (pp. 61–66). Routledge.

Young, M. (2022). Students, teachers thrive when freedom is the norm. *Council Chronicle, 32*(1), 22–25. https://doi.org/10.58680/cc202232052

Ethical Criticism as Pedagogy for the Development of Other-Centric Interpretive Communities in the Literature Classroom

Suzanne S. Choo and Dominic Nah

Introduction: The Rise of Reader-Centric Approaches in Literature

Beginning in the mid-twentieth century, the dominant pedagogical approach to teaching English literature in the United States, England, and England's colonies was New Criticism. New Criticism shared close associations with the movements of Formalism in perceiving the text as a self-contained whole and with Aestheticism in advocating that the text was to be appreciated for its aesthetic qualities rather than any moral value that could be derived from it. New Critics led by literary scholars I. A. Richards and F. R. Leavis, along with poets such as T. S. Eliot and Ezra Pound among others, instituted the pedagogy of close reading characterized by a depoliticized form of distant reading. The objective critic was one who discounted extraneous contexts such as the author's background or impressionistic feelings activated during the reading process (Wimsatt & Beardsley, 2001). New Criticism continued its influence in the 1940s and 1950s in colleges across the United States. In countries colonized by the British, such as India and Singapore, English literature was introduced as a subject that served to perpetuate the values of the Empire, and New Criticism was a key pedagogy that supported this aim. It contributed to a culturally blinkered approach to teaching in which a focus on form and content drew attention away from the politics of curriculum, including such questions about texts selected for study and the kinds of cultural values these promoted (Choo, 2021).

In Singapore, the influence of New Criticism continued in schools in the years after colonization in 1963. This was most evident in the kinds of questions asked in the high school national examinations that ranged from context-type questions, involving short answers on specific details, and passage-based questions, requiring students to examine the significance of a given moment, to lengthier essay questions focusing on the craft of the author. All these influenced the pedagogy of close reading in the teaching of literature. A discernible shift occurred in the late twentieth century when enrollment in the high-stakes national literature examination taken at the end of secondary school fell drastically, sparking intense debates among scholars and educators on the relevance of literature in postcolonial Singapore society. There were calls to broaden the curriculum by including translated works from other ethnic groups, such as Malay poetry (Yeo, 1999), to shift the curriculum from an English to world literature focus (Holden, 1999) and to forge closer connections between literary texts studied and contemporary global realities (Choo, 2013; Liew, 2012; Loh, 2013; Poon, 2010).

More significantly, there was a greater recognition of the need for constructivist pedagogies that lent attention to students' voices and responses. In the literature preservice program at the National Institute of Education, the sole college responsible for preparing and accrediting teachers for mainstream schools in Singapore, New Criticism was now taught along with Reader Response Criticism and Poststructuralist Criticism. A new literature syllabus launched in 2019 pushed for a more holistic approach to literature, emphasizing four desired student outcomes: the development of empathetic and global thinkers; critical readers; creative meaning makers; and convincing communicators. More explicitly, the syllabus mentioned the need for a "mindset shift":

> Students must actively engage with the text. Teachers must take up the mantle of facilitator of learning in place of the traditional roles of information dispenser and opinion provider. This mindset shift must take place in the literature classroom. (Curriculum Planning and Development Division, 2018, p. 7)

Visible thinking, exploratory talk, and dialogic engagement were pedagogies explicitly encouraged in the syllabus, and references were made to prominent American scholars aligned with the Reader Response movement, including Louise Rosenblatt, Judith Langer, Robert Probst, and Sheridan Blau. Blau was invited as a keynote speaker at the Literature Symposium in 2020, a biennial national event for literature teachers organized by the Ministry of Education. His (2003) book, *The Literature Workshop*, provided important glimpses of how teachers can create interpretive communities in the classroom and relinquish their hermeneutic authority to empower students to have critical conversations about literary texts.

At the same time, one recalls Eagleton's (1996) dictum that "Literature, in the meaning of the word we have inherited, is an ideology" (p. 19). Thus, any pedagogical romanticization, even in the name of concepts such as democracy, agency, and empowerment, needs to be interrogated for its cultural assumptions. In this chapter, we discuss some of the challenges of the workshop approach in the context of Singapore as a postcolonial country characterized by a Confucian Heritage Culture (CHC). Singapore's use of English as an official language for administration and instruction in education presents an insightful model for how literature education can be enacted in such postcolonial CHCs. Even though English is an official language and first language in all mainstream schools, Singapore's population is not a "native" English one, comprising about 74 percent Chinese, 14 percent Malays, 9 percent Indians, and 3 percent Eurasians and other minority ethnic groups (Department of Statistics, 2021). Within this multicultural demographic, Wu et al. (2020) observe how Confucian notions of multicultural citizenship—in which humans actively participate and navigate their identities in a pluralistic society—are undercut in Singapore, where a superficial approach to culture is often undertaken in multicultural education. From this context, we highlight three key limitations of the workshop approach based on our observations of literature classrooms in Singapore. We examine how teachers and students negotiate autonomous responses and communitarian values. These limitations lead us to propose that the workshop approach and, more broadly, reader-centric pedagogies be extended with what we term other-centric pedagogies. Based on the principles of Ethical Criticism that emerged in literary studies at the turn of the twenty-first century, we discuss how this approach shifts readers from attunement to self and like-minded peers toward an ethical response and responsibility to others in their society and the world.

Context: Shared Values in Confucian Heritage Cultures

Although Asia cannot be considered a monolithic continent, given its diversity of ethnic groups, languages, and cultures, there are shared traditions arising from interlocking philosophical histories. One example is what is known as CHCs describing countries such as China, Japan, South Korea, Vietnam, and Singapore that, to varying degrees, ground their shared values in Confucianism. The spread of Neo-Confucianism during the Song Dynasty in China (960–1279) led to its influence in the political governance and social ethics of Vietnam, Korea, and Japan (Tu, 2000). Later, the rapid industrialization of East Asian and Southeast Asian countries in the mid-twentieth century led to the fashioning of a pan-Asian identity. In the 1990s, the concept of "Asian values" was advanced by then prime minister of Singapore, Lee Kuan Yew, and gained traction in these countries. It was used by governments to promote social norms favoring loyalty to family and state as opposed to concepts of freedom and autonomy associated with Western liberalism (Barr, 2000). The basis of "Asian values" was connected to Confucianism, particularly the emphasis on the interdependent nature of human relations. Scholars critiqued political uses of "Asian values" to support hegemonic authoritarian rule of the state (Chia, 2011; Englehart, 2000; Wee, 1999), and the concept gradually became less fashionable. The intensification of globalization also led to a wider, more cosmopolitan embracing of plural identities and philosophies.

Despite this, an argument can be made that key Confucian values continue to influence implicitly the cultural ethos of

CHCs. For example, in multicultural Singapore, the mention of Confucian values in official discourse is downplayed by the state, partly in recognition of the diverse ethnic groups and religious beliefs in the country. At the same time, several scholars have observed that Singapore's five shared values correspond closely with Confucian ethics:

1. Nation before community and society above self;
2. Family as the basic unit of society;
3. Community support and respect for the individual;
4. Consensus, not conflict; and
5. Racial and religious harmony. (Englehart, 2000; Tan, 2012)

Other studies on education in CHCs have found a number of common characteristics such as the ways students are reluctant to express personal opinions and are uncomfortable with challenging authority whether in the form of the textbook or the teacher (Durkin, 2008; O'Sullivan & Guo, 2011). One problem is the very notion of CHCs may perpetuate stereotypical binaries such as East versus West, communitarianism versus individualism, and social harmony versus human rights (O'Dwyer, 2017).

Perhaps one way to avert reliance on stereotypical binaries is to perceive the adoption of Confucian values on a spectrum. For example, scholars have distinguished between thick versus thin CHC discourses. The former emphasizes strong continuity with Confucian values observed in official government ideology and in ideological state apparatuses such as education, whereas the latter subscribes to the view that the modernization of Asian societies has led to a shallow Confucian heritage in which residual values of filial piety and harmony continue to be cherished but with superficial connections to Confucianism (O'Dwyer, 2017). Whichever perspective one subscribes to, the question is how Confucian-informed values such as respect, harmony, and responsibility may influence and even challenge the kinds of interpretive, dialogic communities advocated by Blau's workshop approach to literature.

Challenges to the Workshop Approach in Confucian Heritage Cultures

Blau (2003) begins his workshop approach by acknowledging its roots in "the transactional theory and democratic ideology of Louise Rosenblatt" (p. 5) by focusing on process-oriented, collaborative, and learner-centered practices. At the same time, he aims to address the limitations of reader response observed in literature classrooms where discussions seldom go beyond individual responses or may appear more akin to a textual reaction. For him, the workshop approach endorses the development of interpretive communities where individual ideas that are shared become sharpened and clarified among peers, and students apply "evidentiary reasoning" (p. 51) as they negotiate differences in opinions as well as metacognitive thinking as they reflect on their changing ideas emerging from discussions.

While the workshop approach promotes more democratic forms of discussion, its application in CHCs with strong communitarian cultures requires closer examination. In this section, we highlight some of the challenges to the workshop approach based on our observations of two literature classrooms in Singapore. Our data is taken from part of a larger two-year research study on literature education in Singapore high schools. Over a period of six months, we worked with a group of five literature teachers who were interested in engaging students with current local and global issues through poetry. In this chapter, we feature two of these teachers—Katrina and Rosie (pseudonyms)—who worked with us to design a ten-week literature unit titled, "Examining Race and Identity through Singapore Poetry." Both teachers taught in mainstream government schools, and they enacted the unit in their Secondary 4 (grade 10 equivalent) classes at the beginning of 2020 when their students had to take the national high-stakes examination at the end of the year. The teachers were keen to work with researchers to design a unit that would enable students to actively connect literary texts to their familiar world and pertinent issues encountered in their everyday lives. This was despite the pressure of having to prepare students for the literature national examination, which requires students to critically appreciate the style of the author without any engagement with critical-ethical interpretations of the text. While teachers did incorporate close reading skills, they also pushed students to read widely from a diverse range of voices including minority ethnic groups, and there were ample opportunities to include learner-centered pedagogies, particularly personal response, group discussions, and creative writing. In the scenes we describe below, both teachers had students discuss the poem "FAQ" by Luke Vijay Somasundram (2016), which describes forms of racial discrimination experienced by Indian minorities in Singapore (an online version of the poem may be found here: https://www.facebook.com/groups/singpowrimo/permalink/976868739095044/). Despite efforts taken to develop interpretive communities in the classroom, three challenges became evident.

Challenge 1: Tendency for Students to Defer to Teacher's Interpretive Authority Despite Attempts to Create Democratic Spaces of Inquiry

One of the key principles that Blau (2003) advocates in his book is that reading is "a social process, completed in conversation" and that "students will learn literature best and find many of their opportunities for learning to become more competent, more intellectually productive and more autonomous readers of literature through frequent work in groups with peers" (p. 54). Blau adopts the term "co-duction" (p. 54) from Wayne Booth (1988) as a basis for literary conversations. As opposed to induction and deduction, which involve more interior processes, co-duction is a form of reasoning arising through collaborative discourse and negotiation among readers (Blau, 2003; Booth, 1988). Yet successful implementation of collaborative inquiry requires that students are predisposed to engaging with others in literary conversations and can appreciate interpretive ambiguity. However, in CHCs like Singapore and other East Asian contexts, students have largely been acculturated to deferring to teachers' interpretive authority over their own critical analysis of texts (Turner, 2011). In one study conducted in an English as a foreign language class in South Korea, a teacher tried to introduce critical pedagogy and collaborative projects to the class. However, the students resisted this as they were used to drill and practice exercises and teacher-centric instruction (Kim & Pollard, 2017). In another study on Chinese international students in Canada, the researchers highlight these students' discomfort with critical thinking and discussions. They pinpoint the discomfort with critical thinking, which is not just a skill set but "reflects the belief system and cognitive orientation of the thinker" as rooted in ancient Greek philosophy (O'Sullivan & Guo, 2011, p. 69). As the researchers then suggest, the valuing of independent thought and the capacity to debate and question is less valued in Chinese culture and philosophy where more emphasis is placed on harmony and unity.[1]

Students' inhibition towards discussion is also observed in Katrina's literature class. In this lesson, Katrina has just introduced the poem "FAQ." The poem features several stanzas listing questions posed by what is presumed to be the voice of the majority race who expresses ignorant, condescending, and patronizing opinions. As part of the discussion, Katrina asks students to interpret a particular line:

Katrina: What is the implication here? What are they talking about?

Student A: Skin color.

Student B: Race. He is very very Black.

Katrina: Please don't give me these kinds of answers. . . . Your exams are coming.

More details.

Student B: Racism.

Katrina: Wow! Are we doing a one-word thing today in class? Everybody giving one-word answers?

Student A: I think he is trying to say "Why are you so dark-skinned"?

Katrina: Yes, so he is referring to the color of Indians that all Indians are Black.

Are all Indians Black?

Students: No.

Katrina: That's where the racism comes in. Explain it like that. Don't assume everybody knows everything. Your marker cannot go into your brain and understand what you are trying to think.

In the above excerpt, Katrina attempts to generate open-ended discussion by asking questions and by pushing students to go beyond one-word answers. She brings in the expectations of the examination that requires students to provide details to their answers. Despite her efforts, students continue giving self-conscious and limited responses with little elaboration. In these exchanges, her students' limited responses lead her to express frustration several times. One possibility is that the constant reminder about "exams" and "marker[s]" may have caused students to become more conscious about providing the "right" answers to her questions.

The students' short responses lead Katrina to revert to an initiation-response-evaluation (I-R-E) discourse structure in which the teacher would initiate a question, students would respond to the question, and the teacher would then evaluate the response (Cazden, 2001), reinforcing an authoritative pedagogy where the teacher continually checks for understanding of previously transmitted knowledge. Throughout the discussion, Katrina's questions are aimed at eliciting recall, provision of evidence, description of literary devices, and the implications of thematic concerns. The monologic pattern of the I-R-E discourse structure is commonly observed during whole-class discussions in this unit. This constrains students' responses as they inadvertently pay attention to what they think Katrina wants to elicit from them.

Challenge 2: Tendency for Students in Interpretive Communities to Impose Hegemonic Viewpoints of the Majority

Blau's workshop approach has challenged conventional ways of reading centered on literary appreciation that convey the impression that critical interpretation should be best left to experts rather than ordinary readers. Conversely, Blau's workshop approach is ultimately aimed at empowering students to gain confidence in their own interpretations. He (2003) has pushed for what he termed "transpersonal readings" (p. 138) in which the reader's response to the text does not only identify that reader as a member of a group of readers in similar cultural roles but also makes arguments publicly available and persuasive based on evidence garnered. However, within such a democratic space, what appears discounted is the differential power dynamics among students. Within an interpretive group, not all students have equal power or persuasive force to convey their points convincingly. This could be due to different linguistic prowess as well as different socioeconomic backgrounds that may affect access to resources such as reading history, life experiences, etc. Further, one needs to consider not only power differentials among individuals in a group but the group as a whole. A particular race, gender, class, or other identity profile of the majority in the group may overshadow the voices and perspectives of minority students.

Interpretive communities are thus not neutral spaces and students may impose hegemonic viewpoints of a dominant culture in their interpretations of literary texts. Specifically, in the Singapore context, this unevenness in student interpretive communities can be attributed to the "surface culture" (Weaver, 2000) approach in multicultural education from elementary to secondary levels, which celebrates ethnic and cultural diversity by focusing on customs, traditions, music, and cuisine, resulting in Singaporean students' "superficial understanding of and limited interaction between cultural groups" (Wu et al., 2020, p. 504). From this, we show how in two separate moments during a small-group discussion of three Chinese students in Katrina's class, students first downplay patronizing portrayals of stereotypes in texts and later deploy ethnocentric perspectives to imagine the experiences of minorities. In the first moment, Katrina has her students discuss the poem "FAQ" in more detail in small groups. One group consists of three Chinese students and their discussion is focused on five particular lines:

> Do you know my friend Tushar?
> Do you know my friend Viknesh?
> Do you know my friend Pavan?
> Do you know my friend Raj?
> Do you know you look like my friend Raj?
> (Somasundram, lines 20–24)

Students consider whether the stereotype that all Indians look alike is a valid one. At first, they appear to condone this stereotype, justifying this by making appeals to anecdotal evidence from their own experiences. However, they miss an opportunity to critically reflect on the cultural assumptions of their opinions stemming from the prejudicial opinions of a majority race:

Student C: Actually . . . all Indians look alike. Like a little bit. . . . But then is it really a bad thing? Because you know a lot of Indians, they are very connected.

Student D: Yeah, it's true.

Student C: It's like really truth . . . it's like [name of Singaporean Indian schoolmate] knows like the whole world or something. Because they got a lot of family friends.

Having been previously introduced to the phenomenon of casual racism in a separate lesson earlier in the unit on a poem about Malay stereotypes, the three students here do not question their own naïve point of view, which does not appear sensitized to casual utterances of racial discrimination and, conversely, conflates all Indians in Singapore into a homogenous, indistinguishable group. In the course of the conversation, the three students, coming from a majority culture, reinforce a prejudicial perspective, justifying this with reference to their own generalized assumptions of a Singaporean Indian schoolmate's social activity. A second moment later on further confirms the students' inability to recognize their own majority culture perspective. At this point, the three students are discussing the significance of these lines in the poem—"Do you speak Indian? / Why don't you speak Indian? / Is your family sad you don't speak Indian?" (lines 5–7):

Student C: I think they are making him guilty.

Student D: Why would [he] be guilty?

Student E: If I ask you all these and relate it to Chinese, will you [feel] guilty?

Student D: For example he [scored] F9* [in] Chinese, then I ask him, "you're Chinese but you cannot speak Chinese."

Student C: Like you will feel bad about yourself.

Student E: Oh.

Student D: [You would] disappoint people.

*Note: * F9 is the lowest grade that a secondary school student in a mainstream Singapore school can score for a subject.*

Here, as students explore the possible reasons for why the persona would feel guilty when faced with questions about his inability to speak his mother tongue language, Student E transposes the situation to her own ethnic background of being Singaporean Chinese. Here, she invokes her sense of the situation's "transpersonal" (Blau, 2003, p. 138) relevance, one in which Chinese students like her may share a similar experience of not being fluent in their mother tongue language. Student D grasps this proposed analogy and proceeds to reimagine the Indian persona as a Chinese person who has failed his mother tongue language as a subject. This elicits empathetic readings by Student C ("Like you will feel bad about yourself") and Student E ("Oh"). However, even as the students attempt to empathize with the Indian persona's possible feelings of guilt, they do so from an ethnocentric point of view using hypothetical anecdotes from their own shared dominant group experiences to try and understand the experiences of a minority group subject. For this age group, Kohlberg's (1981) typology of moral development would locate them at the stage of "conventional morality" (p. 18) where students would be primarily concerned with acting in ways that measure up to others' expectations. As Kohlberg (1981) explains, "awareness of value conflict is not enough to stimulate movement toward principled morality" (p. 239), which would amount to an "awareness of the feelings and claims of the other people in the moral situation" (p. 188). This developmental tendency, combined with the surface culture approach to multicultural education in the postcolonial CHC context of Singapore, explains why at no point is there any attempt to examine the socio-historical-political pressures that minority Indian communities may face in maintaining their competencies in mother tongue languages nor any attempt to problematize the associations of ethnic identity with a monolithic view of linguistic identity.

Challenge 3: Tendency for Students to Provide Emotionally-Charged Responses without Sufficient Self-Reflexivity

The enactment of the workshop approach requires what Blau (2003) has posited as a pedagogical double bind where teachers seek to "encourage [their] students to trust and deploy their own powers as interpreters of texts" while also exercising pedagogical authority to contest students' inadequate interpretations or misreading of the text (pp. 196–197). These challenges may be substantiated by highlighting inconsistencies in students' use of textual evidence. Blau points out that the concern with challenging students' fledgling practice as interpreters may undermine their confidence as independent thinkers. In response, Blau calls upon teachers to focus on students' processes of producing literary interpretations, distinguishing between their "value" and "authority." For Blau, a reading is "*valuable* insofar as it is the product of a student's own engaged and mindful act and leads to subsequent readings and further reflection on a text in a way that might yield a more adequate or even a confirming interpretation" (p. 198). At the same time, some readings "will be more *authoritative* than others" (p. 199) to the degree they can be defended with supporting textual evidence. Thus, the ideal reader is portrayed as one who is able to produce responses that are high value and engaged while supporting these with authoritative, well-substantiated justifications.

In the context of CHCs, high-value responses presume engaged, autonomous interpreters of texts, which may counter some of the core values of Confucianism. In Confucian thought, the self is not regarded as autonomous but embodied in the world and in everyday relations with others. One important concept is self-cultivation—the morally exemplary person is perceived as one who continually cultivates virtues of goodness and benevolence toward others, beginning with one's family and expanding to the world at large (Tu, 1994). The importance of self-cultivation is closely associated with self-reflexivity. This is also why, in many CHCs, values such as social awareness and respect for others are emphasized in education. While scholars have noted that CHCs have increasingly embraced constructivist pedagogies and promoted learner-centered classrooms (Choo & Quek,

2021; Tran, 2013), tensions arise when teachers feel compelled to intervene when engagement exceeds the boundaries of civil discourse and when emotional responses becomes perceived as individualistic.

We present a scene from Rosie's class that foregrounds this tension. Like Katrina's class, she introduces the poem "FAQ" and has the class discuss it in small groups. In one group, students become disturbed and outraged at the provocative lines in the poem:

Student F: This is stupid [*points to the line*]. "Do you speak Indian?"

Student G: Do you know what is even more stupid [*points to another line*]. "Can you, me, and Raj do Halloween as an Oreo?"

Student H: What the heck.

Student F: They can cook more than just curry!

Rosie: This is not reality.

Student F: [They] can cook prata* what? Oreo [is] not just black, white, black, also got different [colors].

Rosie: [*To Student F*] If you can't calm down, I can't talk about it.

Student G: This is super disturbing.

Student H: [*Points to another line*] "Do they cry into their curry because you don't speak Indian?" Damn stupid, what the hell.

Rosie: Another one is offended. Student H is very offended.

Student G: This is super rude.

Rosie: Wait, no. No, guys. Stop. Okay. . . . When you first [read] the poem, your first reaction as a reader, is how the text wants you to respond. This text was intentionally, artistically created in this particular way to get this kind of strong response from you. Your first response is important. This poem is intentionally provocative. It is meant to provoke. Two, but you are not the average reader. You are the lit student. Your job is to stay above and not be offended.

*Note: *prata refers to "roti prata," an Indian flatbread dish often associated with Singaporean Indian cuisine.*

This scene provides an example of a high-value discussion in which students are engrossed and immersed in the text. One explanation for the intense levels of outrage by the students (especially Student F) can be attributed to how the poem presents outright forms of racial discrimination in Singapore. The teacher interjects at certain points to remind them that the context is fictional, that the poet is being deliberately provocative, and that their role as literature students is to go beyond an emotional response in order to analyze more deeply. In a post-unit interview, Rosie reflected that in the lesson, the class was "so agitated and emotionally trapped in that poem that they couldn't actually analyze it as lit students." She attributed this in part to the emphasis on reader-response practices that have tended to blur the boundaries between subjective reactions and objective criticism:

> [The emotional response] was also in part because a lot of the teaching is reader response, which means we stem from the point of view of a reader. But that particular lesson I had to tell them that, "Yes, I get what you're feeling, and what you're feeling is exactly what the poem wants you to feel, but you are lit students, which means you need to transcend this first emotional response and now actually be that third party that analyzes your emotional response.

Pedagogies such as small-group discussion, exploratory talk and Socratic circles are commonly observed in Rosie's classes. While these have validated students' responses and created a safe space for them to articulate their feelings and opinions, what is apparent is a discomfort with overly engaged responses. Hence, she also finds it necessary to intervene and push students toward more socially conscious responses where they can learn to think and feel beyond their own experiences and culture. Perhaps the teacher's intervention at such emotionally charged moments is also important if students lack sufficient intercultural knowledge and global awareness to qualify their responses. For CHCs, this supports Confucian notions of multicultural citizenship such as "openness to other cultures" and a "shared universal family" (Wu et al., 2020).

In summary, we have described various observed scenes of teaching in Singapore literature classrooms that may challenge some of the assumptions of the workshop approach. The first challenge, related to students' deference to the teacher's interpretive authority, is particularly pertinent for CHC cultures that value harmony and respect. The second and third challenges relate to the imposition of majority views and the need for teacher intervention to encourage more socially conscious interpretations about others, particularly those who are marginalized or from unfamiliar cultures. We argue that the workshop approach and its basis on reader-response pedagogy should be further extended to include the pedagogy of Ethical Criticism. Based on the principles of Ethical Criticism that emerged at the turn of the twenty-first century, we show how this approach shifts readers from attunement to self and like-minded peers toward an ethical response and responsibility to others in their society and the world.

Extending the Workshop Approach with Ethical Criticism

Several literary scholars have observed that the beginning of the twenty-first century effected a turn to ethics. The events of 9/11, coupled with a growing consciousness of the intensification of globalization and the exacerbation of global risks such as terrorism and climate change (Beck, 2007), propelled discussions about the fundamental role of literature in cultivating cosmopolitan empathy and hospitable openness toward others. In the early 2000s, a number of edited volumes were published that sought to map this new ethical emphasis in literary studies. They incorporated the ideas of major scholars in literature and philosophy and included such titles as *The Turn to Ethics* (Garber et al., 2000), *Mapping the Ethical Turn* (Davis & Womack, 2001), and *Ethics, Literature, Theory* (George, 2005). Not surprisingly, its associated pedagogy, Ethical Criticism, received renewed attention. Built on the work of Wayne Booth in the 1980s and Noël Carroll, Marshall Gregory, and Martha Nussbaum in the 1990s, Ethical Criticism has, in fact, a long history dating back to Aristotle, who sought to uncover poetry's potential in eliciting philosophical reflection of universal values about human nature and the world (Choo, 2021; Gregory, 2010; Nussbaum, 1997). As Nussbaum (1997) argues, "the teaching of literature can prepare world citizens better if it becomes more truly Socratic, more concerned with self-critical argument and with the contribution of philosophy" (p. 108). A truly inclusive curriculum would require a pedagogical approach that interrupts the reader's interpretive worldview through the lens of the "narrative imagination" (Nussbaum, 1997), the "hospitable imagination" (Choo, 2016), and by adopting the stance of "planetarity" (Spivak, 2012). These similar concepts center on a cosmopolitan orientation that interrupts the boundaries erected by egoism, ethnicity, nationalism, and forms of parochialism.

At the same time, a parallel turn to an other-centric ethics in literature education from the late twentieth century can also be observed, even if literature educators in anglophone contexts did not directly draw on scholars in Ethical Criticism. Such pedagogies aimed to extend reader-centric approaches to other-centric approaches to studying literature using dialogic approaches not dissimilar to Blau's student-centered workshop approaches. For one, the movement of introducing multicultural literature to students had been gaining prominence in American, Australian, and British secondary-level schools from the 1980s (Gunew, 1987; Johnstone, 2011; Norton, 1990). By exposing students in both text selection and classroom discussion to marginal and marginalized groups in both national and global contexts, teachers sought to broaden adolescents' view of the self in the world and to cultivate students' empathetic feeling and thinking for the other in the process (Dressel, 2005; Landt, 2006). A second movement adopted a critical pedagogy and social justice orientation to teaching literature wherein educators not only lead students to empathize with marginalized others but more importantly to identify and critique ideological beliefs that perpetuate injustice and discrimination. Here, antiracist literature pedagogies also use dialogic approaches to render explicit and problematic the prevalence of dominant racial ideologies that systemically privilege members of a majority-race group (Borsheim-Black, 2015; Borsheim-Black & Sarigianides, 2019; Dyches & Thomas, 2020; Schieble, 2012).

Taken together, these other-centric pedagogical approaches to teaching literature focus on the "empathy-altruism hypothesis"—or the notion that reading literature can elicit a reader's empathy toward others, and that this empathy in turn motivates readers to take up prosocial action to address and remove suffering experienced by similar individuals in real life (Bracher, 2023; Keen, 2007; Maxwell, 2018; Nussbaum, 1997). Through the dialogic practices of perspective-taking, other-oriented literature educators aim to guide students to empathize with another's feelings, to provisionally consider the perspective from another's point of view and value stances, which encourage an appreciation of diversity and difference and a commitment toward equity and justice.

More recently, two movements in Ethical Criticism may be discerned, one emerging from Chinese scholars and the other from European scholars. Chinese Ethical Criticism came to the foreground largely through the work of Nie Zhenzhao, a professor of comparative literature in Central China Normal University. Chinese scholars had observed that Chinese literary criticism from the late twentieth century appeared to be dominated by literary theories from the West such as Structuralism, Deconstruction, Postcolonialism, and Feminism, and they were keen to derive their own brand of literary theory (Tian, 2019; Yang, 2013). During this time, Nie formulated his own conception of Ethical Criticism that he (2021) defines as "a critical theory for reading, analyzing, and interpreting the ethical nature and function of literary works from the perspective of ethics" (p. 189). Nie begins from the premise that literature arises out of human beings' need for moral expression. Literature then represents an expression of morality within a specific historical period. An understanding of the historical context is fundamental because one can only appreciate ethics with an understanding of its situatedness. This approach to Ethical Criticism shares some alignment with the tradition of Historical Criticism associated with Biblical studies during the period of European Reformation and Renaissance. However, unlike traditional Historical Criticism and its various branches that focus on historical sources (Source Criticism), processes of transmission and its influence on structure (Form Criticism), and history of the editorial activity (Redaction Criticism), Nie uses history as a starting point to uncover ethical values as an end goal. In other words, knowledge of the socio-historical-political context of the text and the life world of the author are instrumental means to appreciating ethics conditioned within that time and space. Nie (2021) identifies several important concepts that Ethical Criticism should engage with: ethical environment, ethical identity, ethical choice, ethical taboos, ethical dilemmas, ethical boundaries, ethical ends, deconstruction, and ethical consciousness, among others.

The usefulness of this approach is twofold. First, Nie's Ethical Criticism aligns well with the principles of Confucianism that makes this more palatable to literature education in CHCs. Rather than focusing on the close appreciation of the aesthetics of the text or valorizing the reader's informed responses, this form of Ethical Criticism stresses social responsibility as emerging from the educative value of literary study. Nie's Ethical Criticism aligns with the principles of Confucianism concerned with the role of literature and the arts in cultivating virtues such as benevolence and empathy. It should be noted that the capacity to engage in ethical deliberation and abstract reasoning may require a level of maturity more suited to the period of early adolescence onward (see Inhelder & Piaget, 1982). Throughout the *Analects*, Confucius (2014/497 BCE) reiterates the significance of literature, especially poetry, in enabling one to be more humane:

> The Master said, "My young friends, why is it that none of you learn the Odes? The Odes can give the spirit an exhortation, the mind keener eyes. They can make us better adjusted in a group and more articulate when voicing a complaint. (§17.9, p. 286)

This may account for why this approach has gained popularity and been widely adopted by Chinese literary scholars in examining both classical and contemporary texts from China and other parts of the world (Tian, 2019). Its use shifts attention from interpretation to ethical understanding of others as an end in literary discourse. In the case discussed in Challenge 2, in which students overlook the ethical affordances of the poem to critique casual racism by inadvertently imposing their own ethnocentric views, perhaps the solution may not be to cede interpretive authority entirely to the students as suggested by Blau. His workshop approach advances the value of collaborative peer discussion to affirm the role of working with one another to apprehend a literary work more fully. While there is value in empowering students to gain confidence as interpreters of texts, the measure of its effectiveness is not whether students are actively engaged in interpretation but whether they are pushing one another to bridge historical and empathetic gaps between themselves and the other. In cases where students' background knowledge may be inadequate, the inclusion of extratextual knowledge provided by the teacher or other authoritative texts may be necessary.

Secondly, Nie's Ethical Criticism is helpful in guarding against those who analyze literature from their personal ethical values or the moral principles of their contemporaries. This is the case observed in Katrina's class as highlighted in Challenge 2, in which students from a dominant Chinese majority group impose their stereotypical judgments of the text written from the point of view of a minority persona. As Nie argues:

> [Ethical criticism] does not evaluate a work based on today's moral principles. Instead, it emphasizes "historicism" that is the examination of the ethical values in a given work with reference to a particular historical context or a period of time in which the text under discussion is written. The overarching aim of ethical literary criticism is to uncover ethical factors that bring literature into existence and the ethical elements that affect characters and events in literary works. (Ross, 2015, p. 10)

Nie's historicist principles of attending to the ethical values of the work's prevailing sociocultural milieu can be seen as a further extension of Blau's (2003) dimension of literary competence concerning "intertextual literacy," where knowledge of other texts that is "presupposed by most written texts and without which otherwise simple texts can become unintelligible" (p. 206) can validate or discredit interpretations of texts entirely when the references are made explicit.

Although both Western and Chinese critics have extolled the ethical affordances of Nie's theory and methodology, Nie's Ethical Criticism has also been critiqued by Western and Chinese critics alike. Comparatist Dorothy Figueira contends that Nie's ethical concepts "[impose] a rigid and strict function on our reading of literature. It demands our submission to some transindividual ethical power" (Li, 2017, p. 351), suggesting a passive approach to predetermined notions of ethics. Zhang Jie and Liu Zengmei (2007) have critiqued the didactic nature of Nie's Ethical Criticism methodology and argue instead that a pluralist conception of value judgments should underpin such criticism, thus rendering a more dialogical approach for Ethical Criticism. This would then allow for questions about ethical values to be posed and dialogues with readers to occur. Yang Gexin (2016) further proposes that Nie's approach should strive for a multiplicity of criticisms in which Ethical Criticism can operate in conjunction with other types of criticism such as Poststructuralist Criticism.

How then can Ethical Criticism—following Nie's Ethical Criticism—avoid the trap of historicist subjectivity and didacticism, as well as account for the three challenges mentioned previously (that of relying on the teacher's interpretive authority, reinforcing hegemonic views of the majority, and the lack of mature critical-ethical responses to the other)? This is where Nie's Ethical Criticism can be enriched by another strand that emerged at the turn of the twentieth century: Levinasian Ethical Criticism, which promotes an other-centered orientation toward interpreting literary texts in the classroom that broadens Nie's approach. This approach is based on Emmanuel Levinas's "ethics as first philosophy" (Levinas, 2001), which prioritizes the infinite responsibility to the other that always exists prior to one's own attempts at meaning making.

A French philosopher of Lithuanian Jewish ancestry, Levinas embarked on a philosophical project of foundational ethics formulated largely in response to the radical dehumanization of the other during the Second World War and his experience as a French prisoner of war during the Holocaust. Levinas aimed to critique the tendency in Western philosophical tradition to absorb, appropriate, and reduce the other to easy assimilation to the self's interpretation. Instead, Levinas (2006) anchored his philosophy on concrete and particular encounters with another person, which is core to an ethical response: "the responsibility for the Other, for another freedom . . . commands me and ordains me to the other . . . it provokes this responsibility against my will, that is, by substituting me for the other as a hostage" (p. 11).

How does Levinasian ethics apply to literary criticism and, by extension, literature education? Here, we turn to Derek Attridge, who follows Levinas's (1969) caution against the "imperialism of the same" (p. 39), which refers to the innate tendency for one to impose one's interpretations of the other in order to objectify and dominate another through discourse. Attridge (2015) warns of such self-regarding and self-satisfied reading practices that ". . . glides over the work's challenges, or converts otherness to sameness by imposing a common meaning on an uncommon one, or that disregards the context within which the work is being read . . . refusing to accept the responsibility being demanded" (p. 121). An other-centric encounter with the other in literature can be superficially responded to in the form of cultural appreciation. Nie's historicist approach to ethical criticism goes further by pushing the reader to shift toward contextual understanding. The argument is that we cannot truly understand the other without a deep epistemic study of the worldview of the text and author as informed by their respective histories. But Nie's Ethical Criticism falls short in that it valorizes cognitive engagement with the other and discounts the important place of politics (including its associations with violence, power, and ideology). This is where Levinasian Ethical Criticism can fill the gap. For Levinas, an authentic encounter with the other is deeply affective, leading to an obligation that "culminates in a suffering for another, a suffering for his suffering" (Levinas, 2006, p. 18). One cannot suffer with and for another if one does not first of all engage with the forms of violence (political, systemic, discursive, symbolic) that the other has experienced. In this spirit, Ethical Criticism must necessarily be intertwined with political criticism without allowing the latter to overshadow the existential bond of human affinity.

What would a key aim be for the workshop approach if Ethical Criticism were employed in the interpretive process? For one, the aim of Ethical Criticism would be to encourage an attentive openness to the other and the practice of critical reflexivity to interrupt one's prejudices. In considering Levinas's applicability to education, Sharon Todd (2003) observes that this openness toward learning about the other presupposes two points: "that otherness *can* be understood and that learning about others is pedagogically and ethically desirable" (p. 8). Todd (2003) has suggested refocusing our pedagogical attention away from the acquisition of knowledge and instead "to consider practices themselves as relations to otherness" (p. 9). As such, Levinasian Ethical Criticism would require a dispositional shift for students and teachers from efferent and aesthetic readings (Rosenblatt, 1994) to responsible readings of the other. Indeed, it is the very incomprehensibility of the other that allows for response to be manifested in responsibility. Because the other cannot be completely known or objectified, one is dispositionally oriented to read attentively, to read deeply, and to continually push to disrupt prejudicial interpretations, including one's own. An important role of the teacher is to be sensitive to the kinds of discursive dispositions exhibited by students as they engage in literary conversations and to consider the extent to which these may support empathetic and hospitable understandings.

How can students produce a responsible reading of a text in a way that pushes them to look beyond their own interpretive worldview, itself a product of sociocultural forces that form the individual's system of beliefs and customs? This is evidenced in the example of Rosie's class in Challenge 3 where students respond emotionally to a poem. Here, the teacher has to intervene to reflexively reorient them to the otherness of the work. As such, the aim of building students' ease and confidence in literary conversations should go beyond reader-centric principles. Some of these have been outlined by Blau (2003)—to promote processes of rereading and revision, to encourage frequent peer conversations, and to develop evidentiary reasoning and critical thinking skills (pp. 53–59). These are fundamental skills that are particularly useful for CHCs in pushing students to be less reliant on the teacher and to develop confidence in their own opinions. To these, we add two other principles that are what we term "other-centric" as grounded on the theories of Ethical Criticism.

The first principle is to inquire into ethical values emerging from the sociopolitical and historical contexts of the text and use these as a lens to interpretation. This principle is based on Nie's historicist approach to Ethical Criticism. Using the poem "FAQ" that the students in this chapter discussed, it would mean that literary conversations, which may begin with evidentiary responses to the text, would have to be extended to include such questions as:

- Why does the persona voice these concerns? When and where is the persona writing from? What are some key events or movements beyond the text that may have influenced the persona's worldview?
- What race, gender, religion, or other identity group does the persona identify with? What values does this group subscribe to? How might this be similar or different from your own? How do the values of this group influence their members' perception of issues or conflicts faced?

The second principle is to apply empathetic listening, reading, and writing skills in order to practice dispositions of hospitable openness to the other. This principle is based on Levinasian Ethical Criticism that perceives ethics as fundamentally concerned with the prioritization of the other. Here, the teacher plays an important role in instilling an other-centric ethos through which interpretive communities may operate. Rather than a bystander who gives students complete freedom to converse about the text or, at the other extreme, an authoritarian figure who maintains control over the direction and content of the discussion, the literature teacher is more like a cosmopolitan cartographer (Choo & Vinz, 2017), one who role-models a curiosity and openness about other cultures and, more importantly, charts the course by establishing the tone of the conversation. Setting the tone involves encouraging students to practice other-centric dispositions such as learning to listen to others, learning to suspend judgment, learning to respect the views of another even if they are different. It also involves metacognitive capacities that lend attention not just to how one is reading and interpreting the text but with what ethical values one is applying in the process of interpretation. Using the poem "FAQ" as an example, metacognitive questions would entail asking how one has arrived at a particular evaluation or response to the other and with what values one has deployed in doing so. It would also include questions about how the encounter with the other through the text evokes moments of tension or discomfort and to reflect on why one might feel uncomfortable. In the process, students may consider how such encounters also surface their own cultural prejudices and biases.

The importance of social interactions is an aspect that Confucius recognized, but more important than the interaction itself are the dispositions individuals demonstrate through such social interactions. Two of the most important concepts in Confucianism are *ren* (benevolence or kindness toward others) and *li* (ritual action). Because humans are innately self-centered and consumed with wanting to overpower others, *li* (ritual action) plays an important role in training one to behave respectfully and empathetically toward others (Choo, 2020; Ivanhoe, 2014). As Confucius (497 BCE) says, "Restrain the self and return to the rites. This is the way to be humane" (§12.1, 2014, p. 178). Confucius gives the example of archery, and how, after a contest, the competitors should bow to each other and go for a drink afterward. These social rituals acclimatize an individual to focus not on the product of the interaction but the appropriate character dispositions.

To conclude, we argue that building critical-ethical interpretive communities in the literature classroom requires reader-centric approaches proposed by Blau's workshop approach but should be extended to include other-centric approaches such as Ethical Criticism and routines that foster cosmopolitan empathy. In this way, literary conversations do not become ends in themselves but bridges to creating inclusive and tolerant societies. Students too, as they partake actively in these dialogues, learn to imbibe conversational habits of respect and empathy that are foundational to democratic civil societies.

Note

1. The idea that CHCs do not value critical and autonomous thinkers could itself be a stereotypical view. Scholars have noted that critical thinking is, in actual fact, much emphasized in Confucian philosophy (see Tan, 2015; 2017). For example, Confucius often encourages his disciples to examine arguments and present counterarguments. He highlights the principle of remonstrance or duty of someone junior to correct his/her superior when the latter has behaved unethically.

Acknowledgments

Case studies cited in this chapter were supported by the Education Research Funding Programme from the National Institute of Education (NIE), Nanyang Technological University, Singapore (grant OER 22/17 CSL). The views expressed in this chapter are the authors' and do not necessarily represent the views of the NIE.

Works Cited

Attridge, D. (2015). *The work of literature*. Oxford University Press.

Barr, M. D. (2000). Lee Kuan Yew and the "Asian values" debate. *Asian Studies Review, 24*(3), 309–334.

Beck, U. (2007). *World at risk*. Polity Press.

Blau, S. D. (2003). *The literature workshop: Teaching texts and their readers*. Heinemann.

Booth, W. C. (1988). *The company we keep: An ethics of fiction*. University of California Press.

Borsheim-Black, C. (2015). "It's pretty much White": Challenges and opportunities of an antiracist approach to literature instruction in a multilayered White context. *Research in the Teaching of English, 49*(4), 407–429.

Borsheim-Black, C., & Sarigianides, S. T. (2019). *Letting go of literary Whiteness: Antiracist literature instruction for White students*. Teachers College Press.

Bracher, M. (2022). *Literature, social wisdom, and global justice: Developing systems thinking through literary study*. Routledge.

Cazden, C. B. (2001). *Classroom discourse: The language of teaching and learning* (2nd ed.). Heinemann.

Chia, Y. T. (2011). The elusive goal of nation building: Asian/Confucian values and citizenship education in Singapore during the 1980s. *British Journal of Educational Studies, 59*(4), 383–402.

Choo, S. S. (2013). *Reading the world, the globe, and the cosmos: Approaches to teaching literature for the twenty-first century*. Peter Lang.

Choo, S. S. (2016). Fostering the hospitable imagination through cosmopolitan pedagogies: Reenvisioning literature education in Singapore. *Research in the Teaching of English, 50*(4), 400–421.

Choo, S. S. (2020). Examining models of twenty-first century education through the lens of Confucian cosmopolitanism. *Asia Pacific Journal of Education, 40*(1), 20–34.

Choo, S. S. (2021). *Teaching ethics through literature: The significance of ethical criticism in a global age*. Routledge.

Choo, S. S., & Quek, S. Y. S. (2023). Empowering students through cosmopolitan literacies: Pedagogical examples from classrooms in Confucian heritage cultures. In W. O. Lee, P. Brown, A. L. Goodwin, & A. Green (Eds.), *International handbook on education development in the Asia-Pacific* (pp. 601–620). Springer.

Choo, S. S., & Vinz, R. (2017). The literature teacher as restless cartographer: Pedagogies for cosmopolitan ethical explorations. In A. Goodwyn, C. Durrant, L. Reid, & L. Scherff (Eds.), *International perspectives on the teaching of literature in schools: Global principles and practices* (pp. 1–20). Routledge.

Confucius. (2014). *The analects* (A. Chin, Trans.). Penguin. (Original work published 479 BCE)

Curriculum Planning and Development Division. (2019). *Literature in English syllabus: Lower and upper secondary*. Ministry of Education, Singapore.

Davis, T. F., & Womack, K. (Eds.). (2001). *Mapping the ethical turn: A reader in ethics, culture, and literary theory*. University Press of Virginia.

Department of Statistics. (2021). *Census of population 2020 statistical release 1: Demographic characteristics, education, language and religion*. Ministry of Trade & Industry, Singapore.

Dressel, J. H. (2005). Personal response and social responsibility: Responses of middle school students to multicultural literature. *The Reading Teacher*, *58*(8), 750–764.

Durkin, K. (2008). The adaptation of East Asian masters students to western norms of critical thinking and argumentation in the UK. *Intercultural Education, 19*(1), 15–27.

Dyches, J., & Thomas, D. (2020). Unsettling the "White savior" narrative: Reading *Huck Finn* through a critical race theory/critical Whiteness studies lens. *English Education*, *53*(1), 35–53.

Eagleton, T. (1996). *Literary theory: An introduction* (2nd ed.). Blackwell.

Englehart, N.A. (2000). Rights and culture in the Asian values argument: The rise and fall of Confucian ethics in Singapore. *Human Rights Quarterly, 22*(2), 548–568.

Garber, M., Hanssen, B., & Walkowitz, R. L. (Eds.). (2000). *The turn to ethics*. Routledge.

George, S. K. (Ed.). (2005). *Ethics, literature, theory: An introductory reader*. Rowman & Littlefield.

Gregory, M. W. (2010). Redefining ethical criticism: The old vs. the new. *Journal of Literary Theory, 4*(2), 273–302. https://doi.org/10.1515/jlt.2010.017

Gunew, S. (1987). Why and how multi-cultural writing should be included in the English curriculum. *English in Australia*, *82*(Nov), 29–35.

Holden, P. (1999). The great literature debate: Why teach literature in Singapore? In S. H. Chua & W. P. Chin (Eds.), *Localising pedagogy: Teaching literature in Singapore* (pp. 79–89). National Institute of Education.

Ivanhoe, P. J. (2014). Confucian cosmopolitanism. *Journal of Religious Ethics, 42*(1), 22–44.

Johnstone, P. (2011). English and the survival of multiculturalism: Teaching "writing from different cultures and traditions." *Changing English*, *18*(2), 125–133. https://doi.org/10.1080/1358684X.2011.575244

Keen, S. (2007). *Empathy and the novel.* Oxford University Press.

Kim, M. K., & Pollard, V. A. (2017). A modest critical pedagogy for English as a foreign language education. *Education as Change, 21*(1), 50–72.

Kohlberg, L. (1981). *Essays on moral development: Vol. 1. The philosophy of moral development.* Harper & Row.

Landt, S. M. (2006). Multicultural literature and young adolescents: A kaleidoscope of opportunity. *Journal of Adolescent & Adult Literacy*, *49*(8), 690–697. https://doi.org/10.1598/JAAL.49.8.5

Levinas, E. (1969). *Totality and infinity: An essay on exteriority* (A. Lingis, Trans.). Duquesne University Press. (Original work published 1961)

Levinas, E. (2001). *Alterity and transcendence* (M. B. Smith, Trans.). Columbia University Press. (Original work published 1995)

Levinas, E. (2006). *Otherwise than being, or beyond essence* (A. Lingis, Trans.). Duquesne University Press. (Original work published 1974)

Li, J. (2017). Ethical literary criticism and comparative literature: An interview with Professor Dorothy M. Figueira. *Forum for World Literature Studies, 9*(3), 347–354.

Liew, W. M. (2012). Valuing the value(s) of literature. *Commentary, 21*, 57–71.

Loh, C. E. (2013). Singaporean boys constructing global literate selves through their reading practices in and out of school. *Anthropology & Education Quarterly, 44*(1), 38–57.

Maxwell, B. (2018). The link between fiction and empathy as a trait of moral character: A pedagogical legend? In T. Harrison & D. Walker (Eds.), *The theory and practice of virtue education* (pp. 126–139). Routledge.

Nie, Z. (2021). Ethical literary criticism: A basic theory. *Forum for World Literature Studies, 13*(2), 189–207.

Norton, D. E. (1990). Teaching multicultural literature in the reading curriculum. *The Reading Teacher, 44*(1), 28–40.

Nussbaum, M. C. (1997). *Cultivating humanity: A classical defense of reform in liberal education*. Harvard University Press.

O'Dwyer, S. (2017). Deflating the "Confucian heritage culture" thesis in intercultural and academic English education. *Language, Culture and Curriculum, 30*(2), 198–211.

O'Sullivan, M. W., & Guo, L. (2011). Critical thinking and Chinese international students: An East-West dialogue. *Journal of Contemporary Issues in Education, 5*(2), 53–73.

Poon, A. M. C. (2010). Constructing the cosmopolitan subject: Teaching secondary school literature in Singapore. *Asia Pacific Journal of Education, 30*(1), 31–41.

Rosenblatt, L. M. (1994). *The reader, the text, the poem: The transactional theory of the literary work*. Southern Illinois University Press.

Ross, C. (2015). A conceptual map of ethical literary criticism: An interview with Nie Zhenzhao. *Forum for World Literature Studies, 7*(1), 7–14.

Schieble, M. (2012). Critical conversations on Whiteness with young adult literature. *Journal of Adolescent & Adult Literacy, 56*(3), 212–221. https://doi.org/10.1002/JAAL.00130

Somasundram, L. V. (2016). F.A.Q. In J. Ip, R. Tang, & D. Q. Yam (Eds.), *SingPoWriMo 2016: The anthology* (pp. 128–129). Math Paper Press.

Spivak, G. C. (2012). *An aesthetic education in the era of globalization.* Harvard University Press.

Tan, C. (2012). "Our shared values" in Singapore: A Confucian perspective. *Educational Theory, 62*(4), 449–463.

Tan, C. (2015). Beyond rote-memorisation: Confucius' concept of thinking. *Educational Philosophy and Theory, 47*(5), 428–439.

Tan, C. (2017). A Confucian conception of critical thinking. *Journal of Philosophy of Education, 51*(1), 331–343.

Tan, C., & Tan, C. S. (2014). Fostering social cohesion and cultural sustainability: Character and citizenship education in Singapore. *Diaspora, Indigenous, and Minority Education, 8*(4), 191–206. https://doi.org/10.1080/15595692.2014.952404

Tian, J. (2019). Nie Zhenzhao and the genesis of Chinese ethical literary criticism. *Comparative Literature Studies, 56*(2), 402–420.

Todd, S. (2003). *Learning from the other: Levinas, psychoanalysis, and ethical possibilities in education.* State University of New York Press.

Tran, T. T. (2013). Is the learning approach of students from the Confucian heritage culture problematic? *Education Research for Policy and Practice, 12*(1), 57–65.

Tu, W. (1994). Embodying the universe: A note on Confucian self-realization. In R. T. Ames, W. Dissanayake, & T. P. Kasulis (Eds.), *Self as person in Asian theory and practice* (pp. 177–186). State University of New York Press.

Tu, W. (2000). Implications of the rise of "Confucian" East Asia. *Daedalus, 129*(1), 195–218.

Turner, J. (2010). *Language in the Academy: Cultural reflexivity and intercultural dynamics.* Multilingual Matters.

Weaver, G. R. (Ed.). (2000). *Culture, communication and conflict: Readings in intercultural relations.* Pearson.

Wee, C. J. W.-L. (1999). "Asian values", Singapore, and the third way: Re-working individualism and collectivism. *Sojourn: Journal of Social Issues in Southeast Asia, 14*(2), 332–358.

Wimsatt, W. K., & Beardsley, M. C. (2001). The intentional fallacy. In V. B. Leitch (Ed.), *The Norton anthology of theory and criticism* (pp. 1374–1387). W. W. Norton & Company. (Original work published 1946)

Wimsatt, W. K., & Beardsley, M. C. (2001). The affective fallacy. In V. B. Leitch (Ed.), *The Norton anthology of theory and criticism* (pp. 1387–1403). W. W. Norton & Company. (Original work published 1949)

Wu, S. P., Tan, C., & Ng, C. S. L. (2020). Educating multicultural citizens from a Confucian heritage: Examples from Singapore. In E. J. Delgado-Algarra & J. M. Cuenca-López (Eds.), *Handbook of research on citizenship and heritage education* (pp. 501–525). IGI Global.

Yang, G. (2013). Ethical turn in literary studies and the revival of American ethical criticism. *Foreign Literature Studies, 35*(6), 16–25.

Yang, G. (2016). *American ethical criticism: A survey.* Central China Normal University Press.

Yeo, R. (1999). National education in Singapore: Promoting NE in the literature curriculum in secondary schools and junior colleges. In S. H. Chua & W. P. Chin (Eds.), *Localising pedagogy: Teaching literature in Singapore* (pp. 68–78). National Institute of Education.

Zhang, J., & Liu, Z. (2007). Interpretation of the ethical literary criticism from the perspective of pluralism. *Foreign Literature Studies, 5*, 137–143.

Chapter Eight

The Disputatious Personality and the Value of Listening

Peter Smagorinsky

In the 1990s, my university career began with my appointment as assistant professor in the College of Education at the University of Oklahoma. I also became involved in the Oklahoma Council of Teachers of English (OKCTE), the state's affiliate organization of the National Council of Teachers of English (NCTE). I served on their Executive Board, and during our planning of the annual convention one year, I thought it would be stimulating to invite a couple of people from different positions and perspectives to discuss and debate policy issues surrounding public education. I hoped that attendees would benefit from the exchange of ideas coming from people whose experiences and dispositions led to different understandings and approaches and that the discussion would prove stimulating beyond the confines of the conference.

I had two people in mind. One was Julius Caesar "J. C." Watts, a conservative Oklahoma Republican Congress representative. Watts had played quarterback for the Oklahoma Sooners, a position where he had to make immediate recognitions based on film study and coaching to note defensive tendencies and real-time speed-reads of a constantly changing, often disguised defensive formation. It's a smart man's position, and I admired Watts's intelligence and fortitude in becoming the first African American Republican US Representative from south of the Mason-Dixon Line since Reconstruction. I disagreed with him on just about every political issue, and so I thought he might make a good participant on a convention panel.

The other person was someone I'd met through NCTE, Sheridan Blau. At the time, he was director of UCSB's South Coast

Writing Project (SCWriP) and a veteran of many policy wars in California over the teaching and assessment of literature and writing. Sheridan was, like Watts, a smart guy. He was famously well-versed in the issues and loved a good disagreement. He seemed the ideal person to match wits with Watts in a discussion about how to conduct schooling in the early 1990s, when the Culture Wars were kicking into high gear and education was serving as a principal theater for playing out ideological battles across US society.

But when I approached Sheridan about coming to Oklahoma to discuss education with Watts, he said something like, "Sorry, I don't want to debate another politician." My understanding of his reluctance, and his decline of the invitation, was that politicians don't engage with opponents' ideas. Rather, they argue to win or to assert an ideological perspective on reality rather than to learn from or to even listen to what their opponent is saying. Simply having two people state and defend opposing points of view without recognizing and addressing their areas of difference, and possibility for synthesis, is not a worthwhile debate. For an exchange to succeed in advancing understandings, the antagonists need to listen to one another. If they simply talk past each other, they advance neither their own position nor that of the people in attendance. Without good listening and an ego that accommodates growth over certitude and victory, such a debate would have little value.

Sheridan's point was substantiated in another debate I did successfully organize for the OKCTE convention. I persuaded people from two very different perspectives on the teaching of high school English language arts to talk about the profession's purposes and practices. One set of speakers consisted of teachers who voiced a classroom perspective grounded in their experiences with adolescents and the structural constraints of working within public schools. I matched them with a university English professor who believed that secondary school teachers weren't preparing students well enough for college studies. The session went about as well as Sheridan would have predicted: The teachers emphasized the challenges faced in public education, the professor spoke from the ideal perspective of the university, neither side listened except to refute, and the hour ended with far more frustration than fruition. So much for my ability to plan for a compelling conference experience.

These stories help me reflect on the theme of this essay, the disputatious personality as exemplified by Sheridan and the value of productive dispute to the advancement of ideas. They also demonstrate how simply planning for idea exchanges based on the presentation of opposing views does not necessarily produce anything new, satisfying, or compelling. I next ground this dynamic tension in a construct that was central to the worldview of L. S. Vygotsky, a Soviet psychologist whose short, mercurial career spanned the early 1920s through his death at age 37 in 1934 from tuberculosis. From there, I move to a review of dialectics, the engagement of opposing ideas to produce something new in contrast with the tendency for opposing views to clash and remain unchanged. I explore the role of productive disagreement and inherent contradiction in teaching English language arts, focused on teaching writing and literature. Each field has grown through the engagement of opposing views, a phenomenon that characterized the National Writing Project's challenge to formalist orthodoxies that have often followed from socialization processes. Teaching literature has also involved competing philosophies that position teachers in their midst, resulting in contradictory practices that appear relationally and situationally, often without resolution. I conclude with an argument that a deep immersion in contradictory environments, aided by a disputatious personality, requires listening to advance the field beyond irreconcilable differences and toward synthesis and progress (Smagorinsky, 2023).

Vygotsky: Very Disputatious, Very Stimulating

Vygotsky argued with a lot of people through deep engagement and disagreement with the ideas of his day, often those of the era's most respected and titanic figures. He took on Freud, Pavlov, Piaget, and many others, disagreeing with a chutzpah that in a sense was shocking for a young man born and raised within the lowly social position limited to the Jewish people on the margins of Tsarist Russia. Vygotsky and other Jewish people had been confined to the Pale of Settlement in Belarus, both to preserve the Christian purity of Russia and to make them easy targets for the deadly pogroms of the era.

Vygotsky survived the antisemitism of his day and region and the obscurity of his origins to rapidly ascend the ranks of psychology in the newly formed Soviet Union. He did not do so by being quiet and compliant. Even as a young outsider, he took on any idea he found inadequate. He led a movement that forced psychology to be more comprehensive in its scope, to become more historical in understanding the social conventions framing human development, to attend to the cultures produced by historical activity and how they shape societal and individual frames of mind, and to see any individual mind as situated within the contours provided by societies and communities.

Vygotsky typically presented his understandings in contrast with those of a contemporary giant. He would begin by reviewing someone's account of a psychological phenomenon in painstaking detail, engaging carefully, analytically, and thoughtfully with their stated understandings. From there, he enumerated the flaws in the conception to build an alternative based on what he considered better research. In doing so, he implemented a way of thinking typically ascribed to Georg Wilhelm Friedrich Hegel, a Prussian philosopher who lived from 1770–1831.

Hegel was a major influence on Karl Marx, who in turn provided the critical foundation for Soviet society and psychology; ironically, the Soviets in short order shut down dialectical thinking, imposing instead state dogma. What is often known as Hegel's dialectical formulation relied on the union of opposites, with a thesis-antithesis-synthesis process for development of productive human conceptions. Hegel never actually used the three terms in this fashion, leaving Marx to popularize them in his name (Benson, 2003). I next turn to dialectical materialism to illuminate the value of how I see Sheridan Blau's disputatious personality serving to advance understandings rather than, as is often the case in a polarized society, to leave two opposing camps shouting into the night and only producing more noise. Being disputatious does not mean someone is disagreeable or unpleasant. Rather, I use the term to characterize those who, like

Blau and Vygotsky, see disagreement as stimulating and formative in the development of their own perspectives. It is a quality that, channeled through productive discourse, advances not only oneself but potentially a field of scholarship and endeavor.

Dialectics

Dialectics involves the logic of change. The universe is not a static place but is always in flux. Not only is the material world continually shifting in relation to natural elements and human activity, but ideas are always evolving through the influence of volcanic cognitive eruptions, the erosion of established understandings, shifts in the ideological winds, and other factors. These environmental changes challenge the notion that knowledge is fixed and ready-made for people to accept wholly and without contestation, as claimed by those who assert that their positions are based on "settled science" (e.g., Stukey et al., 2019), a claim that is easily debunked by reading the history of any science as it has evolved over time.

Rather, the mind is always in action, along with everything else (Wertsch, 1999). Engels, Marx's intellectual companion, pithily states the issue when he characterizes dialectics as "nothing more than the science of the general laws of motion and development of nature, human society and thought" (quoted in Miller, 1982, p. 106). There might be moments of apparent equilibrium and stasis, but these conditions are temporary lulls in the general turmoil of change and development, illusions that suggest greater stability than has ever actually occurred. One needn't be a Marxist in other respects to accept this axiom.

With nothing fixed and everything in motion, multiple ideas and realities can exist at the same time. They might appear in conventional argumentation or in narratives and their counternarratives. This multiplicity of perspectives provides the dynamic tension upon which dialectic materialism is coiled. Often, the ideological basis for contradictory ideas provides for more head-butting than interpenetration of minds. The Soviet insistence on the superiority of socialistic/communistic national means of economic organization and the Euro-American insistence on the merits of capitalism have rarely come into true dialogue. Rather, the two positions' adherents argue that there is a forced choice between two incommensurate opposite conceptions. The merits and ideals of each are juxtaposed without engagement or respectful acknowledgment, at least among those voicing ideologies. This type of oppositional thinking, absent engagement, tends to reinforce ideologies rather than allowing them to evolve. Opposition remains firmly in place with each side seeking total victory.

Soviet architect Vladimir Lenin (1914/1965) characterized the dialectic approach as "the doctrine of the unity of opposites." Vygotsky (1999) described this union of opposites by saying, "great genius develops with the help of another great genius not so much by assimilation as by clashing. One diamond polishes another" (p. 121). The sort of unity available through the engagement of opposites has rarely been achieved in ideological conflicts, which often produce more wars than understandings. These wars might be armed conflicts or might be the sort of Culture Wars that undoubtedly led Sheridan Blau to assume that it would not be possible to have a productive exchange with a politician of contrary ideology, one whose discourse community is driven by winning more than learning, a problem not confined to any political party. As my own experiences can testify, it's also often the case among academics and educators to take hard and fast positions that confirm their expertise and support their egos rather than to engage thoughtfully with people they see as antagonists. As a result, the field has Reading Wars, Culture Wars, Math Wars, Science Wars, and wars for pretty much everything else that happens in school, often accompanied by the claim that one perspective is based on "settled science" that wins the day for its adherents. This sort of victorious stance represents the kind of disposition rejected by dialectical thinking.

Few of these conflicts create space for nonbinary thinking. The Reading Wars tend to align antagonists according to either a nature position or a nurture position (Yaden et al., 2021). The "Science of Reading" camp is largely biological, studying the brain to determine how to teach reading. The sociocultural camp is largely environmental, looking outside the human head to consider how to shift settings to better enable reading.

Advocates of both perspectives tend to talk past rather than with each other, resulting in binaries from which the wars are launched and conducted. Meanwhile, both the brain and the environment continue to matter in how people learn to read.

Polarized ideological positions too often do not provide the paradox available in dialectics that allows for contrary perspectives to coexist in a synthetic formulation. Not all perspectives, I should note, require careful listening and respectful attention. If you approach me with the argument that the earth is flat because it sure seems that way to you, then I will refer you to someone else for a discussion, because I've seen photographs, and the earth is round. The opposing perspective needs to have merit in order to provide the basis for a synthesis, and decisions about merit are often subjective. These perspectives might be fortified through argumentative moves, with evidence such as a photograph from space sustaining a position. They might be fortified with experiential stories whose resonance demonstrates a point, including anecdotes, thought experiments, and other narrative means. What matters is putting different reasonable understandings in dialogue to emerge with something more complete than either is alone.

The decade of the 2020s is deeply divided, suggesting that no middle ground—or more ideally, no new ground built on the shifting foundation of the old—is possible. A society rent by binary positioning cannot manifest the unity of opposites in either the material or the ideological world. If anything, it is designed to produce a winner whose scorched-earth tactics obliterate the enemy, allowing for no contrariness or dissent and creating the illusion of permanence. The world of the 2020s provides little space for growth in schools or society. It is an era of entrenchment from which little positive development is available. What follows is likely a continued state of stasis, albeit a temporary holding pattern that inevitably will shift as the environment changes its currents and contours over time.

The thesis-antithesis-synthesis is, in contrast, productive. Dialectical thought requires an understanding of both the thesis and the antithesis, the contradictory points in play, no matter what genre they appear in. It also requires practical evidence to support claims, which may come from conventional argumentation or the force of a narrative presentation. Thinking thoughts alone is insufficient for promoting change; change requires activity in material contexts. Vygotsky (1987) was adamant on this point, while also valuing the abstraction available through education and other means of formal learning. But without practical application and empirical validation, abstract thinking is hollow and useless. At the same time, without abstraction, everyday conceptions are stuck in the context of their learning, with no way of extrapolating to new-but-similar circumstances. Both "scientific" (academic) and "spontaneous" (everyday) conceptions can guide life, especially when they work in tandem, in a dialectical relationship.

Vygotsky (1997) held views that no doubt run against some current conceptions but that fit with his emphasis on the unity of opposites and his understanding of the process of human development. For instance, he asserted that learning should not be too easy but rather benefits from overcoming impediments: "it is necessary to take care to create as many difficulties as possible in the child's education, as starting points for his thoughts. . . . If you would like a child to learn something well, take care to place obstacles in his path" (pp. 174–175). Contrast this view with the breezy understandings of the zone of proximal development in which teachers make learning smooth and direct via "scaffolding," Bruner's term for structuring learning activities to produce increasing independence after initial support (Wood et al., 1976; see Smagorinsky, 2018, for critiques of ZPD misinterpretations). To Vygotsky, however, overcoming obstacles is an important part of learning.

Dialectic Thinking in the English Language Arts

This excursion into the role of dialectic materialism comes in the context of my reflections on Sheridan Blau's career. Sheridan has always been a ready disputant with a challenging stance in high-stakes discussions. The field has often embraced cooperative and collaborative approaches under the assumption that they are nicer and more affirming than sharply argued counterpoints or challenging counternarratives. They are also prone to the manipulations of people who know how to operate in groups while maintaining a patina of collegiality, but that's another story.

Sheridan is not uncooperative, but he is argumentative, and that's a good thing. He made his most important contributions by questioning conventional wisdom and the passing fads of education. He left this legacy both in his interpersonal engagement with people and on the pages of books or articles (e.g., Blau, 2003). Such a disposition can be destructive to groups when the argumentative sort is a poor listener with an ego too great to create space for accommodation and respectful disagreement. When ideas clash, when iron sharpens iron or diamonds polish diamonds, they can't simply collide and bounce back to their points of origin. They need to emerge all the better for the confrontation via a new understanding grounded in a synthesis. I think that Sheridan has succeeded in policy discussions because he is both assertive and open-minded in considering whether a unity of opposites might be possible, pushing hard against received wisdom to see how it manages when under stress. As a literary scholar, he was conversant with both argumentative and narrative modes of ideation. They needn't be considered mutually exclusive, as Bruner (1986) positioned them. Rather, they often work in tandem, with argumentative evidence provided by stories and stories implying arguments.

Teaching Writing

I suspect that Sheridan was attracted to the field of English education because of its practical nature. Like many people of his generation, his doctorate and early scholarship were in the area of literary analysis, dissertating on "Texts and Contexts: Studies toward a Reading of George Herbert." People are often surprised to find that George Hillocks, Charles Bazerman, and other writing researchers of their era had no formal training in writing theory and research. Rather, they did conventional critical studies of literary texts and authors in graduate school. When I got my master's degree under Hillocks in 1976–77, I was often treated to his views based on his 1970 dissertation, "The Synthesis of Art and Ethic in Tom Jones," the novel by Henry Fielding.

To generate a field of composition theory and research, these scholars and teachers had little precedent. There was such a dearth of formal research that, until 1963, it had never been organized into a comprehensive body of work. At that point, Braddock, Lloyd-Jones, and Schoer combed through widely scattered writing studies, many of which were unpublished dissertations, to draw conclusions about the research base and to create a foundation for a formal field of study. Virtually all writing research to that point had been conducted on the teaching of writing in schools and first-year composition courses in college. The pioneers of writing theory, research, and practice launched their antithesis against the thesis of formalism, the dominant approach to that point that emphasized the imitation of models, instruction in rules of grammar and usage, and other formalist values underlying much school instruction. The process movement that emerged in the wake of Braddock et al. included both formal research that relied on experimental studies and methods adapted from anthropology, communication, and other fields; and teachers' "lore" (North, 1987) based in experiential knowledge, working from testimonials, narratives, and inquiries to challenge the assumptions and norms of formalism.

The launch of the National Writing Project in 1974 was among the largest and best-networked efforts designed to challenge the dominant orthodoxy of the era. It was practitioner-driven, urging teachers to become one another's critical friends and colleagues in identifying effective ways to teach writing. If anything, university-based people were marginal to this effort beyond orchestrating sites within which teachers were elevated to the status of the most knowledgeable and respected authorities about how to teach writing. At the time, experimental research dominated the investigative world, and Graves's (1979) admonition that "research doesn't have to be boring" characterized how many classroom teachers felt about the sterile tone of the research reports, which seemed stale and lifeless in contrast with the teeming, fecund vitality of classrooms. These tensions were among many that emerged when I began teaching in the mid-1970s, and many remain in play a half-century later.

The formalist monolith provided the established base that needed to be displaced in order for students to become liberated from the constraints of correctness and rigid, mimetic roles. Both traditions and teachers themselves were considered the problem to be overcome. Elbow (1973) argued that students might be better off without teachers, writing themselves into their own process instead of following instructional dictates. Graves (1983) described himself as damaged by negative feedback from his teachers. Emig (1971) described teachers as "neurotic" practitioners of the five-paragraph theme and other strict forms (p. 99). They were among many who questioned both the traditions governing the English language arts and the people who taught it as they sought alternatives to the stultifying effects of the formalist emphasis. Their general solution was to emphasize "the writing process"—only one—consisting of a series of steps that writers go through regardless of the task or setting. These views became part of the new orthodoxies developed within the National Writing Project and among its advocates, the antithesis to the formalist thesis.

Yesterday's antithesis becomes today's thesis. The assumptions behind both formalism and the mimetic tradition, and the new orthodoxies about a single writing process, provided the thesis that I was educated to question through my studies with George Hillocks (1986; 1995). George was concerned that this general teaching approach was insensitive to the specific demands of tasks such as argumentation, narrative, and other genres (Smagorinsky & Smith, 1992). Like the NWP architects, he believed that an exclusive emphasis on formalism was somewhere between ineffective and damaging to writers. Where he departed was in his view, which he developed as a junior high school English teacher in the 1950s and 1960s in Euclid, Ohio, that one general process does not take into account the particular strategies that benefit writers engaged with a writing task like personal narrative or extended definition. Simply knowing "the writing process" formula of prewriting, drafting, etc. was inadequate to specific tasks. This insight became the basis for my own doctoral dissertation (Smagorinsky, 1991).

This brief historical review suggests how in the field of writing theory, research, and practice, movements have developed in dialogue with prior movements. More recent challenges to the perspectives developed in the 1960s–1980s, regardless of which process theory one followed, would emphasize such factors as social positioning, racialized means of engagement with ideas, cultural discourse conventions, gendered ways of experiencing schooling, and other issues that originate outside the building and surface in classroom life. The hegemony of classroom instruction as the focus of writing studies, designed to find "what works" in writing instruction regardless of context, further encouraged the study of writing in the professions, in communities, in everyday activities, and in other settings. The assumption behind this expansion of sites for writing research was that knowing how people write outside school should help direct writing instruction in school (Smagorinsky, 2006).

Since the 1990s, various semiotic conceptions have shifted attention away from writing altogether and toward other sign systems, especially but not limited to those afforded by technology. After a few decades in which the seductive lure of multimodality took over composition studies, a refocus on verbal writing has emerged, as indicated by a 2022 communication from the Writing and Literacies Special Interest Group of the American Educational Research Association in which the leadership encouraged their membership to pay more attention to writing. Each of these shifts has served as the antithesis to an established thesis, helping to produce a new synthesis that provides a provisional state of stability awaiting the next challenge and development.

The National Writing Project and the Challenge to Orthodoxy

Sheridan Blau played a key role in the emergence of the National Writing Project through his founding and directing—with his colleagues Carol Dixon, Stephen Marcus, and Jack Phreaner—the South Coast Writing Project (SCWriP) at UCSB in 1979. It was among the original sites in what became a national network of writing teachers. Like other NWP sites, SCWriP challenged the orthodoxies of the day, a task well-suited to the eminently argumentative Dr. Blau. One doctrine of the day was that expertise resides in university professors, with teachers positioned as empty vessels waiting to be filled with the nectar of university research.

The investment of authority in teachers was a major departure from that historical set of relationships, and Sheridan's role in this shift suggests his interest in and ability for crossing boundaries and building communities, along with an emphasis on practical application of the abstractions and ideals that typify university thinking. The hierarchy placing universities above schools diminished teachers' knowledge and experience. This arrangement was predicated on the assumption that the best information about classrooms comes from detached outsiders with formal research training who drop in to study them, then drop out and rarely return to share their findings or have them validated by those whose work produced them. Spending time in schools after the data are collected carries no reward in the university evaluation system. Prestige and promotions follow from publications, so there's no reward-incentive to motivate a return to share and discuss findings with the people whose teaching and learning enabled the study and to get insights from the people responsible for the data.

NWP sites further contested the instructional dominance of formalism, replacing it with a process model associated with Elbow (1973) and others who argued against teacher direction and for uninhibited student-directed composition available through "the writing process." These centerpieces of NWP workshops and institutes even reached the contents of writing textbooks, which began including some attention to brainstorming, drafting, response, revision, and publication while maintaining a foundation of formalism to satisfy the dominant tradition. The two often rested together uneasily, but the insistence by many in the profession that formalism was insufficient provided one avenue toward breaking up its monopoly. The synthesis available in textbooks, and no doubt classrooms, was a bit lumpy, but it was a start.

There is a danger when new orthodoxies emerge. Egotism, consulting fees, fame, and other benefits become available to those who propound the new truths. But those truths are not always so self-evident, and they benefit from skepticism from a committed, disputatious sort of person. Sheridan Blau never got too comfortable with the doctrines that replaced the straightjacket of formalism. I always admired the way he was intellectually restless and didn't rule out a perspective just because of the location of its source. This disposition no doubt helped him to elevate teachers in the SCWriP to the highest levels of authority. But that didn't lead him to reject other sources of knowledge, including university writing researchers. He went to the conferences and didn't just bask in his own celebrity but stuck his head into the mouth of whatever lion he thought might be worth a closer look. I first met him at an annual meeting of the Conference on College Composition and Communication, a place far removed from the task of teaching writing and engaging with literature with adolescents in public schools. He went because it was a site where ideas came into contact, where engagement with contrasting views permeated the program and conference hallways, albeit with various orthodoxies in the air that stunted rather than stimulated new thinking.

Socialization and Orthodoxy

Pushing forward can require questioning accepted wisdom, including your own and that of your tribe. I once introduced George Hillocks by reflecting on a principle from his teaching, "Always examine assumptions, especially your own." I was socialized into Western conventions for argumentation derived from the Age of Reason and its presumed enlightenment via rational, scientific thought. This tradition valorized logical argumentation at the expense of narrative modes of thinking, even as literary study tends to involve both. My own socialization in university studies, however, emphasized formalism, first the New Criticism permeating the Kenyon College faculty and then the neo-Aristotelian formalism of the University of Chicago department of English, whose courses I took as a master's student (Smagorinsky, 2024). I brought this value into my initial teaching before broadening my appreciation for other ways of engaging with literature, even as I'd been taught by Hillocks other ways of engaging with literature: writing alternative endings to stories, rewriting a literary narrative from another speaker's perspective, producing a parody of an author, and so on. Socialization can run pretty deep in one's soul.

I learned argumentative conventions within the tradition captured by Toulmin (1958), who formulated argumentation as involving claims that something is so, data that supports the claim, warrants that render data into evidence for the claim, backing that supports the warrant, a modality that establishes the certainty of the argument, and the rebuttal of counterarguments. The idea of rebutting counterarguments might fit with the dialectical value of listening, depending on how a counterargument is treated. If it's summarily dismissed, then the speaker or writer is probably less interested in listening and more interested in winning, and a synthesis will be sacrificed to the need for the rewards following from victory.

I relied on Toulmin, who influenced Hillocks (e.g., Hillocks, 2011), when I taught argumentative writing to students. Toulmin's claim-data-warrant model is built into the American Psychological Association (APA) text structure (Bazerman, 1988) and has provided the basis for major studies of the teaching of argument in schools (Newell et al., 2015). It is the general means by which I've mounted scholarly arguments in my career, at least when writing for journals and book publishers. But it's not how every culture engages in argumentation, a problem when a cultural approach to persuasion is considered un-Toulminian and therefore dubious in logic. As is often the case, the nondominant culture is at the mercy of the gatekeepers of the institution, and other ways of being are considered intellectually weak.

Although I tend to avoid gross cultural generalizations, I have been persuaded that African American discourse genres do not necessarily follow the conventions of Western academic knowledge displays. I will use what I know of this genre to illustrate the notion that not all groups of people do things the same or according to dominant culture traditions, even as ethnocentrism often produces the assumption that my people and I represent the crown of creation. African American argumentation outside the academy may involve different procedures from those described by Toulmin. Lee (1993; cf. Gates, 1989) relates how one such tradition involves signifying, the exchange of ritual insults, a way of making a point that violates the culture of politeness that governs US schools and is considered by some as a form of bullying (e.g., Rivers & Espelage, 2013). Kochman

(1981) found that in public forums involving Black and white community residents, Black speakers were more passionate and considered the more reserved white speakers to lack commitment; in the same discussions, white speakers were more detached and interpreted the more emotional Black speakers as being illogical. Majors (2015) found that in community settings, Black speakers tend to justify their beliefs through personal narratives of their experiences, call-and-response patterns originating in Black churches that include others as participants, the signifying practices described by Lee and Gates, performative presentations of views and narratives, and other aspects of African American cultural norms.

Arguments in this sense don't follow Toulmin's reliance on detached analysis but value passionate, performative, story-driven, experiential expression of a perspective on social issues. In school, this means of argumentation tends to be viewed as irrational, overly emotional, and inappropriate, such that students from outside the dominant culture are obligated to check their socialization at the door and act like a different sort of person in order to be recognized as academically sound. This structural bias is built into schools and society and is among the means by which white ways are reified and other ways are penalized, another example of the institutional racism that puts students on unequal footing in school (Crenshaw et al., 1996).

If Western conventions are the thesis, and the African American discourse genre is the antithesis, is a synthesis available? Not in current times, when white supremacy is reinforced through the national uprising against Critical Race Theory, the Diversity-Equity-Inclusion movement, the presence in libraries and curricula of books that present a Black perspective, and other challenges to the established hierarchies that have long governed schools. This problem illustrates the ways in which entrenched battles between polarized positions work against the sort of synthesis that characterizes a dialectic society in which growth and change are understood as normal, and stasis is mistaken for established knowledge or eternal truth or settled science that must not be violated.

Two issues emerge from this contrast. First, it's very challenging for a nondominant perspective or set of practices to make headway against an established culture's orthodoxies, making it difficult for these African American discourse practices to be valued and rewarded in school. That is, a deeply embedded thesis may be difficult to challenge in institutions with a viable antithesis offered by a minoritized population. Second, without that challenge, conventional wisdom can never be questioned, rather serving as the only option within a doctrinaire system. How one argues or how one narrates is a point to be argued, and by listening to a perspective that ran contrary to what I had been taught to value, I broadened my understanding of educational and societal processes through which advantages are maintained and alternatives rejected. My synthesis from listening has, I hoped, broadened my mind and opened me to ways of being that schools have rarely endorsed or rewarded.

Teaching Literature

A major tension in the teaching of literature has long bedeviled the field. It is typically represented as a binary choice between strict formalism, as available in New Criticism and its emphasis on close reading of the technical structure of a work, and reader-response theories that make the reader's subjective experiences the most critical factor in a literary reading. Studying form is regarded by many as passé, an artifact of the days of structuralism and formalism's hold on school and university literary teaching. The reader-response alternative in its most radical forms makes the text almost incidental to the more important processes occurring when readers look inward to explore their feelings, stimulated by something in the text (e.g., Bleich, 1975). The polarity has often produced an imperative to make a choice between analyzing the text and analyzing the self. This tension has produced in many teachers and readers a contradiction: They believe in the reader's need to personalize readings while simultaneously pulled by the gravity of tradition to emphasize conventional readings based on the arrangement of textual signs and structures so as to understand the author's intentional orchestration of features (Rabinowitz, 1987).

What is a teacher to do when forced to choose between seemingly incommensurate options positioned as polar opposites? In practice, they typically do both, with or without a formal resolution. In the 1990s, I was part of a project in which such inconsistency was characterized as "doubleness," with the suggestion that such inconsistencies indicated a dim mind, a bad compromise, almost a moral failure (Marshall et al., 1995). Teachers who emphasized conventional readings while also saying that they valued open-ended, student-generated responses in the constructivist tradition appeared to be unreflective, professing to honor two conflicting paradigms at once, often without recognizing the contradiction. Rather, we assumed, it was more responsible to teach in one way or the other, preferably in student-centered, constructivist ways.

That was then. This is now. I see it differently these days after spending several decades studying how teachers account for their instruction and reading more extensively in various fields taking a cultural-historical approach (synthesized in Smagorinsky, 2020). Those experiences have taught me that human contradiction is to be expected, not criticized. Walt Whitman wrote in "Song of Myself," "Do I contradict myself?/Very well then I contradict myself;/(I am large, I contain multitudes.)" As do I, and as do you. People are contradictory, not because of intellectual feebleness but because they are immersed in contradictory social and ideological environments. Evolutionary biologists Dutton and Heath (2010) conclude that

> multicultural individuals are able to shift between multiple cultural frames depending on which one is cued by their current situation. Interestingly, even monocultural American individuals shift their self-construals, value endorsements, and social judgments depending on situational cues . . . . [I]t is computationally impossible for an individual to ensure complete coherence among any reasonable number of elements. (pp. 60–61)

Cultures, they argue, are always in flux, producing shifting environments that cue a variety of responses that may not be consistent with one another, no matter how principled a person might try to be. This acknowledgment of the inevitability of human contradiction in the face of multiple environmental forces is available through Bakhtin's (1986) notion of heteroglossia, the streams of discourse that infiltrate people's minds and shape their thinking without being consistent. It is also aligned with the assumption in dialectical materialism that the world is always in flux and that it is possible for more than one thing to be true at the same time.

The human world is thus contradictory, and people are inevitably involved in competing theses about the most fruitful way of understanding human action, both as individuals and as part of cultural groups and their histories and traditions. Teachers of literature might take comfort in this fact, given that they might have been exposed to a number of critical traditions that suggest very different ways of engaging with texts, each providing its own lens and assumptions. They are also caught amidst competing settings, such as the tendency for their university training to emphasize progressivism and constructivism and their school environments that tend to require formalism and conventional interpretations of texts. It's common for school mission statements to state the importance of recognizing individual differences while imposing rules that require conformity. It's not fair, I think, to criticize teachers who are caught in these ideological clashes for doing contradictory things. It's computationally impossible for them to do otherwise.

Vygotsky (1971) provides additional insights that suggest contradiction is not simply a byproduct of heteroglossic conflicts but a fundamental property of literary art (cf. Smagorinsky, 2011). Traditionally, he argued, critics had sought to explain "the harmony of form and content" in artistic works, as formalists do in resolving tensions. In contrast, Vygotsky argued that "form may be in conflict with the content, struggle with it, overcome it" to produce a "dialectic contradiction between content and form" that provides an inherent paradox, the "inner incongruity between the material and the form" (p. 160). This internal contradiction is what produces conflicting emotions in the reader. A work of art produces to Vygotsky "a state of emotional and philosophical complexity which does not succumb to rational analysis" (Van der Veer & Valsiner, 1991, p. 28).

This very early scholarship by Vygotsky—his dissertation on *The Psychology of Art* with an emphasis on literature—relies on the thesis-antithesis-synthesis formulation to account for two seemingly contradictory issues at once. First, he attends to the formal structure of a text, without which there is no art from which to generate a response. The task of the reader is not so much to resolve contradictions between content and form or within content or form. Rather, it is to experience emotions that follow from these contradictions and to have an emotional experience he calls a *catharsis*, which follows from the ways in which a person generalizes from personal emotions to higher human truths; it is different from Aristotle's construct of a cathartic purge or purification. "The emotions caused by art," Vygotsky says, "are intelligent emotions" (p. 212). The formal properties of a text are critical factors in producing this emotional response.

Catharsis involves "an affective contradiction, causes conflicting feelings, and leads to the short-circuiting and destruction of these emotions" (Vygotsky, 1971, p. 213). This emotional response produces "a complex transformation of feelings" (p. 214) and results in an "explosive response which culminates in the discharge of emotions" (p. 215). Art, he asserts, "complements life by expanding its possibilities" (p. 247) as one overcomes, resolves, and regulates feelings through a process of generalization of those feelings to a higher plane of experience.

Teaching literature is thus an inherently contradictory act. Texts are internally contradictory, which provides them with the potential for elevating a reader's emotional response and producing "intelligent emotions." Teachers may have been socialized to respond to multiple competing traditions that produce tensions in how to teach properly. They may be under pressure to teach toward formalism for standardized assessments and to teach toward constructivism to serve the ideology of progressive organizations and other sources. Policies and practices designed by different people produce different influences on teachers' work with students. People with no stake in actual school teaching but great interest in selling products and consultations need to promote their own services by caricaturing other approaches as foolhardy and counterproductive. Teaching consistently within such an environment is likely to be virtually impossible.

A disputatious personality can serve this conundrum in different ways. Those who argue to win are likely to occupy polarized ground, making little effort to listen to and engage with opposing ideas. Rather, they tend to identify a potential weakness and use it as the synecdoche for the whole of an opposing position. What remains is a thesis and an antithesis, with no synthesis possible because nothing new is sought; the goal is to win, not to enrich a perspective. In such a case, there are only winners and losers. When educators butt heads only to bounce back from one another to their original positions, the field gets stale. The disputatious personality who listens and sees argumentation as a means for both persuasion and personal development—traits I admire in Sheridan Blau—has a much better possibility of advancing knowledge, their own and that of others.

Sheridan's legacy is indebted to his ability to hold multiple views at once, to embrace contradiction and interrogate it, to recognize the merits of seemingly incompatible traditions, and to emerge from contentions with a clearer understanding. We could all benefit from such a disposition. I'm glad to have had Sheridan as an inspiration to try to develop it in myself.

Works Cited

Aristotle. (2022). *Poetics* (S. H. Butcher, Trans.). The Internet Classics Archive. http://classics.mit.edu/Aristotle/poetics.html (Original work published ca. 350 BCE)

Bakhtin, M. M. (1986). *Speech genres and other late essays* (C. Emerson & M. Holquist, Eds.; V. W. McGee, Trans.). University of Texas Press.

Bazerman, C. (1988). *Shaping written knowledge: The genre and activity of the experimental article in science*. University of Wisconsin Press.

Benson, P. (2003). Hegel and the Trinity. *Philosophy Now*, *42*, 23–25. https://philosophynow.org/issues/42/Hegel_and_the_Trinity

Blau, S. D. (2003). *The literature workshop: Teaching texts and their readers*. Heinemann.

Bleich, D. (1975). *Readings and feelings: An introduction to subjective criticism*. National Council of Teachers of English.

Braddock, R., Lloyd-Jones, R., & Schoer, L. (1963). *Research in written composition.* National Council of Teachers of English.

Bruner, J. (1986). *Actual minds, possible worlds.* Harvard University Press.

Crenshaw, K., Gotanda, N., Peller, G., & Thomas, K. (Eds.). (1996). *Critical race theory: The key writings that formed the movement.* The New Press.

Dutton, Y. C., & Heath, C. (2010). Cultural evolution: Why are some cultural variants more successful than others? In M. Schaller, A. Norenzayan, S. J. Heine, T. Yamagishi, & T. Kameda (Eds.), *Evolution, culture, and the human mind* (pp. 49–70). Psychology Press.

Elbow, P. (1973). *Writing without teachers.* Oxford University Press.

Emig, J. (1971). *The composing processes of twelfth graders* (NCTE Research Report No. 13). National Council of Teachers of English.

Gates, H. L., Jr. (1989). *The signifying monkey: A theory of African-American literary criticism.* Oxford University Press.

Graves, D. H. (1979). Research doesn't have to be boring. *Language Arts, 56*(1), 76–80.

Graves, D. H. (1983). *Writing: Teachers and children at work.* Heinemann.

Hillocks, G., Jr. (1986). *Research on written composition: New directions for teaching.* National Conference on Research in English; ERIC Clearinghouse on Reading and Communications Skills.

Hillocks, G., Jr. (1995). *Teaching writing as reflective practice.* Teachers College Press.

Hillocks, G., Jr. (2011). *Teaching argument writing, grades 6–12: Supporting claims with relevant evidence and clear reasoning.* Heinemann.

Kochman, T. (1981). *Black and white styles in conflict.* University of Chicago Press.

Lee, C. D. (1993). *Signifying as a scaffold for literary interpretation: The pedagogical implications of an African American discourse genre* (NCTE Research Report No. 26). National Council of Teachers of English.

Lenin, V. I. (1965). *Lenin: Collected works* (C. Dutt, Trans., Vol. 38, 2nd ed.). Marxists Internet Archive. www.marxists.org/archive/lenin/works/1914/cons-logic/summary.htm

Majors, Y. J. (2015). *Shoptalk: Lessons in teaching from an African American hair salon.* Teachers College Press.

Marshall, J. D., Smagorinsky, P., & Smith, M. W. (1995). *The language of interpretation: Patterns of discourse in discussions of literature* (NCTE Research Report No. 27). National Council of Teachers of English.

Miller, J. (1982). *History and human existence: From Marx to Merleau-Ponty.* University of California Press.

Newell, G. E., Bloome, D., & Hirvela, A. (2015). *Teaching and learning argumentative writing in high school English language arts classrooms.* Routledge.

North, S. M. (1987). *The making of knowledge in composition: Portrait of an emerging field.* Heinemann.

Rabinowitz, P. (1987). *Before reading: Narrative conventions and the politics of interpretation.* Ohio State University Press.

Rivers, T., & Espelage, D. (2013). Black ritual insults: Causing harm or passing time? In s.j. miller, L. D. Burns, & T. S. Johnson (Eds.), *Generation bullied 2.0: Prevention and intervention strategies for our most vulnerable students* (pp. 75–84). Peter Lang.

Smagorinsky, P. (1991). The writer's knowledge and the writing process: A protocol analysis. *Research in the Teaching of English, 25*(3), 339–364.

Smagorinsky, P. (Ed.). (2006). *Research on composition: Multiple perspectives on two decades of change.* Teachers College Press.

Smagorinsky, P. (2011). Vygotsky's stage theory: The psychology of art and the actor under the direction of *perezhivanie. Mind, Culture, and Activity, 18,* 319–341.

Smagorinsky, P. (2018). Deconflating the ZPD and instructional scaffolding: Retranslating and reconceiving the zone of proximal development as the zone of next development. *Learning, Culture and Social Interaction, 16,* 70–75.

Smagorinsky, P. (2020). *Learning to teach English and language arts: A Vygotskian perspective on beginning teachers' pedagogical concept development.* Bloomsbury.

Smagorinsky, P. (2023). Arguing and listening for civic engagement. *English Journal, 112*(3), 57–63.

Smagorinsky, P. (2024). Emotions, empathy, and social justice education. *English Teaching: Practice & Critique.* Advance online publication. https://doi.org/10.1108/ETPC-06-2023-0055

Smagorinsky, P., & Smith, M. W. (1992). The nature of knowledge in composition and literary understanding: The question of specificity. *Review of Educational Research, 62*(3), 279–305.

Stukey, M. R., Fugnitto, G., Fraser, V., & Sawyer, I. (2019). *The settled science of teaching reading*. Center for the Collaborative Classroom. https://socal.dyslexiaida.org/wp-content/uploads/sites/21/2020/10/MKT4419_The-Settled-Science-of-Teaching-Reading_whitepaper_final_REV.pdf

Toulmin, S. (1958). *The uses of argument.* Cambridge University Press.

van der Veer, R., & Valsiner, J. (1991). *Understanding Vygotsky: A quest for synthesis.* Blackwell.

Vygotsky, L. S. (1971). *The psychology of art* (Scripta Technica, Trans.). MIT Press.

Vygotsky, L. S. (1987). Thinking and speech. In R. Rieber & A. Carton (Eds.), *The collected works of L. S. Vygotsky: Vol. 1. Problems of general psychology* (N. Minick, Trans., pp. 39–285). Plenum Press.

Vygotsky, L. S. (1997). *Educational psychology* (R. Silverman, Trans.). St. Lucie Press.

Vygotsky, L. S. (1999). *The collected works of L. S. Vygotsky: Vol. 6. Scientific legacy* (R. W. Rieber, Ed.; M. J. Hall, Trans.). Plenum Press.

Wertsch, J. V. (1998). *Mind as action.* Oxford University Press.

Wood, D., Bruner, J., & Ross, G. (1976). The role of tutoring in problem solving. *Journal of Child Psychology and Psychiatry, 17*(2), 89–100.

Yaden, D. B., Reinking, D. P., & Smagorinsky, P. (2021). The trouble with binaries: A perspective on the science of reading. *Reading Research Quarterly, 56*(S1), S119–S129.

III

"Thus the places where [a text] seems weakest in its logic or where its drama seems either least believable or most at odds with its own doctrinal claims become the places that hold the greatest promise for teaching us what we do not yet understand."

—Blau interview, 2021

Chapter Nine

The Literature Workshop: *A (Surprising) Treatise for Teaching Struggling Readers*

Cheryl Hogue Smith

When the editors of this volume approached me about writing a chapter related to Sheridan Blau's professional contributions, the first idea that popped into my head was to write about a friendly argument Sheridan and I had early in my career about how I was "misusing" his work. "Your work helps teachers of basic writers learn how to better teach their struggling students," argued I. "My work is about teaching students of literature," argued he. This argument stemmed from my using the ideas in *The Literature Workshop* (2003) to help explain counterproductive reading habits my struggling students often exhibited in my developmental writing classes, even though Sheridan never refers to struggling students or developmental writing classes—or any writing class, for that matter. Our argument was not settled that day; in fact, it was not until several years later that Sheridan finally came to believe that *The Literature Workshop* is as much about teaching struggling readers/writers as it is about teaching successful students of literature. I have always been intrigued by how Sheridan was, for so long, unable to see the wider application of his work and have wondered how his ideas about the teaching of reading may have evolved since he began to appreciate his broader influence. Since the only way to discover what Sheridan knew or felt was to ask him, I requested an interview whereby we could discuss my "misuse" of his work and explore his ideas about the teaching of reading more broadly. That interview[1] is the bulk of this chapter.

Before I get to that interview, however, let me first discuss what he calls the "learning theory" that undergirds his dramatized workshops in *The Literature Workshop*, the theory I first applied to my own pedagogical choices for my struggling students in developmental writing classes. In both his book and his workshops, Sheridan leads readers through a set of tasks designed to help students recognize and work through the confusion and questions they encounter when reading difficult literary texts. The undergraduate and graduate students in the classes where he developed his workshops over the years were typically highly successful and well-prepared students who were all ready for or already exercising to some degree the kind of dispositions and thinking that his workshops are designed to foster and that together define what he called "performative literacy," which are dispositions or capacities that he defines in terms of seven traits: "(1) capacity for sustained, focused attention; (2) willingness to suspend closure; (3) willingness to take risks; (4) tolerance for failure; (5) tolerance for ambiguity, paradox, and uncertainty; (6) intellectual generosity and fallibilism; [and] (7) metacognitive awareness" (2003, p. 211). Collectively, performative literacy

> refers to the kind of knowledge that enables students to perform as autonomous, engaged readers of difficult texts at any level of education. These are readers who, in encounters with difficult texts, demonstrate a particular set of attributes or dispositions that may seem more like character traits than academic or literary skills. Yet this set of attributes or habits of mind can be said to constitute the foundation for a related set of literary actions or an intellectual discipline that expert adult readers characteristically exhibit and readily recognize as the discipline and behaviors of the most accomplished student readers. (2003, p. 210)

Sheridan always saw his workshops and all his literature instruction as designed to strengthen the typically underdeveloped literary behaviors of the top-level high school graduates who entered the highly selective university where he taught mostly English majors. He wasn't working with students who had long histories of struggling to read difficult texts and who needed to overcome counterproductive reading habits based on long-standing feelings of inadequacy or expectations of imminent failure. (For more about struggling readers, see Smith, 2012, 2017.) Thus, when I discussed in my own work how I teach to encourage my struggling students to adopt his performative literacy traits, he couldn't see how the work he was doing with his high-performing students would be appropriate for my struggling students.

It wasn't until a few years after our argument began, when I described the distorted version of his performative literacy traits that seem to be the operative traits of many of my struggling students, that Sheridan fully appreciated the applicability of his work to the pedagogical theory and practice in the field of basic writing. In fact, he was excited by the degree to which his theory could be used as the basis for my own theory of a counterproductive set of dispositions and traits that account for the limitations and misguided behaviors of many struggling students:

> [S]truggling readers have the ability to exercise the traits defining performative literacy, but they often do so in ways that sabotage rather than enable learning. For example, readers who adopt [counterproductive reading habits] often show a capacity for "sustained and focused attention," but employ it counterproductively when they listen carefully in class to find in the thinking of other students the one "correct" interpretation of a text that they then choose to adopt. Also, because struggling readers often lack sufficient vocabulary, cultural knowledge, and background information, they find much that they don't understand even at the literal level in the texts typically assigned in college and accept their condition of only half understanding what they read. In that sense, many struggling readers show their capacity to "tolerate ambiguity and uncertainty" without showing any concomitant sense of responsibility for trying to resolve their uncertainties or figure out how to disambiguate what confuses them. For such students, "paradoxes" seem the norm because often when they do interpret texts and others' interpretations run counter to their own, they deliberately and perfunctorily defer to those other interpretations. In fact, because of their acceptance of ambiguity, paradox, and uncertainty, they are more than happy to be "intellectually generous," believing in and deferring to others' interpretations rather than their own. (2017, pp. 32–33)

And so I made the case for all seven of Blau's performative literacy traits I had observed in the struggling readers in my classes. Struggling students in college classes—developmental or otherwise—usually don't struggle because they can't read; they struggle for a host of reasons that interfere with their capacity (or willingness) to work through difficult texts, a fact well documented in my own and other basic writing scholars' work.

Sheridan's work is built around helping skilled readers become more engaged, autonomous readers of difficult texts. I use his work to help struggling students first learn how to identify healthy learning habits from counterproductive ones so they can work through any reading difficulties they encounter. Because my struggling students often have many issues that can affect their reading habits, I most want them to develop a metacognitive awareness so they are able to monitor their thoughts and emotions as they try to develop a tolerance for failure and become willing to take risks. If they can adopt those three performative literacy traits, I know they will be more apt to eventually adopt the others. In fact, I have documented how students who feel success with one assignment can transfer those feelings of success to the next assignment, which leads them to continue to succeed with reading events and adopt more of Sheridan's performative literacy traits (Smith, 2017).

As readers will see, the following interview demonstrates how Sheridan learned to accept how some, like me, appropriately believe that *The Literature Workshop* can stand as a treatise for teaching struggling readers. More importantly, however, the interview also demonstrates how a humble giant in the field of teaching literature views (and misunderstands) his contribution to a larger field.

The Interview

Cheryl: As you know, I invited you to meet with me today to discuss how your ideas about reading have evolved over time. To begin, I want to talk about a conversation we had early in my career about how my struggling readers could benefit from your ideas in *The Literature Workshop* as much as your literature students do. But you thought I was misusing your work in my developmental writing classroom. Can you explain why you thought your work was relevant only within the boundaries of a literature classroom?

Sheridan: It's hard for me to believe that I was so wrong about it. I remember feeling that, not only was I not talking about struggling readers but my whole theory of literacy was about what it meant to be a highly competent reader. What troubles me now is it's so obvious: People who are basic readers need to become highly literate readers. But I thought that I was addressing people who are already acceptably literate by school standards and needed to become highly literate as English majors. Most of my workshops come from teaching a sophomore-level literature class at UC Santa Barbara. So, I'm teaching students who were in the top 5 percent of their high school class and are highly literate, actually, compared to the population in general. And many of them were or were about to become English majors. So, these students were already pretty good readers. And the issue was what it really means in an advanced literary community to be a good reader of literature. I think it was a kind of snottiness on my part that I apologize for now, because you're very sensibly wanting to use the ideas in my book in a basic writing class when that seemed to me that's not who I'm writing for.

Cheryl: When you moved to Teachers College (TC), you discovered your colleagues were using *The Literature Workshop* in the reading course, and you didn't understand why they were doing so. Can you say a little about why you felt they shouldn't use your book?

Sheridan: When I came to TC and found out that John Brown, Pat Zumhagen, and other people were using my book in their class on the teaching of reading, I said, "Why are you using my book in the teaching of reading classes? It's not about reading; it's about reading literature." And I was partly right, because I do think one of the problems with the TC reading class is that they were talking about reading literature, almost always. And we have, of course, a class in the teaching of literature that I teach. I thought in the reading class they'd be addressing reading problems rather than literature problems. I didn't fully recognize how my book is really about teaching the reading of literature. The issue, for me, was that students weren't actually experiencing the texts, which meant really, deeply and empathically, reading them, taking them in as an aesthetic experience [á la Rosenblatt]. And I saw all the failures as problems with reading, but I still thought of them, somehow, as connected exclusively to the reading of literature. I did not recognize how much my book was about a reading pedagogy and how much, therefore, it would be useful to people who are struggling readers. And also—and I don't like to think this—I think I was unable or unwilling to move beyond the perspective of my identity as someone in an English department more than someone who's working more broadly in education.

Cheryl: Let's switch gears a little bit: Not too long ago, you realized that your commentary project [an extended exercise that helps students become interpreters of texts through commentaries and replies within a community of learners who function as both apprentices and guides] was more about reading than it was about writing. Can you talk a little about that realization and about how it contributed to your understanding that your work is, in fact, universal in that it speaks to the teaching of reading at all levels and courses?

Sheridan: I borrowed my commentary idea from my English department colleague, Steve Allaback, who had his students keep reading logs in his American literature course. Steve had his students turn in their entries from their reading logs each week. Then he'd read through all their reading logs and pick some log entries that he would use in his lecture. I liked Steve's idea, and I wanted to refine it. So, I then called the weekly writing "commentaries." The log is sort of a record, and I wanted something more academic than the log, something more formal. I define a "commentary" as a contribution to a discussion that is advancing some idea. And so, it's different in lots of ways. It is written for other students; it's part of a conversation. I'm not sure how much I knew that when I started doing my commentaries.

Cheryl: When did you come to realize, or why even, that the commentary project really is as much about reading as it is about writing?

Sheridan: I don't know. But I don't think I mentioned it as a reading exercise the first time I wrote about it in *What Is College Level Writing?* [2010]. I think I started to recognize how it was about reading just as much as writing when I was regularly doing workshops for Writing Project sites. I don't think I recognized it in my classes. But at some moment in a workshop for teachers, I realized that what was happening in the commentary workshop was that the participants were seeing in the different ways that other people were writing about the story or poem how they, too, might talk about a literary text. One of my favorite workshops in my 2003 book is called "What's Worth Saying about a Literary Text," where I attempt to find an answer to that question. But what I didn't recognize for a while about my commentary workshop is how effectively it functions as another way that students can discover what's worth saying. What are the things you can talk about? And it wasn't until the last essay that came out in the second volume of *Deep Reading* [2023] that I wrote about the commentary project as a reading apprenticeship and not just an approach to academic writing.

Cheryl: Pat Zumhagen, John Brown, I, and others who "misused" your work challenged you to really look sort of introspectively to realize how much bigger you are than teaching literature. The title of this article, by the way, is "*The Literature Workshop:* A (Surprising) Treatise for Teaching Struggling Readers." I don't think you would ever in a million years have imagined that's what your book is, but it is.

Sheridan: Yes, that's good, right? When you say "misuse," yes, I've had to discover the ramifications of my own theory. On one hand, I'm embarrassed that I didn't see all the ramifications earlier. But I'm proud that I now see them. Ironically, I actually had a sense of their broader applicability earlier but saw that as somehow rendering my theory or model of competence less relevant to literary study. When I first elaborated what you are calling my "theory of performative literacy" and what it takes to read well, I remember recognizing at some point this is just a description of mental health. And it embarrassed me. And I thought, "Maybe I can't use this model of literary competence." In fact, I think that's why I originally called the model "personal literacy," and that's the way I presented it in workshops and early publications. But I always worried that my name for it and the traits I described were too touchy-feely. So, in the final draft of my book, I called it "performative literacy." I love your point that I didn't see its wider significance. It's a kind of learning theory. And I finally saw that I liked it, especially as I saw other people make use of it.

Cheryl: So, coming to the realization that your work is as applicable to students who struggle as readers as well as to typical college students of literature must have made you see the teaching of reading in a different way. Can you describe how you now view the teaching of reading? And how that viewpoint has changed from the time when you were insisting that your book was not about reading?

Sheridan: I'm not sure it has. The question is how can I give a course in reading that is not unrelated to my initial complaint about John Brown and the others? Because I was saying my book is not about reading; it's about literature. And my criticism of them was that they should be addressing the more basic problem, the fundamental problem that they get in secondary schools with students who can't read. It's not that they don't know how to read literature; it's that they can't read. You give them a newspaper or something, and they're not going to be able to read it very well. And I was saying that's the kind of problem they should be addressing in a reading course. They shouldn't be overlapping with me. But I can now see why they are, and it's a legitimate thing.

Cheryl: You have talked about retiring for several years now. What do you want your legacy to be?

Sheridan: Why is legacy important? Legacy is important because, in a certain way, it keeps you from dying. So, you're fighting against death. My children and my grandkids are my legal and genetic heirs, and I love and cherish them for who they are and have become—not just because I am their father and helped to raise them. But my students are my heirs because they carry on my ideas and practices. That feels to me at least as important as the preservation of my genes.

Cheryl: Your students are your intellectual heirs.

Sheridan: Yes. And that feels to me more about me. My children are biological heirs, which is less about me than my intellectual legacy. That's interesting.

Cheryl: Even when they "misuse" your work?

Sheridan: [*laughs*] Yeah. So I think about legacy and wonder, "What ideas or practices do I want to make sure are carried on?" It's an approach to teaching, which has to do with the importance of asking questions, but John Dewey says that, too, doesn't he? I'm inclined to say I want my legacy to include my mistrust of teaching, even of my teaching. My argument is that teaching is the enemy of learning. So what am I doing, then? I mean, I do believe teaching is the enemy of learning, but maybe it has to do with a definition of "teaching." And that kind of brings us to my obsession with the idea of apprenticeship (which is itself a way of ensuring a legacy). I guess I feel that I'm doing something worthwhile with texts, trying to make sense of them, trying to make them real and doing something with Milton, for example, that I would hope to preserve. I'm reading Milton (especially *Paradise Lost*) and taking very seriously what I will learn from it. And I'm doing this work with students. So, there's one sense in which I'm modeling a method. And there's also a sense in which I'm pushing them, so I am teaching them that this isn't just a Bible story; this is about their life. It's an insistence about the status of the text, which, perhaps, isn't the same as interpreting it. What I'm really after, I think, is for them to experience Milton for themselves.

You know, I once took a class fairly rapidly through a poem. At the end, a student said, "Well, I hear what you said. I hear your interpretation. But, you know, it feels to me like something that's yours. And I'm going to buy it because it is convincing. But I don't really know it for myself." And then, as they were leaving the room, she said, "This feels to me like what you're teaching against. And we don't want that." *We don't want it*, she said. She had learned from me not to want that. So, what do we do about that? What do *I* do about it? I think what is endlessly exciting about teaching is that you're still always trying to figure out how to do it.

Cheryl: I think this very well may be the perfect place to end.

A Not-So-Surprising Treatise for Teaching Struggling Readers

In the end, I'm appreciative of the years-long argument Sheridan and I had about the applicability of his work to my struggling readers in a writing class. Those debates not only helped Sheridan see the wider implications of his work but they also shaped much of my own thinking about teaching. I was reminded in the interview how Sheridan's teaching experience with the college students he taught throughout his career made it difficult for him to see the relevance of his work to students in quite different academic settings.

I want to be clear, though, that I don't think Sheridan's reluctance for so long to embrace the wider applicability of his work derived from any elitism on his part about the students he has taught or about the superiority of literary discourse over the discourse of reading instruction. Instead, I think it came from his almost missionary focus on saving literature and the intellectual and spiritual benefits that literature confers on readers from the typical kinds of teaching that render the literature taught in schools and colleges irrelevant and meaningless to most students. In fact, he has shown that his loyalty is to literature, including the problem of reading it even outside literature courses, by publishing an essay in 2017 (in a book on reading in the composition classroom) that suggests well-prepared teachers of writing might be more fit as instructors of literature than literature professors because they have a long history of caring more about learning than about teaching. In his article "How the Teaching of Literature in College Writing Classes Might Rescue Reading as It Never Has Before," Sheridan argues that the best way to strengthen the reading proficiency of college students is to reinstate literature as the reading that students do for all or most of their writing in first-year composition courses.

In Sheridan's eyes, he wrote *The Literature Workshop* to help teachers of literature become the kinds of teachers who are friends—not enemies—to learning, but he also worried that his book could be taught in ways that run counter to the pedagogical ideas he expresses. Sadly, Sheridan's friend and former student

Noah Gordon demonstrates this to be true when he recounts his first experience with *The Literature Workshop*: His teacher not only reduced the "workshops [in the book] into a bullet-pointed list of instructions with the nuanced scripts, pedagogical notes, and explanations of principles removed" (p. 205) but also asked him to write an antithetical midterm that merely compared the book to several other texts (pp. 199–205). It's not difficult to see why Sheridan was, at first, resistant to anyone's "misuse" of his work.

Given Sheridan's focus on reconstructing the standard model for the teaching of literature, it took some effort on my part to convince him that the principles of learning and the theory of reading that inform his workshops can also apply to teaching struggling readers. However, I still feel he has a diffidence to some of the wider uses of his book, leading him to resist that his book can act as a sort of treatise for teaching struggling readers. Yes, he has encouraged me to use his work to write about helping struggling readers succeed, but, at its core, *The Literature Workshop* is about teaching literature. Yet his own words actually describe the broader applicability of his theory: "Performative literacy refers to the kind of knowledge that enables students to perform as autonomous, engaged readers of difficult texts *at any level* of education" (2003, p. 210, my emphasis). As he acknowledged to me, the "level" he refers to in that sentence would include elementary, middle, high school, or college, but he unwittingly opened the door for "level" to also include what he would want as a goal for struggling readers in the different levels of developmental and first-year composition classes. After all, primary or secondary students don't enter their classes having already acquired mastery of all the performative literacy traits, any more than struggling students do; they develop those traits by participating in the kinds of workshops Sheridan encourages teachers to conduct. In that sense, all students who experience variations of his workshops that foster performative literacy are probably underprepared before they participate.

Sheridan would certainly not argue with Berthoff's claim that "what is good for the best and the brightest is essential for students who have difficulties" (1981, p. 73). While she is talking here about the quality of texts and assignments struggling readers and writers deserve to read and write, her statement also holds true for any theory of learning or pedagogical practice. After all, wouldn't teachers want their students to have, as Blau (2003) theorizes, "a capacity for sustained, focused attention; a willingness to suspend closure; a willingness to take risks; a tolerance for failure; a tolerance for ambiguity, paradox, and uncertainty; an intellectual generosity and fallibilism; [and] a metacognitive awareness" (p. 211) when they read or write?

To help teachers achieve their goals, Sheridan provides in *The Literature Workshop* step-by-step instructions that demonstrate for teachers how to conduct workshops that can help their students develop the performative literacy traits. Take, for example, Chapter 2, "From Telling to Teaching," in which Sheridan outlines a workshop whereby students read a poem three times, each time underlining what they don't understand and each time rating their understanding of the poem on a scale from 1–10. Not only does this workshop encourage rereading, it also encourages students "to look more honestly and critically at the state of their own understanding, to make distinctions between what they do and don't understand, and to note qualitative differences in the kinds of understandings they themselves possess" (2003, p. 56). In other words, it asks, at the very least, for students to have a sustained, focused attention; a tolerance for failure; a tolerance for ambiguity, paradox, and uncertainty; and a metacognitive awareness. I adapted this particular workshop into one I call "Interrogating Texts," a small-group activity that frequently directs students to first read a portion of the text, write down their response to the question/direction, wait for their group members to write their responses, read aloud what they actually wrote (the most important step), and discuss their responses only after everyone has read aloud what they wrote. When students follow the protocols for this workshop and actually read their responses before any discussion begins, they work together as a group to discover the value of their own interpretations to the thinking of other readers as well as the value of alternative interpretations to their own thinking. Since almost every question on any "Interrogating Texts" exercise asks students to reread the text again, the activity engages students in such a way that they learn to read with a confidence that allows them to expand, rather than limit, their attention so they can adopt some of Sheridan's performative literacy traits and become more sophisticated thinkers about texts. (For more about this activity, see Smith, 2012.)

In short, teachers of struggling readers benefit from the same theories and effective practices as those who teach successful readers; they just need to adapt those theories and practices to their own students and institutional contexts. The workshops in *The Literature Workshop* promote the kind of thinking teachers of struggling readers want their students to engage in, and Sheridan's careful explanations about the theory that undergirds each workshop, chapter, and section create a blueprint of sorts for teachers of struggling readers to easily adapt his workshops for their students. This, combined with Sheridan's unique style of inspiring teachers to encourage their students to embrace confusion, helps *The Literature Workshop* stand as a not-so-surprising treatise for teaching struggling readers after all.

Note

1. After editing the interview for brevity, I sent the interview portion of this chapter to Sheridan in case he wanted to revise his statements. The interview presented here is his minimally revised version.

Acknowledgments

I would like to thank Sheridan for his time, the interview, and his subsequent revisions to the interview transcript. But most of all, I want to thank him for his ideas that have underscored my pedagogy for decades.

Works Cited

Berthoff, A. E. (1981). *The making of meaning*. Boynton/Cook.

Blau, S. (2003). *The literature workshop: Teaching texts and their readers*. Heinemann.

Blau, S. (2010). Academic writing as participation: Writing your way in. In P. Sullivan, H. Tinberg, & S. Blau (Eds.), *What is "college-level" writing? Vol. 2. Assignments, readings, and student writing samples*(pp. 29–56). National Council of Teachers of English.

Blau, S. (2017). How the teaching of literature in college writing classes might rescue reading as it never has before. In P. Sullivan, H. Tinberg, & S. Blau (Eds.), *Deep reading: Teaching reading in the writing classroom* (pp. 265–290). National Council of Teachers of English.

Blau, S. (2023). On not teaching college-level reading in order that students might learn it: Honoring our pedagogical legacy in the composition classroom. In P. Sullivan, H. Tinberg, & S. Blau (Eds.), *Deep reading, deep learning* (Vol. 2, pp. 299–314). Peter Lang. https://doi.org/10.3726/b19104

Dewey, J. (1991). *How we think*. Prometheus Books.

Rosenblatt, L. M. (1981). On the aesthetic as the basic model of the reading process. *Bucknell Review, 26*(1), 17–32.

Smith, C. H. (2012). Interrogating texts: From deferent to efferent and aesthetic reading practices. *Journal of Basic Writing*, *31*(1), 59–79.

Smith, C. H. (2017). Aesthetic reading: Struggling students sensing their way to academic success. *Journal of Basic Writing, 36*(2), 26–53.

Chapter Ten

Paradise Regained: Sheridan Blau and the Future of English Education

Andrew Rejan

> *"They, looking back, all th' eastern side beheld/Of Paradise, so late their happy seat/ . . . The world was all before them."*
>
> —Milton, *Paradise Lost*, 12.641–646

Contributions and Discussions

I can conjure the scene of the commentary workshop in my head like a highlights reel, the familiar words repeating with shifting backdrops. Maybe Sheridan is wearing a wool jacket and tie or perhaps a dapper blue blazer. He could be at a writing project in California or a high school classroom in New York City or an NCTE convention hall anywhere or even in a conference room overlooking a koi pond at a brand-new school building in Shanghai, China. Maybe we see only Sheridan's face, wearing the professorial beard that he waited until he was 80 to grow out, as he teaches on Zoom from his Upper West Side apartment through the worst of the pandemic that ravaged New York City.

Or maybe I have cast myself in the role of Blau—minus the jacket and tie—as I utter the words that now feel almost like my own, drawing my tenth-grade students into an experiment in which we'll write commentaries on *Frankenstein* or *Song of Solomon*. I could use the script that Sheridan provides in his invaluable 2011 book chapter "Academic Writing as Participation," but I prefer to recite the words as I remember them. "A commentary is . . . a *contribution* to a *discussion* of a literary text."

"A commentary" is exhaled faster than you'd expect, with more air in the "ary" and less pop on the "comment." A small pause after the "is," holding you in suspense. A *contribution*. This word is the key, the sacred word; it rises up like a prayer. And *discussion*! A word to savor, all the stuff of a life well lived can be tasted in that word. Not so lofty as "contribution"—but the perfect answer to it, the ideal mate, earthy and wondrous. Oh, you thought *contribution* was the end of it? The *discussion* is the embodiment of the principle, what we can actually *do* with literature. "Literary" is the gentlest word in the cue, fast and delicate, and "text" the most guttural, swallowed as if out of breath after the majesty of all that has preceded it.

The first time I participated in Sheridan's commentary workshop, the idea of the literature classroom as a site of public writing and authentic discourse was new to me. The words I scrawled in my notebook as Sheridan spoke—"activity theory," "genre theory," "identity theory," and "apprenticeship"—did not yet hold meaning.

I remember the question that I raised my hand to ask before the end of Sheridan's workshop. What about the special, sacred relationship of teacher and student, sanctified through the epistolary exchange of papers submitted privately to the teacher and the teacher's attentive comments in response?

I would arrive at my own answer to that question a few months later in Sheridan's writing class, which remains the most influential course I've ever taken. During that fall semester, I found myself wearing new identities, shedding a sense of myself as primarily a student and gradually seeing that, underneath school's protective cocoon, I was a writer and learner. That semester, my peers became my teachers, and my teacher, Sheridan, became my peer. Sheridan taught me, by example, to live a life of *contribution* and *discussion*.

The Parable of False Knowledge, Part I

I read *Paradise Lost* with Sheridan twice. In the spring of 2011, as a master's student facing a classroom of my own students for the first time, I enrolled in Sheridan's *Paradise Lost*-centered literature course. Seven years later, in the spring of 2018, as a PhD student under Sheridan's advisement, I took another version of the Milton course. My first *Paradise Lost* class with Sheridan was held in a large basement room with harsh fluorescent lights, with the students spread out in rectangular tables throughout the room like stations in a science lab. My more recent Milton class was in a smaller, brighter room, where the class sat elbow-to-elbow around a wood seminar table; the room was fortunately located across the hall from Sheridan's office so that he could retrieve the books, papers, and handouts that he was always forgetting to bring with him. Wherever one reads Milton with Sheridan, I think that the ethos of both of these spaces—the warm seminar room and the laboratory site—becomes palpable.

From my two readings of *Paradise Lost* with Sheridan, one phrase stays with me more than any other: "False knowledge." One might imagine that Sheridan shouts the phrase, his whole body shaking in outrage, one of his visceral, uncensored responses to educational injustice. But when I think of Sheridan speaking of "false knowledge," the phrase is more likely to be whispered, a curse so vile that he can barely bring himself to utter it. The concept of false knowledge is derived from Sheridan's reading of *Paradise Lost*, and here I must tread cautiously, for if I allow Sheridan's interpretation to substitute for my own embodied, internalized experience of the poem, I too will have fallen to the vice of . . . (whisper) *false knowledge.*

Sheridan uses the false knowledge of *Paradise Lost* as a metaphor for any literary knowledge that has not been attained experientially:

> Indeed, one of the reasons that a borrowed interpretation often deserves to be classified with what Milton calls "false" knowledge (*Paradise Lost*, XI, 412–14) is that it becomes an obstruction to learning in the sense that it is what a student holds onto and insists on dogmatically and uncritically as constituting knowledge (even against contradictory evidence), precisely because it was borrowed and therefore not arrived at experientially through a process of evidentiary reasoning. That is, insofar as the borrowed knowledge takes the place of what might have been accrued for the student through his own intellectual work and experience of a text, the recitational

> knowledge itself often becomes what the student takes to be a source of intellectual power and efficacy and thereby becomes a possession that the student (or, unfortunately, sometimes the teacher) must protect in order to preserve his own power and efficacy. (*Literature Workshop,* p. 198)

Sheridan's classes won't always stick to the syllabus, and, if you're reading *Paradise Lost* with Sheridan, you might spend weeks on Book 9, putting off all the rest of the assignments as long as possible. Sheridan, you will learn, lives in and for Book 9 of *Paradise Lost*—the book that, in enacting the perils of false knowledge, makes available to its readers the truest, fullest, purest knowledge that literature can offer.

So, let's take a field trip to the Garden of Eden. We land in a verdant grove at the center of which stands "the Tree of Life/ High eminent blooming ambrosial fruit of vegetable gold./And next to Life/Our death, the Tree of Knowledge grew fast by" (Milton, 4.218–221).

When Satan, disguised as a serpent, claims that he has attained the power of speech by consuming the fruit of the tree (a lie), Eve accepts this testimony without any evidence. Recognizing that the serpent's flattery casts doubt on his reliability, Eve briefly reevaluates her assumptions. Her skepticism—the doubt that nearly causes her to overturn her initial conclusion about the "virtue" of the fruit—suggests that reason might prevail, but "credulous" Eve all too quickly sets aside her skepticism and accepts as "proved" what has never been proven at all (Milton, 9.616, 9.644). Making a variety of arguments about the wisdom of ignoring God's commands, Satan urges Eve to consider "these, these and many more causes import your need of this fair fruit" (Milton, 9.729–730). The fact that Satan persuades Eve to act on the basis of "causes" not only unobserved but also unmentioned shows that Eve has abandoned any pretense of rational inquiry.

After Eve has succumbed to Satan's temptation and consumed the forbidden fruit, she first praises the Tree of Knowledge and then praises "Experience" (Milton 9.807–810). Some have argued that the tragic results of Eve's "experience" should be understood as Milton's warning about the limitations of experiential knowledge (Major, p. 39). Sheridan, though, sees Eve's fall not as a sign of

Milton's suspicion of empiricism but instead as evidence of Eve's misunderstanding of genuine experiential learning.

What Eve imagines to be her "experience" of the fruit—and the knowledge it supposedly contains—may be a flight of fancy: "Eve/Intent now wholly on her taste naught else/Regarded, such delight till then as seemed/In fruit she never tasted whether true/ Or fancied so, through expectation high/Of knowledge" (Milton 9.785–789). The phrase "as seemed" places a veil of uncertainty over the effects of the fruit; the exceptional sensation it produces may be mere illusion, "fancied so, through expectation high/Of knowledge." She is singularly focused not on the taste of the fruit but on "her taste" so that Eve's encounter with the fruit becomes a solipsistic counterpart to the earlier scene when she gazes at her own reflection, except this time Eve's self-reflection is displaced by the imprint of Satan's false experience. With the phrase "whether true/Or fancied so," Milton uses the possibility of truth to tempt the reader to join Eve in accepting the fruit as a true experience of knowledge before the enjambed sentence turns to point out the falseness of Eve's vision.

When Eve convinces Adam to join her in consuming the fruit, she adopts Satan's role as the purveyor of false "experience" (Milton 9.989–90). Adam is urged to substitute for his own knowledge a secondary source (Eve's "experience," which is merely the blind acceptance of Satan's illusory claims). In yielding to Eve's argument against his "better knowledge," Adam turns to borrowed interpretation and dubious evidence instead of the embodied knowledge that has been confirmed by his own reason and experience. Adam's fall, like Eve's, is precipitated not by an overreliance on experience but instead by the failure to commit to what Sheridan calls *experienced understanding* ("Literary Competence," p. 45).

When the business of an English class is the dispensing of a teacher's interpretations, which may have been purloined from the teacher's own teachers, the resulting knowledge is counterfeit. Despite good intentions, teachers and students often find themselves cast in the role of Satan, peddler of false knowledge, or of Eve, secondhand redistributor of knowledge falsely acquired. Yes, I am repeating some of Sheridan's reading here, but I embrace it as the one authoritative reading that paradoxically opens up infinite possibilities for divergent readings—of *Paradise Lost*, of any text, and of the world. The commentary workshop offers an alternative to false knowledge by disrupting traditional hierarchies and creating a community of practice in which students and teachers are empowered to create and share their own ideas.

Just as humankind may never return to prelapsarian bliss, students and teachers in any literature classroom, even Sheridan's, inevitably exist in a fallen world, where a teacher's authority, no matter how wise, gentle, or judicious, mediates the literary experience. Yet for all the reasons Sheridan gives us to maintain a healthy dose of skepticism toward any educational institution, including his own classroom, he also shows us that the literature classroom can be a place for wonder, curiosity, and measured outrage, where the impossibility of true knowledge doesn't make the pursuit of it any less delightful.

Teacher participants in the commentary workshop sometimes ask how they might respond to a recalcitrant, disaffected student—the one who says, "I hate this poem!" Sheridan coaches the teacher to accept the student's response—with a smile, showing, in fact, that the subversive student within him relishes the "I hate this!" opener. The next step, Sheridan would say, is to use the context of the discussion to compel the student to say *why*. "I hate this because . . ." and voila! A commentary! Not a graphic organizer or a five-paragraph essay outline or a sample topic sentence generator. Just "I hate this because . . ." The student's own words become a source of power. As Sheridan writes, "The best assistance that the teacher can provide . . . is the assistance of assuring the student that his or her own questions about the text are resources for making advancements in understanding the text" ("Fostering Authentic Learning," p. 12).

To provide the assurance that one's own questions are the most valuable resource: Sheridan has given that gift so many times, to the angry senator he met in the antechamber and to generations of students. On the subway after class one evening, I found myself standing with a group of Sheridan's students. Each of us had a story about telling Sheridan our idea for a paper topic and watching his eyes light up with wonder as he blurted out, "This idea could change the field!"

"I was so excited," one of Sheridan's students said. "I didn't realize then that he acts like that all the time." And yet, for every person in the group, the paper proposal that had garnered Sheridan's excitement ended up becoming a published article.

Sheridan never forgets that his own boundless curiosity sometimes led to collisions with his teachers and that he discovered his love of literature through reading the philosophically rich but profanity-filled *The Naked and the Dead* by Norman Mailer, which he came across in a box of books inherited from an older cousin. That experience helped awaken him to the possibility of an intellectual life and inspired him to give up his cleated shoes and ducktail haircut to join the Forum Club with his more academic peers (Gordon, pp. 192–193).

For Sheridan, the literature classroom is a space for the sacred and the profane, a place where we can worship literature—or shit on it. The literature classroom manages to be a secular church, a speakeasy, and the backroom of a tailor's shop. Saying "what the hell," as the senator did, is welcome, yet Sheridan seeks to foster the conditions in which his students are able to believe in texts as well as to doubt them. Drawing on Peter Elbow's practice of believing and doubting and Stanley Fish's reader-focused interpretation of *Paradise Lost*, Sheridan exhorts his Milton students to "approach the poem under the assumption that it is poetically and humanly and universally true as the greatest works of literature are also true, and that we have much to learn from its wisdom, that it will continue to reward study and re-reading with additional insight over a lifetime of readings . . ." ("Believing and Doubting," p. 10).

The point of advocating for this worshipful relation to the text is not, in the end, to promote blind obedience but instead to raise the stakes of reading and deepen critical reflection. As Sheridan explains, "What I hope I am really doing is urging student readers, first, to respect their doubts by acknowledging and articulating them at least for their heuristic value, and then to . . . treat their doubts provisionally as an index of the degree to which they remain learners who may not yet have arrived at an entirely adequate understanding of the conceptual system they are obliged as students of Milton (and of mine) to try to understand" ("Believing and Doubting," p. 11).

Confusion as an Advanced State of Understanding

Of all Sheridan's maxims, one stands above the rest. "I have come to believe," I tell my students, borrowing the sacred phrase, "that confusion can be an advanced state of understanding." I watch the miracle unfold: their skeptical, incredulous looks metamorphosing into a sense of recognition—and then, relief. Here, at last, is the moment of anagnorisis and *peripeteia* in the Greek tragedy of an education that systematically robs students of agency and dignity. I'm trying to dismantle the "anxiety of the right reading" that plagues students—and sometimes their teachers, too—the belief that success only comes through performing a singular, teacher-authorized interpretation and that doubt, skepticism, uncertainty, or difficulty are signs of failure (Blau, *Literature Workshop*, p. 147).

This year, for the first time, I am teaching Vivek Shanbhag's novella *Ghachar Ghochar* in my senior Literature of Suspense class. Translated into English from the Kannada dialect by Srinath Perur, *Ghachar Ghochar* is taut, dark, and perplexing, both psychological thriller and social critique, the work of an Indian writer influenced by Hemingway and Chekhov. The reader's understanding of the story hinges on the testimony of an unreliable narrator, and the novella returns to problems of interpretation, taking as its title a nonsense phrase the meaning of which is entirely contextual. Many of the students who signed up for my suspense class were hoping for Stephen King and Alfred Hitchcock, and the rambling opening chapter of *Ghachar Ghochar* tests their patience.

"I'm so confused!" I hear a student say as I open the door. Cue the magic phrase. I tell the students that focusing on confusion will be our method for discussing the book. Each class will start with writing a brief response to a moment of confusion in the text, and the students' writing will provide the material for discussion. With the opportunity to talk about confusion opened, everyone has something to say.

"I was confused about the ending. When the narrator shatters the glass, and Vincent says there's blood on his hand, I don't understand what he means."

"I'm confused about the ants. They go on and on for pages about hating the ants. Where is this coming from?"

"What happened with Amma and the woman in the green sari? I don't understand why the situation escalated so quickly."

"Most of the ending confused me because there was so much talk of murder. Did someone actually commit a murder, or is it just suggesting that they would be capable of it? Does it connect to the narrator being uncomfortable about blood?"

I point the students back to a particularly thorny passage that many of them brought up in their writing and encourage them to work with a partner on the difficulty. When the energy in the room begins to fade, I raise my tingsha meditation bells, another homage to Sheridan, and a resonant ring directs everyone back to the full-class discussion.

I think back to my multiple *Paradise Lost* classes with Sheridan, in which he modeled the role of expert reader as one who seeks rather than holds all the answers. Working among a class of apprentices, the expert teacher can recognize the limitations of his own knowledge—and devote a lifetime (in Sheridan's case, literally a lifetime) to the exploration and conversation that gradually expands it.

Confusion, Sheridan will admit, is not *always* an advanced state of understanding, but the brazenness of the principle is a powerful subversion, letting students know that the rules of the traditional literature class—where the work of real minds and hearts is sometimes suppressed—need not apply. As Sheridan explains, "the student who is confused is frequently the one who understands enough to see a problem, a problem that less perceptive students have not yet noticed or arrived at," and therefore we might structure the literature class to "welcome and even foster among readers the experience of confusion" because this confusion is often manifested by the interpretive complexity that distinguishes the great literature that is worthy of discussion (*The Literature Workshop,* p. 21). I hold on to Sheridan's words as an antidote for the ingrained anesthetic (rather than aesthetic) approach to literature that school sometimes reinforces. And if I consider my own teaching life as a kind of text, I remember that attending to the problems, the vexations, the confusion, and the frustrations is not only what allows me to learn and grow but also what elevates me out of the static and the banal—toward a sense of fullness and meaning akin to what I find in a literary experience.

The Parable of False Knowledge, Part II

Sheridan sometimes will remark that most of what he wants to say, Louise Rosenblatt already has said before him. The bible of English education just might be Rosenblatt's *Literature as Exploration*—or perhaps the collected works of John Dewey, upon whose foundation Rosenblatt builds. Moffett's *Universe of Discourse* and Lave and Wenger's *Situated Learning* could also be contenders for this title, given their importance in Sheridan's teaching and learning life. But I believe that the urtext for English education is, for Sheridan, a work of literature, Milton's *Paradise Lost*, which defines the problem of false knowledge—and its alternative, learning through experience—with extraordinary power. At a time when the discourse of politics and the methods of the social sciences sometimes reign supreme in the field of education, Sheridan reminds English teachers and teacher educators to look to literature as our guide.

With the tradition of devotional reading in mind, Karen Edwards suggests that Milton's *Paradise Lost* represents an "experimental" reading of the Bible and that Adam and Eve's interpretive activities within *Paradise Lost* also embody seventeenth-century "experimental reading":

> Traditional exhortations to read the book of the world mean by read something akin to "repeat the lessons learned by rote." The new experimental reading, which Milton makes central to Adam and Eve's lives in paradise, demands a creative and ongoing engagement with the text. Thus Raphael does not interpret the minims' script for Adam and Eve; they must interpret it for themselves—and continue to review and perhaps revise their interpretation. Construing meaning is a labor that is coterminous with life. (Edwards, p. 69)

What Edwards describes sounds like Blau and Rosenblatt and Dewey—but conceptualized centuries earlier by Milton! The words "experience" and "experiment" were, in Milton's time, virtually interchangeable. In the terms of Louise Rosenblatt, "experimental" reading stands in contrast to efferent reading—the pulling out of facts or lessons that could be acquired outside the context of a textual experience—and instead corresponds to aesthetic engagement with a text. The experience/experiment of reading the world within the poem becomes a model for the external reader of *Paradise Lost.*

Although Sheridan ultimately chooses the term "workshop" to describe his preferred literary pedagogy, partly to show his indebtedness to the National Writing Project, he acknowledges that he is sometimes tempted to think of his teaching as based in "experiments": "And in my own classes (as on occasion here) I sometimes do identify activities of the kind I dramatize as experiments, and I sometimes speak of class sessions as laboratories" (*The Literature Workshop,* p. 14). Sheridan's literary experiments always serve to reposition participants as more active, self-aware readers and learners, more deeply engaged in literary experience.

Sheridan's radical vision of the classroom as a place of experimentation and conversation has roots in a Miltonic view of learning. The biography by Milton's nephew, Edward Phillips, highlights Milton's work as a tutor, depicting a "pedagogical environment in which students, seated together in Milton's home, take turns reading from his annotated books, sharing their translations aloud, and participating in a conversation with and about the text that involves Milton's written memoranda and, certainly, his oral instruction" (Festa, p. 26). I love how much this little snapshot of Milton's pedagogy resembles Sheridan's teaching, in which we are always invited to participate "in conversation with and about the text" and make contributions to an evolving discussion.

Thomas Festa suggests that Milton's annotations on the works of Euripides do not constitute authoritative pronouncements so much as they represent records of a personal transaction with the texts and contributions to an ongoing conversation (Festa, p. 44). Milton's experimental or experiential margin notes frequently begin with *puto ego* ("I think" or "I consider")—first person interjections that distinguish his voice from other commentators and the text itself. These same words have been the start of so many commentaries written in Sheridan's classes.

With the allure of Satanic borrowed knowledge ever-present in school, students and teachers of literature in the twenty-first century continue to face a Miltonic problem—how to bring real experiences and experiments to the center of the interpretive project. And in all of my attempts to shape pedagogical spaces that are hospitable to literary experience, Sheridan's reading and teaching are with me. So, with *Paradise Lost* in one hand and *The Literature Workshop* in the other, I "with wand'ring steps" make my "[not so] solitary way" (Milton, 12.648–649).

Looking Forward

Lately I've been thinking about artificial intelligence and its implications for the future of writing and, especially, the implications for the ways students interact with and write about literature in schools. In January 2023, I was among over 3,000 attendees at a webinar titled "ChatGPT and the Future of Writing Instruction," cohosted by National Writing Project and the WRITE Center of UC Irvine. By the end of 2022, headlines like "The End of High School English" and "ChatGPT Wrote My High School English Essay" had gone viral.

Facing an existential threat to their profession, my colleagues are responding with equal measures of excitement and doom, and the faculty room has been pulsating with the tension of a Samuel Beckett production: *Waiting for the End* (of High School English).

"Tests, tests, tests. Enough with the writing that students can cheat on. We need objective tests. Content that students learn and perform their understanding of under test conditions, just like other disciplines."

"We need to talk about going beyond the five-paragraph essay. I used to think that we were giving kids training wheels. But did you know that training wheels actually don't help with learning to ride a bike? We now know that they interfere with learning the most important skill: balance. It's not about taking the training wheels off. It's not using them to begin with."

"The pendulum has swung too far toward process. And toward technology. This all goes to show that there are situations where we need to give students blue books and have them perform a task."

"Everywhere I look I'm reading about the end of the English major. Students are going into STEM. We have to get past writing about literature. They aren't going to be English majors, and these kinds of assignments aren't going to be relevant for them."

To all of these understandable responses, I want to shout, "Sheridan Blau! *The Literature Workshop*!" With his graceful blend of theory and practice, Sheridan gives us a way forward for working with literature in an AI-filled world.

The powerful data-scouring and text-predictive capacities of machine learning, Noam Chomsky writes, are fundamentally different from the human process for acquiring language. Without an ability to construct possible explanations—different from descriptions or predictions—and the related mechanisms of fallibility and error correction, AI may patch together sophisticated parodies of human thought but can't actually execute a human process. That is, the textual product of AI often will amount to . . . (whisper) *false knowledge.*

I'm reminded of Sheridan's observation that the principles of language acquisition may provide a model or metaphor for many forms of authentic learning. Pointing to the work of Jerome Bruner, Sheridan has noted that the adoption of academic discourse in a classroom community mirrors "the same kind of process that defines the learning of language and thought by children in their interactions with parents and older siblings" (*The Literature Workshop,* p. 160). The miracle of human language acquisition is fundamentally different from machine learning, making it all the more valuable as a blueprint for the immersion in various discourses that can take place in re-humanized and humanistic schooling.

Moreover, Chomsky demonstrates that AI, at least at present, lacks moral intelligence. As a hedge against generating morally objectionable content, ChatGPT's creators have severely constrained the chatbot's creativity so that it avoids offering a personal perspective or "contributing anything novel to controversial—that is, important—discussions" (Chomsky,

2023). Although I fully expect that ChatGPT will become an increasingly sophisticated text generator, it cannot act with the rhetorical intentionality, situatedness, and truthfulness of a human *contributor.*

After my tenth-grade students finish reading and writing about *Othello* (and performing original monologues that extend or modify Shakespeare's vision), I run some experiments with the students in which we challenge ChatGPT to respond to various prompts: Write a five-paragraph, argument essay (with textual support) responding to the question "Is *Othello* a racist play?" Write from the perspective of an actor discussing the challenges that would be confronted and interpretive choices that might be made by portraying Iago in a production of *Othello.* Write a monologue from the perspective of Emilia, coming back from the dead as a ghost and confronting Iago. ChatGPT completes each task, more or less, filling up the page with coherent sentences and paragraphs. It even improves its writing somewhat in response to follow-up directions. Although my students can identify features they like in some of the chatbot's text, they find the writing to be lacking.

"It doesn't take any risks," one student says.

"It doesn't do anything besides what you asked it to do, following the prompt literally."

"It repeats itself, and there's not much analysis of the text."

"There's no feeling, no perspective, no voice."

On the other hand, in my college-prep senior class, when I compel ChatGPT to churn out a five-paragraph essay on the American Dream and *The Great Gatsby*, one student's eyes widen with amazement. "It's too good to be a student essay. Too perfect. I could never write something like that."

Another student says, "It would take me hours to write an essay like that. And what's the point? A computer can do the same thing in thirty seconds."

To value robotic writing processes and products—in the context of tasks that fail to inspire an authentic sense of purpose for the writer—feels increasingly perverse when real robots can achieve a comparable or superior result so much more efficiently. Noah Gordon, whom I met in Sheridan's commentary workshop and who was my colleague in both of the Milton classes I took with Sheridan, anticipated the rise of AI's capacities in composition long before the release of ChatGPT-3. Recently, he posed the problem of AI poignantly: "What troubles me is that machines are learning to compute and to create and to compose in ways that are far more humane than the tasks my students complete for their online credit recovery courses. We're teaching our computers like children and making our children into machines" (p. 302). In order to get out of this bind, we have to find ways to reimagine school as more than "dummy runs" and "didactic caretaking" (Britton et al., p. 130).

I turn to near the end of *The Literature Workshop*, where Sheridan offers seven dimensions of performative literacy that provide what he characterizes as the antithesis of Miltonic false knowledge:

1. Capacity for sustained, focused attention.
2. Willingness to suspend closure.
3. Willingness to take risks.
4. Tolerance for failure.
5. Tolerance for ambiguity, paradox, and uncertainty.
6. Intellectual generosity and fallibilism.
7. Metacognitive awareness. (*The Literature Workshop*, p. 211)

These principles of performative literacy are not necessarily what is taught in school, but they are precisely what is most human about reading and writing—and least possible for machine learning to effectively execute. If we can someday train AI to truly emulate human thinking, we'll be assessing the value of its output based on these traits.

Literacy, as Sheridan's NWP and NCTE colleague Miles Myers argues, refers not to a fixed set of skills but rather to a set of socially and culturally constructed practices. Writing in 1996, Myers is especially concerned with the transition between what he calls "analytic/decoding" literacy and "critical/translation literacy." In "translation/critical literacy," Myers posits, cognition is no longer defined by skills acquired through "school drills, exercises, and sequenced assignments" but instead through "participation in socially organized practices" (p. 157). Perhaps AI can nudge literacy education more fully into the "translation/critical literacy era," rendering the decontextualized kind of literacy largely futile as a human pursuit because it can be so effectively replicated by machines. Or perhaps AI marks the beginning of a new era of literacy entirely, in which humans will often be consuming AI-generated text and cocreating their own texts with AI. As I confront these new realities, I know that I will be holding Sheridan's principles and practices close to heart.

The commentary project is not a panacea for all that has gone wrong in literature education—like any other teaching practice, it can falter, stagnate, and sputter over time; it can be reinvented for good and for ill. But the way the initial commentary workshop shifts the script of the classroom is always worthwhile. Content informs form instead of being controlled by it; students become aware of the way genre conventions are socially constructed rather than being enslaved to the teacher's rubric; writing about literature has audience and purpose; real thoughts and feelings are embraced rather than suppressed; voice, sometimes vernacular, is vital; and the teacher, too, becomes a learner as part of an ongoing academic apprenticeship.

Despite the inherent limitations of literary learning in a school setting, Sheridan's commentary workshop remains powerful because it brings people together in human conversation. At the heart of Sheridan's career has been his ability to create connections between people who come to see themselves as participants in communities powered by human curiosity and generosity. In his account of the unique power of the National Writing Project model for teacher education, Sheridan writes, "Schools . . . for a variety of cultural and sociological reasons, are notoriously anti-intellectual places and have traditionally possessed no institutionalized mechanisms for nurturing and sustaining communities of teachers who wish to explore pedagogical and substantive ideas" ("The Only New Thing," p. 4). Nurturing and sustaining communities of teachers who explore and experiment has been Sheridan's life work, and I've been honored, in the later stages of Sheridan's career, to participate in just a few of the countless communities he has cultivated, made up of exemplary teachers who "are by definition exemplary learners and are therefore eager to share and explore ideas" ("The Only New Thing," p. 4).

Telio

Three hours ago, the conversation began in the lower level of Sheridan's apartment, buttressed by the two-story bookcase that is the pillar of a literary life, its shelves lifting up skyward, far out of reach, like a beacon toward the light. Now we are seated outside at Telio, the Greek restaurant down the block. How appropriate, I think, that a Greek restaurant would be the site of our Socratic dialogue, my friend Noah Gordon and I savoring every moment of our role as Platonic interlocutors. We are there as apprentices to the master, but Sheridan, mostly, wants to learn from us. When we arrived at Telio, Sheridan asked, as always, to sit at the large round table at the center of the restaurant, the one that resembles a seminar table. But the waiter insisted that it was a table reserved for five, and our party had only three, so we were relegated to a small table outside, where a humid summer afternoon has given way to an evening chill.

During our meal, we talk about lecturing—Sheridan forswears it, but Noah insists that Sheridan does lecture sometimes and proposes that Sheridan's lectures have had a transformative impact on him. We talk about the difference between open and closed texts, and whether all knowledge is created aesthetically. We talk about intuition and reason, about algorithms and heuristics, about problems and experiments. We trade stories about the joys of learning and the horrors of schools. Discussing the field of English education, about which Sheridan encourages us to be suspicious, we trace intellectual lineages.

We are sharing a piece of baklava, and the sugar and oil provide a brief rush—a ritual consecration of the evening's intellectual pleasures—and though the taste of this sweet offering may soon fade away like an Edenic apple, the promise of remembering and reconstructing this spirited dialogue leaves a more enduring afterglow.

The conversation turns, as it often does, to Milton. "You were talking about experiential knowledge," Noah says, "the kind of knowledge that comes from reading literature."

Sheridan continues. "Well, for Milton, wisdom is how you conduct your life, and knowledge is what you understand. Wisdom is a guide to action; knowledge is an understanding of Truth."

The word TELIO glows on the restaurant's signboard. Telio means perfect, and the elation I feel after a conversation with Sheridan surely approaches perfection, yet telio also refers to completion, to an ending. And though we'll soon rise, bellies full, minds swirling, walking our separate ways through the New York City night, the conversation never really ends. I reach for the last sliver of baklava.

"Isn't Adam's claim to wisdom the ultimate sin?" Noah asks.

"By saying 'I know myself,' Adam sins," Sheridan replies. "Unless he knows his Nature, which is to say, he knows himself always to be changing. To be the self that doesn't change is a sin. No knowledge is ever finished."

Works Cited

Blau, S. (1999). The only new thing under the sun: 25 years of the National Writing Project. *The Quarterly of the National Writing Project*, *21*(3), 2–7, 32.

Blau, S. (2001). Politics and the English language arts. In C. Dudley-Marling & C. Edelsky (Eds.), *The fate of progressive language policies and practices* (pp. 183–208). National Council of Teachers of English.

Blau, S. (2003). *The literature workshop: Teaching texts and their readers*. Heinemann.

Blau, S. (2009). Believing and doubting as hermeneutic method: Reading and teaching *Paradise lost*. *The Journal of the Assembly for Expanded Perspectives on Learning*, *15*, 8–15.

Blau, S. (2010). Academic writing as participation: Writing your way in. In P. Sullivan, H. Tinberg, & S. Blau (Eds.), *What is "college-level" writing? Vol. 2. Assignments, readings, and student writing samples* (pp. 29–56). National Council of Teachers of English.

Blau, S. (2011). Fostering authentic learning in the literature classroom. In J. Milner & C. Pope (Eds.), *Engaging American novels: Lessons from the classroom* (pp. 3–17). National Council of Teachers of English.

Blau, S. (2014). Literary competence and the experience of literature. *Style*, *48*(1), 42–47.

Britton, J, Burgess, T., Martin, N., McLeod, A., & Rosen, H. (1975). *The development of writing abilities (11–18)*. Macmillan.

Chomsky, N., Roberts, I., & Watumull, J. (2023, March 8). The false promise of ChatGPT. *The New York Times*. www.nytimes.com/2023/03/08/opinion/noam-chomsky-chatgpt-ai.html

Conservative groups throttle pioneer California student test. (2021, August 9). *Chicago Tribune*. www.chicagotribune.com/news/ct-xpm-1994-08-29-9408290093-story.html

Dewey, J. (1998). *How we think*. Houghton Mifflin.

Edwards, K. L. (1999). *Milton and the natural world: Science and poetry in* Paradise lost. Cambridge University Press.

Festa, T. (2006). *The end of learning*: *Milton and education*. Routledge.

Fitzgerald, F. S. (1925). *The great Gatsby*. Charles Scribner's Sons.

Gordon, N. H. (2022). *Unanswered questions: An educational autobiography of endless apprenticeship* [Doctoral dissertation, Columbia University]. Academic Commons. https://doi.org/10.7916/191z-s819

Huang, K. (2023, January 16). Alarmed by A.I. chatbots, universities start revamping how they teach. *The New York Times*. www.nytimes.com/2023/01/16/technology/chatgpt-artificial-intelligence-universities.html

Lave, J., & Wenger, E. (1991). *Situated learning: Legitimate peripheral participation*. Cambridge University Press.

Major, J. M. (1970). Eve's "experience." *Milton Quarterly*, *4*(3), 39–40. www.jstor.org/stable/24462773

Milton, J. (2005). *Paradise lost* (G. Teskey, Ed.). W. W. Norton & Company.

Moffett, J. (1968). *Teaching the universe of discourse*. Houghton Mifflin.

Morrison, T. (1977). *Song of Solomon*. Knopf.

Myers, M. (1996). *Changing our minds: Negotiating English and literacy*. National Council of Teachers of English.

Rejan, A. (2017). Reconciling Rosenblatt and the New Critics: The quest for an "experienced understanding" of literature. *English Education*, *50*(1), 10–41.

Rosenblatt, L. M. (1978). *The reader, the text, the poem: The transactional theory of the literary work*. Southern Illinois University Press.

Chapter Eleven

Creatures Again: What ELA Teachers Discover Reading in Community

Kathleen (Buchan) Kelly

"This is a battle, a war, and the casualties could be your hearts and souls," declares John Keating as he instructs his students to rip out a section of their literature textbooks (in the "Understanding Poetry" introduction written by J. Evans Pritchard). "We will not have that . . . in my class, you will learn to think for yourselves again."

The "again" of Keating's remarks from this memorable scene in *Dead Poets Society* always stays with me, as it presupposes that somewhere along the way, students are told how to think in a way that perhaps robs them of an autonomous self, in a way that prevents them from being creatures capable of discovery. What Peter Weir's film explores is something Walker Percy took up in the 1950s in his essay "The Loss of the Creature." Percy ponders whether humans can function as "sovereign persons" as they confront a modern world of technical and technological advancement. Percy maintains that as people encounter the objects in their lives, they must grapple with seeing "the thing as it is" versus seeing the thing as it has been "appropriated by the symbolic complex which has already been formed in the seer's mind" (p. 47). In Percian terms, the reader's battle for discovery or seeing a text "as it is" amounts to an independent, close reading, absent interference from other secondary sources; conversely, the symbolic complex already formed in readers' minds consists of interference such as a told-to-you-by-an-"expert" interpretation.

I begin with this scene from a 1989 film and hearken back to a 1954 essay because the issue both address is, amazingly, still prescient, for the battle over telling readers exactly how to "rightly" understand poetry, and really all literature, persists. In a twenty-first-century world, the Pritchards of today are many, offered by both human and artificial intelligence. Within this landscape, how might we resist the educational packaging of ideas that Keating and Percy warn against?

By way of learning more about this tension that readers may experience, I invited a small group of ELA teachers at an independent school in Southern California, all Harkness practitioners, to gather and read three short literary works together. I was particularly keen on knowing how they would approach texts commonly taught and read in schools. I also wondered whether reading in community might function as a type of interference for readers in "seeing the thing"—the literary work—as it is.

Thirty years ago, Sheridan Blau suggested a reading group *could* play a pivotal role in a reader's experience. In his work with an NEH-sponsored Literature Institute for ELA Teachers, Blau reported on the complaints several participating teachers made about their experience in working with reading groups. Many noted that in contrast to their experience in National Writing Project (NWP) writing-response groups, "discussions in their small reading/writing groups were competitive rather than collaborative and led them to feel discounted rather than affirmed, ignored rather than heard, and alienated rather than affiliated in a collegial community" (Blau, 1993, p. 9). I understood what these teachers had already experienced in writing institutes. What they describe in reading groups seemed diametrically opposed to what I myself have felt as the magic of summer writing workshops with fellow teachers—the encouragement, the camaraderie, even the transformation that's possible when people write together. Is reading together really so different? In what follows, I report on what happened in my study, what I learned about Harkness discussion, its rewards and challenges, and the possibilities for discovery when reading literature in community.

The Site of Exploration

To better understand what happens when ELA teachers read literature together, I decided to explore this question at an independent school in Southern California that practiced and trained their faculty in conference-style discussion, Harkness Pedagogy. Harkness Pedagogy is an approach to discussion that takes its name from philanthropist Edward S. Harkness, who gifted millions to Phillips Exeter School with the caveat that it dream up something that would radically change the nature of education at Exeter and the whole "educational system in secondary schools" (Phillips Exeter Academy, 2006). The Harkness Table was key to the radical change; the thinking was that students seated across a table would no longer be talked *at*; they would have a stake and a voice in their own learning. The Harkness approach is guided by the assumption that knowledge is co-constructed within the educational setting. In fact, the number-one rule of Harkness is collaborate, don't compete. This pedagogical approach positions students at the center of their own learning with teachers functioning as facilitators or coaches to support student discussion.

Confronting the Thing to Be Known

In an ELA Harkness classroom, literature is what spurs discussion. That literature is thought to provoke a particular response in readers is essential to our work here. To better understand the Percian notion of "the wonder and delight" as a result of "penetration of the thing itself" (Percy, 1), it is helpful to review the contributions of those scholars who have theorized reading as experience.

Reader-response theory is thought to be born out of the work of Rosenblatt (1938, 1978), yet some might even go farther back to I. A. Richards's *Practical Criticism* (1929) or farther back even to Husserl's (1913) *Ideas* to get a sense of how objects "constitute themselves in consciousness." Influenced by Richards's work as well as that of Dewey's *Democracy in Education* (1916) and *Experience in Education* (1938), Rosenblatt advances the Deweyan focus on human nature. Her *Literature as Exploration* raises an essential question: What can we gain from reading literature? She claims literature "makes comprehensible the myriad ways in which human beings meet the infinite possibilities that life offers" (p. 6). But the text on its own cannot do that—isn't even a text without the reader, so Rosenblatt argues. What gives language meaning is "the essential third element"—"the human being" (p. 25). In her 1988 "Writing and Reading: A Transactional Theory," Rosenblatt famously sketches the distinction between two kinds of reading stances: 1) efferent: the kind of reading in which attention is centered predominantly on what is to be carried away or retained *after* the reading event, and 2) aesthetic: the kind of reading in which the reader adopts an attitude of readiness to focus attention on what is being lived through *during* the reading event.

How else to explain what happens when a reader encounters a literary work? We might look at Reader Reception theories since Rosenblatt. We could consider Fish's claim (1970; 1976) that language "ought to be thought of as an experience rather than as a repository of extractable meaning" (*Literature in the Reader,* p. 161). Or we might look to his suggestion that a text, "because it has been a part of a reader's experience, . . . means" (Variorum, p. 470). Or we could follow Holland, who sees multiplicity of readings as a given. Holland (1975) suggests it is the reader's identity and not the text that fuels the interpretation. Maybe we agree with Bleich (1975; 1978; 1981; 2019), who explores reader response as subjective, suggesting that interpretation of what we read hinges not on the text but on the conceptual experience we each create in our minds. Or perhaps we look to Probst (1994) who echoes his predecessors' interest in Reception Theory in suggesting "Meaning lies in that shared ground where the reader and text meet" *(English Journal,* p. 38) More, we could try to understand the reading experience by considering more recent work on Transactional Theory, which has considered the ways readers experience events through the symbolic fantasy of the text and the role these experiences play in shaping identity (Haruna & Abd Aziz, 2019).

Beyond an individual's reading experience, for this study, we also need to consider the role of a reading community in shaping reader response. Thus, we would do well to recall Fish's (1980) notion of "interpretive communities." Fish suggests that it's the community, not the text or the reader, that influences members' interpretations and accounts for similar readings of texts. Because this study involves Harkness teachers who have been trained in the pedagogical approach, we may want to be mindful of the work of Lindlof (2002), who conceives of the interpretive community as a "a collectivity of people who share strategies for interpreting, using, and engaging in communication about a media, text or technology" (p. 64). And we would do well to think about the work of Brooks and Browne (2012), who consider reader response within a culturally-situated context, arguing that cultural practices enable literary interpretations of texts. It's possible that some discussion and school norms may inform how the ELA teachers in this study read literature together.

The dialogic classroom may also inform reader response, as the co-construction of knowledge is the lynchpin of this kind of learning environment. The boons of such a classroom setting are many. As Fecho (2011) has observed: "From such communities comes the willingness to risk and honor diverse perspectives, to shift the class from one that keeps all participants safe from the discomfort of self-reflection to one in which it is safe to work through the discomfort" (p. 50). Yet the creation of such a community requires intentional planning and establishing of a culture of inquiry. Because we're looking to see whether reading in community can interfere with discovery, we ought to consider Alexander's (2017) five principles of dialogic teaching, which are designed to both create a culture of collaboration between teachers and students as well as invite discussion and dialogue that will advance students' ideas on a given topic. Per Alexander, dialogic teaching is: 1) collective; 2) reciprocal; 3) supportive; 4) cumulative; and 5) purposeful. According to Alexander, the first three principles establish the classroom culture; the last two address the content of the "talk." Taken together, these scholars detail what is possible when people talk to each other within classroom spaces designed for meaningful discourse.

Now that we know the site of exploration, are aware of factors that may inform the Percian notion of sightseeing, and have a few ways to consider Blau's suggestion of a reading group's pivotal role in a reader's experience, we'll next meet the sightseers and detail their journey to discovery.

Gazing Directly at the Thing Itself

Sightseers

The study itself involved ten teachers—three middle school (grades 6–8), six upper school (grades 9–12), and one crossover (grades 6–12). There were eight females and two males. These teachers ranged in age from thirties to fifties. Their respective ages are only important in relation to participants' exposure to texts that continue to be taught at the high school, college, and graduate school levels. If schools still embrace particular curricula, i.e., certain canonical authors' works, then the teachers in my study would be more likely to have been exposed to these works along the course of their respective educations.

Avoiding the Approved Confrontation of the Tour

This small group of ELA teachers knew nothing of what they would read, what I hoped to study, and had no knowledge of my research question. Teachers were handed a packet of texts with instructions. I asked the group to read, consider, and discuss three literary works. Then, I asked them to respond to a brief questionnaire that invited reflection on the experience of reading and discussing the texts on their own and with the group. This study took place in an extended block class period in May of 2022.

The Things Themselves

Within the packet I handed to the teachers were two poems by Emily Dickinson from her 1924 *Complete Poems*: "Much Madness is divinest Sense" and "Success is counted sweetest." The third text was a novel excerpt—the epigraph of Toni Morrison's *The Bluest Eye*. After the study concluded, I distributed a

"Reading Study Reflection," a set of questions that functioned as the title suggests.

Since I wanted to try and replicate some of what Blau had done in his 1993 study on reading communities, my text selection was informed by his. I knew that the teachers in the NEH Institute studied Dickinson's poetry and Morrison's *Beloved.* Given my time constraints, I opted for two Dickinson poems and the opening of *The Bluest Eye.* Another reason for my text selection was my assumption of familiarity. These works are widely taught in schools; thus, I thought it possible the teachers may have been exposed to all three works.

Preformulation

Once everyone was gathered in a classroom around a Harkness Table, I distributed the packet of literary works. The instructions for engagement with each text were the same:

1. Please read each of the literary works that follow. We will read a total of three, but we will consider them one at a time.
2. First, read the text to yourself. As you read on your own, feel free to take notes in the margins on what sentences, lines, or phrases in the text you find interesting or compelling, troublesome, or perhaps confounding.
3. Then, we will do a jump-in reading two times. If it helps to continue taking notes as we read, do.
4. After we've had some time for you to read the text on your own and then together with the group, let's engage in a discussion.

As people were preparing to participate, I was asked to clarify the term "jump-in reading." I did. The group read and discussed the texts in order. They began with Dickinson's "Much Madness is divinest Sense," next explored "Success is counted sweetest," and ended with the epigraph to Morrison's *The Bluest Eye.*

Once we were underway, my role was to observe, take notes, chart the discussion, serve as timekeeper, and cue transitions. I will next share what happened within the two poetry discussions, since the group ran short on time and was unable to fully discuss Morrison's epigraph to *The Bluest Eye.*

Encounters

The data for this study are my own classroom observations and notes from charting the participants' discussions. It also consists of participants' answers to a series of reflection questions.

The Dialectic of Sightseeing

Teachers read the two Dickinson poems. They did so first by reading silently. I invited them to take notes on the page if they desired. After time was allotted, about 5–8 minutes, I asked for volunteers to read the poems aloud two times. They did. The group went on to discuss the poems one by one. I next share the poems and report on what happened within this reading community. All names are pseudonyms.

Sightseers Encounter Dickinson

Text #1

Emily Dickinson (1830–1886). *Complete Poems.* 1924
Part One: Life
XI

MUCH madness is divinest sense
To a discerning eye
Much sense the starkest madness
'Tis the majority
In this, as all, prevails
Assent, and you are sane;
Demur,—you're straightway dangerous,
And handled with a chain.

Discussion #1: Dialectical Movements

The first conversation was a quiet start. The second reader filled the silence by asking the group "Who pronounced it better?" He was referring to his reading of line 4 "'Tis the majority.'" Rather than reading it as "tis" as in an abbreviated form of "it is," he read it as "T is." This made 'T the subject of a clause and the reading rather comical. Though this reader was self-conscious, he was still game to participate. The group giggled as he paused at the line and read it a few different ways. After the laughter and smiles from this awkward moment, Bonnie said she had "read this poem before." Yet she found herself "reading it so many times, with each one offering a new noticing." This got the discussion underway. I offer it below.

Bonnie: This poem is comprised of sentences and stanzas. Reading the poem a few times highlighted that. The next sentence straddles.

Cora: Rhyme offers a completion. . . . There seems a counteracting completion here.

Kanda: I am struck by ambiguity.

Joanne: There is an entering through a process of assent.

Ronald: The majority decides on ascending.

At this point, Ronald confused "ascent" with "assent." His comments about climbing rather than giving in to public opinion seemed to stall conversation at the table. Soon after . . .

Kanda: Does second person feel more personal?

Kanda: Who is "I"? Is this also "eye"? Are people seeing this?

Anita: The first half of this poem seems a proclamation or an edict. The second seems fulcrum, a decision.

Bonnie: This poem is concrete. God is there in the first line . . . I am wondering—What is assent? Is it verbal or nonverbal?

Maya: There is no majority without.

Elaine: The you is personal. . . . Demure suggests—

At this point, I stepped in to correct the error in conflating "demur" with "demure."

Anita: The majority decides . . . it's a verbal not getting in.

Reflections on the First Dialectic

Virtually every comment in this discussion is a reference to the text or a textual feature. Comments about structural elements, syntax, pronouns, and diction dominate. The classroom became a space to voice ideas, a place to try to arrive at some clarity as individual thinkers by saying aloud what textual elements they noticed.

Observations rank second in group participant comments. There are six from Cora, Bonnie, Maya, Elaine, and Anita. As a result of their remarks, we hear about how "Rhyme offers a completion"; the fact that "this poem is concrete"; that "the you is personal"; and we learn "there is no majority without." The other prominent kinds of remarks are theories and questions. We see three each in the discussion. Anita theorizes early on, "The first half of this poem seems a proclamation. . . . The second seems fulcrum"; Elaine later starts a hypothesis, "The you is personal. . . . Demure suggests—"; and Anita finishes with her second theory, "The majority decides . . . it's a verbal not getting in." Whether the tie between theories and questions is significant, I am not sure, yet I also noticed the ways that questions don't necessarily yield answers and theories don't necessarily get built together. For instance, we see in the exchange between Joanne and Ronald that Joanne opines, "There is an entering through a process of assent," and Ronald follows this up with his own observation, "The majority decides on ascending." Also significant is the fact that there is only one answer to a question posed. Bonnie's "What is assent? Is it verbal or nonverbal?" seems to be answered by Maya's "There is no majority without." This absence of a steady stream of Q-and-A seems noteworthy. Perhaps people were searching for larger explanations or broader interpretations during the discussion and hoped for a more capacious reading as they listened to one another. Maybe a single answer seemed too narrow in the moment. Or, people may have been thinking about their own theories that never got aired. Another possibility is that some did not answer questions due to confusion or a lack of mental focus in the moment.

Kanda and Bonnie's comments are outliers. Kanda outwardly verbally engaged in a reader-response approach to the literature with her peers. Her remarks seemed to vocalize her experience of the text, made clear on what she was "struck by," what she wondered "feel[s] more personal," and by her implicit declaration of what she saw. Kanda also invited the reading community to think with her by posing a question to the group: "Are people seeing this?" She seemed interested in building an interpretation with others. Bonnie's remarks also suggest an experiential approach to reading. She airs her experience, indicating structural elements she says were "highlighted" from "reading the poem a few times."

Overall, the set of remarks from the group suggests that this literary discussion hinged on making mention of and offering suppositions about textual features. Seeing the text as it is and then moving on to meaning making is one possible path these readers took en route to discovery. The questions raised all followed from several instances of text references plus observations. And the theories came much later in the discussion. That people had questions and theories afterward may suggest these as higher-order thinking moves. Also, based on this discussion, attempts at making meaning within a reading community seem to hinge on explicitly stating what participants saw as noteworthy in the text. This led to some co-construction of an interpretation as the discussion developed.

Finally, I offer a confession. I jumped in and clarified that Dickinson's word was "demur" and not "demure." After the correction, one participant echoed my point. I noticed my remark was a discussion killer and wondered whether it may have hindered others' discovery.

After the first conversation seemed over, we transitioned and read the second Dickinson poem.

Text #2

Emily Dickinson (1830–1886). *Complete Poems.* 1924
Part One: Life
I

SUCCESS is counted sweetest
By those who ne'er succeed.
To comprehend a nectar
Requires sorest need.

Not one of all the purple host
Who took the flag to-day
Can tell the definition,
So clear, of victory,

As he, defeated, dying,
On whose forbidden ear
The distant strains of triumph
Break, agonized and clear.

Discussion #2: Dialectical Movements

After time was allotted for silent reading and note-taking, I again prompted volunteers to read the poem aloud. Two readers did. This conversation was livelier than the first. At this point, people seemed comfortable working alongside each other. As before, there was a comment about the reading process that kicked things off. Cora said, "I got it when I heard it the second time." This remark got the discussion underway. It appears below.

Bonnie: Comprehension is need?

Ronald: So, this is comprehension of need? I was trying to make sense of the soreness of need. Triumph is visible, in painful need to have it. I see that in the first and third stanzas . . . I don't know what to do with the middle.

Bonnie: I think that's how he hears it.

Latisha: It feels like no one ever tells us.

Elaine: I am reading Christianity into it—the regal colors, the purple, the host, what is forbidden.

Cora: I see academic language versus emotional language. We get "comprehend" and "brain" and then "Sorest in body." The distinction is clear in those uses of language.

Kanda: I notice the repetition of "clear." The center seems to be about the center. It is not linked to heady participation.

Cora: OOH! That's really spooky!

Anita: Comprehend is linked to taking in . . . I see this poem as a Venn diagram. The middle fits with both. Success is a zero-sum game at expenses. . . . Why "forbidden"? Forbidden from?

Adrian: Do you comprehend nectar?

Bonnie: One question I have is about "comprehend." Does it mean value or understand? And, first of all—success—what a weird word. I wrote never, ever?. . . . Is there an underclass?

Joanne: That's what I thought. Knowing the pain to get to the nectar . . .

Adrian: You do get the militarized colors, flag. . . . What's the speaker's definition of success?

Joanne: If this is militaristic, we're not fighting for it, and he knows what success is.

Latisha: This is my first time reading this poem. The last line is bothering me. Why?

Reflections on the Second Dialectic

This time around, the primary way people are engaging in discussion is by posing questions. Within this data set, we have eight. Bonnie, Anita, Adrian, and Latisha all pose questions to the group. In fact, questions frame this discussion. Bonnie's "Comprehension is need?" begins the conversation, and as the discussion unfolds, we see people interrogating the text aloud with remarks such as Anita's "Why 'forbidden'? Forbidden from?" and Adrian's "Do you comprehend nectar?" Latisha's wrestling with text ends the conversation: "The last line is bothering me. Why?"

Also noteworthy is that there are many more questions that get answered in this discussion. We see four explicit Q-and-A exchanges as the discussion unfolds. Ronald looks to address Bonnie's opener by way of recasting her question; Bonnie and Latisha look to answer Ronald's query; and Joanne responds affirmatively to Bonnie's question about "the underclass." What is also interesting about these data beyond the number of questions are the new categories of remarks that arose around trying to answer questions such as: statements of confusion like Ronald's "I don't know what to do with the middle"; speculative remarks like Bonnie's "I think that's how he hears it"; and questions for clarification like Bonnie's "Does [comprehend] mean value or understand?" and Adrian's "What's the speaker's definition of success?" Too, we see people asking questions throughout.

As before, statements about or references to text features figured prominently in participant comments. We hear people voicing what they notice about structural elements of the poem, such as Ronald's remark about syntax, "I see that in the first and third stanzas," and Cora's comments about diction, "We get 'comprehend' and 'brain' and then 'Sorest in body." This time we also hear about literary techniques, such as Adrian's observation, "You do get the militarized colors, flag," and Kanda's "I notice the repetition of 'clear.'" In this discussion, the number of participant comments regarding textual references is tied with theories—there are seven of each of these. Thus, early and often, people are spinning yarns, such as Ronald's "Triumph is visible, in painful need to have it."; Kanda's "The center seems to be about the center"; and Anita's "Success is a zero-sum game at expenses."

This time, reader response figures much more prominently in the discussion. As contrasted with the outlier remarks of the first discussion, here we get six comments. In fact, personal reactions are the bookends to the discussion. Cora's report on "getting" the poem after hearing it a second time starts things off. Ronald's explanation of his thinking process—that he was "trying to make sense of the soreness of need" continues that trend. Cora's reports on what she "sees"; Kanda's comment about what she "notices"; Joanne's confession "that's what I thought"; and Latisha's declaration of the ways the poem was "bothering" her all evidence people's public airing of their reading experience. We also get some descriptions of people's reading processes.

Observations are also noteworthy within participant remarks. We get four, seen in Ronald's "Triumph is visible"; Cora's comment on "academic and emotional language"; Elaine's pointing to "regal colors . . . purple"; and Kanda's remark about "the repetition of clear." This discourse showcases Harkness practitioners endeavoring to engage in a genuine discussion. They look to co-construct meaning based on observations, questions, and theories. Bonnie's opening question, "Comprehension is need?," is one others take on and try to deal with. We hear some analytical remarks and suppositions in efforts to understand the text. Ronald's question of "what to do with the middle [of the poem]" is something Kanda takes on and Cora finds "spooky." In fact, in some ways, the entire conversation is still looking to understand what Dickinson means by "comprehend." Adrian wonders how this word functions in relation to "nectar." And as late as Bonnie's comment, we still see people struggling to get at the denotation of the word in this context.

As a collective, the data from these two conversations seem to suggest that making meaning from a text within a reading community hinges on explicitly stating what participants saw as noteworthy textual features. And meaning making may follow a pattern: in both discussions pointing to the text often preceded a theory. However, unlike the first discussion, the second one actually begins with Ronald theorizing in response to Bonnie's question. And many questions followed theories. Also, sometimes theories were posed as kinds of interpretive questions, such as Bonnie's "Comprehension is need?" One possibility emerges from these data: Questions beget more questions, and these lead to meaning making.

How else might we account for the many theories and questions in this second discussion? We might note that participants vocally speculated about and deconstructed the text. Their observations, voiced personal reactions, and explicit descriptions of thinking processes all contributed to a collective endeavor and a livelier intellectual exchange. Is there a causal connection? This is too limited a set of data to say for sure. What we can say, though, is that in this discussion, people seemed comfortable sharing their aesthetic experience of the text. They described their reading processes as well. And we see more involvement here from the group as a whole; there is much more thinking out loud and together than in the first discussion. Is comfort a factor? Perhaps. It may be that they began to see the classroom space as a safe one to think out loud the more time they spent together. Maybe this is a necessary precursor to what I witnessed. Maslow would tell us yes. I also wondered if perhaps Alexander's "1) collective; 2) reciprocal; 3) supportive" standards had established the classroom culture so the talk could then thrive.

To further explain the ways the group engaged with the literary works, we might consider the genre and the subject matter of the respective Dickinson poems. It's certainly possible that not everyone is entirely comfortable discussing poetry. And it may be that different subject matters resonate with different readers. Beyond the subject matter, we might also wonder about the difficulty level of these respective poems. Could we say the second was easier than the first when comparing poetic devices? These are questions that are worth posing, given the nature of this study and the real-world implications for ELA teachers and their students.

As a result of my work here, I see several boons of reading literature in community. In each conversation, I saw participants listening to one another, using each other's names (omitted for anonymity), responding to one another, asking clarifying questions when required, pointing to particular lines within the literary works, and wondering aloud. There seemed to be a sorting out of thought within each discussion. Moreover, the back-and-forth in the building of an interpretation seemed clear in both conversations. I paid witness to the co-construction of knowledge. I also saw evidence of the advantages and possibilities of the dialogic classroom. And I observed what Fecho describes: "the willingness to risk and honor diverse perspectives." In the questions people asked, the ways they built on one another's answers and theories, and the confessions of being troubled or confused by certain elements of the text, it seemed people felt safe to work through discomfort. Though it's difficult to know how tolerant participants were in dealing with uncertainty, their comments, especially regarding the second poem, demonstrated an awareness of ambiguity. And I paid witness to some frustration with lines that people could not quite get a handle on. These wrestling-with-the-text remarks seemed to run counter to what some scholars say is a benefit of discussion. For instance, what happened here may go against the findings of Brookfield and Preskill (1999), who have argued for the many benefits of discussion, among them increased awareness of and tolerance for ambiguity and complexity.

In terms of involvement in the discussion, every person in the group participated at least once, some more than others. As a group, they ran the Harkness Table. Edward S. Harkness's vision that "learners would have a stake and a voice in their own learning" was also readily apparent to me. And in their laughter, concerns, uncertainty, and trying, I saw what researchers claim Harkness makes possible—its effects on cognitive and interpersonal skills. I saw Boadi's (2015) suggestion of Harkness's positive effect on developing nuance and humility. Too, I saw Pettigrew's (2015) suggestion that Harkness cultivates the art of listening. These people seemed attuned to one another.

Also clear is Rosenblatt's idea of literature as experience. Participants' comments about what happened as they read on their own, as well as what they reported happened as they listened to and reconsidered the texts during the jump-in reading, made evident that texts were "being lived through *during* the reading event." And teachers' remarks reflected the individualized experience that seems to occur when people read literature. These individual experiences were also made visible in the questions and comments on compelling and confusing aspects of the text. Something else that seems clear from these two discussions is Fish's notion of language "as an experience rather than as a repository of extractable meaning" (p. 67). People commented on particular words that struck them or phrases or repetition or stylistic elements that they noticed. Not everyone read the same way.

One issue I have yet to consider is Percy's idea of theory and his claims about what theories do to our experience of the world. Percy suggests that "in the transmission of scientific theory from theorist to layman, the expectation of the theorist is reversed. Instead of the marvels of the universe being made available to the public, the universe is disposed of by theory" (p. 63). For Percy, theory can rob people of an actual experience because the objects become specimens of a larger concept and are no longer viewed in ways that honor and recognize their very essence. In my coding of the participants' remarks, I also use the term "theory." And here I must clarify. What I mean by "theory" in my charting of the Harkness discussion is supposition; speculation; voiced ideas; and explanations proffered to better understand the text at hand. I did *not* pay witness to people superimposing a framework such as a feminist or a psychoanalytic lens onto the poetry they read. Therefore, I do not see what these readers did as somehow "disposing" of the literature by theory in the ways Percy describes theory can. Rather, I paid witness to these readers working to see the thing itself.

I have no way of knowing, of course, based strictly on my own observational and empirical evidence whether or if participants struggled to see if the poetry was "measuring up to the criterion of the preformed symbolic complex" (p. 47). However, one of my reflection questions might shed some light on this issue.

Transmission of Scientific Theory from Theorist to Layman?

After the conversations ended, I asked the participants to sit and reflect on what had just happened. And I asked them to put these reflections in writing. My reflection questions prompted participants to comment on several factors that I imagined might inform how they accessed the literature we studied, such as the role of multiple readings of a text, both silent and jump-in; note-taking prior to and during discussion; and feelings of obligation to arrive at a "right" reading, to name a few. Since the parameters of this study do not allow for a look at every query or response, I will focus on that which is most relevant to my work here: on the ways schooling might play a role in participants' reading process. Below, I present one question from the reflection questionnaire. Then I offer nine anonymous responses to the question. (Only nine participants returned their responses to me.) After that, I present some discussion.

Q #3) How much of a role did your own schooling in studying these texts play in your reading process? (Circle all that apply, and please elaborate as you see fit.)

A. Did you approach the text in the same way you were taught to in school?
B. Did you recall a reading you had previously done in school and activate that one?
C. Do you think your reading process was or may have been informed by previous instructors' guidance and interpretation of the literary work?
D. Another factor?

Responses

P1: "This makes me wish I read all of the questions before responding."
P2: No answer.
P3: "Probably all of the above!" [A–C]
P4: B
C, both (instructors' guidance and interpretation);
D, too "years of following students through this process."
The same respondent also put a question mark (?) beside A and wrote "Too long?"
P5: A
P6: A
C with a clarification under "interpretation of the literary work": not this one but I often think of this one lecture from grad school and a Frost poem
D, teaching this poem to 11th graders
P7: A & C
P8: A, B & C; For D—teaching the text, hearing students discuss it. Also, in one case, writing about the text in school

P9: D, "I have taught two of three texts here. I was transported back to the time in a way that felt nostalgic—the texts felt special"

Knower Confronts the Thing to Be Known

If the question is *How does schooling affect how we read and whether we can see a text anew when reading in community?* a few answers emerge. Here, I first offer the responder totals and then offer some discussion of these data. Of the nine participants, five selected (A); three selected (B); five selected (C); and four selected (D); another factor. These four responses were 1) "following students through process"; 2) "teaching the poem"; 3) "teaching the text; hearing students; writing about it in school"; and 4) "having taught the texts [in the past]." There was one blank response and no real response from "P1."

The data reveal that most participants (5/9) selected "A" and in effect said they approached the texts the same way they were taught in school. I took their answers to mean that they read the literary work and/or tried to render an interpretation using a certain strategy their teachers previously instructed them to do. This seems important to note and bears upon how readers may go about cognizing a text—approaches seem to become fossilized. Essential to note is that more than half (5/9) also said by choosing letter "C" that their reading process was or may have been informed by previous instructors' guidance and interpretation of the literary work. This set of responses suggests that discovery within a reading community, or at least within this one, was not entirely available to readers, as they confess they were influenced by a past reading or perhaps by comments from past instructors on how to go about accessing a text. This may have implications for the extent to which they could "see the thing as it is," as in see these texts with fresh eyes. I wondered if this outcome might be possible at the outset of this study and was curious how or if people would let go of those ideas and instead experience the text anew with the reading group. These findings reveal that people admit to relying on past resources to read literature. Also important to note is the one third of the group who indicated that they recalled and activated a previous theory

(3/9 who chose letter "B") handed down from an instructor. If we assume it's possible that people read letter "C" as repeating a former teacher's guidance and interpretation, then the numbers for "B"—activating a former reading—may be even higher.

Though participants may have interpreted letter "C" in question number three to refer to pedagogical strategies and ways to access literature that they were taught long ago, it may also be the case that these readers have held on to former teachers' and professors' readings of texts years after they've left those classrooms. Thus, perhaps readers cannot see the text on its own, absent the lens they have been given. And maybe we now find ourselves back with Percy's dyad: "the thing as it is" versus seeing the text as it has been "appropriated by the symbolic complex which has already been formed in seer's minds."

The Road to Recovery by a Dialectical Movement

Percy offers a way to help perhaps explain the above responses, especially the selection of response "C"—the possibility that a reading process was or may have been informed by previous instructors' guidance and interpretation of the literary work. He blames it on consumerism, which, he claims, affects the way educational institutions are organized. Rather than function as learners, instead, students are cast into the role of consumers of a particular form of educational packaging, and this packaging is what robs them of authentic discovery. The predicament, per Percy, is one in which every individual finds him/herself in a modern society:

> a society, that is, in which there is a division between expert and layman, planner and consumer, in which experts and planners take special measures to teach and edify the consumer. The measures taken are measures appropriate to the consumer: the expert and the planner *know* and *plan*, but the consumer *needs* and *experiences*. There is a double deprivation. First, the thing is lost through its packaging. The very means by which the thing is presented for consumption, the very techniques by which the thing is made available as an item of need—satisfaction, these very means operate to remove the thing from the sovereignty of

> the knower. . . . The second loss is the spoliation of the thing, the tree, the rock, the swallow, by the layman's misunderstanding of scientific theory. (p. 63)

The application of Percy's idea here is obvious: any reader cannot see the literature in front of her because of the educational packaging in which it has been delivered—a textbook, a teacher, a theory, or, to make this more current, a bot, or another kind of source that provides "truths" to readers about the things they are interested in studying. This lens obscures an individual's ability to truly see the text. These packages keep knowledge at a distance from learners. Percy points out that so much of our society is designed this way on purpose. And people are used to it, even expect it. We have grown comfortable with "a generalized surrender of the horizon to those experts within whose competence a particular segment of the horizon is thought to lie" (Percy, p. 56). What Percy suggests here has me curious about whether readers are even conscious of the lenses through which they see and interpret literature. Do we notice Percy's experts and planners in our lives? Though the Rosenblattian aesthetic experience was clearly happening in the study I conducted, I wonder if it isn't also the case that people activate ideas that already take lodging in their brains about what a text "means." Participant responses in selecting letters "A" and "C" to question number three offer an affirmative answer. These folks did recall and perhaps lean into earlier readings and training. And perhaps this is a part of what each individual reader does when recognizing a work of art. Perhaps this is a learned behavior that we, all of us, engage in. Moreover, maybe this is evidence of educational institutions' effectiveness in training people to recall what readers ought to value when reading literature. And perhaps that is what school has taught people that studying literature entails—handing down interpretations from one generation to the next. Certainly, literature can serve as a cultural artifact, and so why not accept this relaying of interpretation as normative, even celebrate it? Why not join Barbara Tuchman in her acknowledgment that "books are the carrier of civilizations"?

Blau also provides a way to think about the role that schooling plays in people's reading processes. He claims that schools do train students of literature to think of "learning" it in precisely the ways we have recently discussed. Blau's concept for it is "false knowledge"—a term that is linked to readers arriving at a "normative" or "authorized" interpretation of a text—something akin to what college professors may offer students in a lecture, that "may provide readers with literary knowledge in the sense that it offers them information on what constitutes a right reading, but insofar as it invalidates their own experience as readers, it disables their capacity to function as authentically literate persons" (Blau, 1993, p. 12). According to Blau's theory, literature is taught in schools in what amounts to handing down information in a patterned cycle: professor imparts interpretation to teacher, teacher passes this on to her own students, and the cycle repeats. The result, per Blau, is a reading that may result in little or no genuine understanding of *what* and, to borrow from Ciardi, *how* a text means. This is, thus, an echoing of an interpretation of a text. Blau's label for this approach to literary study is a term he borrows from Milton in *Paradise Lost*. For Blau, this kind of "knowledge" is "that which opens [readers'] eyes but closes their minds" (Blau, 1993, p. 12). His argument is not unlike Percy's—institutions' tendency to rob individuals of their agency and possibility of discovery.

The group of teachers in my study engaged in a spirited conversation with one another by taking turns talking and simultaneously searching, speculating, and listening. They seemed to be engaged in and open to constructing meaning together. They were, ostensibly, looking to discover what they did not know. If there were a sense of confusion or alienation, a kind of packaging that got in the way of what they were able to cognize or interpret, it was not immediately apparent; but that does not mean it was not there. Some participant responses indicated that people went quiet when an alternate reading than their own came to light. Thus, one is left to wonder what becomes of a quiet participant's comprehension of the text. This is a question that requires further research.

One thing that seems clear from this study is that in contrast to the teachers *at the start* of Blau's NEH Institute, these study participants worked together and allowed for various interpretations of the literature they studied. Given what we see here, Harkness pedagogy seems to support collaboration over competition. Brownback's (2015) idea that Harkness enables the construction of "truth" was evident in the work people did together to try to arrive at a sound, legitimate interpretation of the poems. And in the give-and-take, questioning, pointing, wondering, searching, and speculating as a community, I paid witness to ways Harkness has a positive effect on developing discernment, nuance, and humility. I might also explain this outcome by pointing out that these educators are Harkness teachers, that they are colleagues, and that they are already part of a school community.

Circumstances through which the Thing May Be Restored to the Person

Ultimately, this study offered a window into how a small team of ELA teachers approach literature and think about it together. They demonstrated that a community approach to reading together is a legitimate way to access literature.

The ease with which I saw people engaging with one another's ideas was important, earnest, real, and generous. They were enacting the bedrock principle upon which Harkness pedagogy was founded—the Emersonian idea—respect the pupil. This is a group of people invested in learning and invested in each other. In one of the reflection responses (and there were many like this one), a participant commented, "I love and respect my colleagues and trust them—and want to know what they think." Here may be a moment where we can see Clark and Soutter's (2022) findings at work: they claim Harkness can positively impact learners' civic and intellectual character strengths. It's worth noting that those teachers in the Blau NEH Institute eventually did work through their discomfort by engaging in many of the strategies employed in this study: "reading aloud, using collaborative reading and interpretation groups, attending to a variety of interpretive perspectives, and using various strategies to encourage hermeneutic generosity" (p. 18). It's also likely their own teaching contexts helped things along. Both narratives of teachers reading and working together—Blau's and my own—show me what's possible for educators and, by implication, for students in learning environments that celebrate inquiry, invite curiosity, and model encouragement.

I leave this study hopeful that collaboration can serve literature students well as they lean into their own uncertainty as readers. I also recognize that the struggle to be free of educational packaging is real, and yet I am inspired by the mission of education Percy defines: "The highest role of the educator is the maieutic role of Socrates: to help the student come to himself not as a consumer of experience but as a sovereign individual" (p. 63). Percy is right. Students deserve to experience conditions that support genuine discovery. They ought not have to be *re*trained to think for themselves, or as the instructor John Keating puts it in *Dead Poets Society*—"to think for themselves again." The real work of the ELA teacher is to create conditions that enable readers to locate the thing in itself, to bring latent ideas into clear consciousness on their own, absent the symbolic complex. Though what Percy suggests may alter the way some educators view their role in the classroom, this is what all learners deserve to be: true creatures, makers of their own ideas about the world and the literature they experience.

Works Cited

Alexander, R. J. (2017). *Towards dialogic teaching: Rethinking classroom talk* (5th ed.). Dialogos.

Blau, S. (1988). Teacher development and the revolution in teaching. *The English Journal*, 77(4), 30–35. https://doi.org/10.2307/819300

Blau, S. (1993). *Building bridges between literary theory and the teaching of literature*. National Research Center on Literature Teaching and Learning.

Bleich, D. (1975). *Readings and feelings: An introduction to subjective criticism*. National Council of Teachers of English.

Bleich, D. (2019). *Subjective criticism*. Johns Hopkins University Press.

Boadi, K. (2015). A meeting point of ideas. In J. S. Cadwell & J. Quinn (Eds.), *A classroom revolution: Reflections on Harkness learning and teaching* (pp. 105–107). Phillips Exeter Academy.

Brookfield, S., & Preskill, S. (1999). *Discussion as a way of teaching: Tools and techniques for university teachers.* Society for Research into Higher Education; Open University Press.

Brooks, W., & Browne, S. (2012). Towards a culturally situated reader response theory. *Children's Literature in Education, 43*(1), 74–85.

Brownback, K. (2015). In pursuit of truths: An exploration of Harkness in the humanities. In J. S. Cadwell & J. Quinn (Eds.), *A classroom revolution: Reflections on Harkness learning and teaching* (pp. 119–125). Phillips Exeter Academy.

Cadwell, J. S., & Quinn, J. (Eds.). (2015). *A classroom revolution: Reflections on Harkness learning and teaching.* Phillips Exeter Academy.

Ciardi, J., & Williams, M. (1975). *How does a poem mean?* Houghton Mifflin.

Clark, S. & Soutter, M. (2022). *Growth Mindset and Intellectual Risk-Taking: Disentangling Conflated Concepts.* Kappan Online. https://kappanonline.org/growth-mindset-intellectual-risk-taking-soutter-clark/

Cole, D. B., & Cornell, R. H. (Eds.). (1981). *Respecting the pupil: Essays on teaching able students.* Phillips Exeter Academy Press.

Dewey, J. (1938). *Experience and education.* Free Press.

Dewey, J. (1964). *John Dewey on education: Selected writings* (R. Archambault, Ed.). Modern Library.

Dickinson, E. (1924). *The complete poems of Emily Dickinson.* Little, Brown and Company. www.bartleby.com/lit-hub/complete-poems

Emerson, R. W. (2015). *Education: An essay and other selections.* Forgotten Books.

Fecho, B. (2011). *Writing in the dialogical classroom: Students and teachers responding to the texts of their lives.* National Council of Teachers of English.

Fish, S. (1970). Literature in the reader: Affective stylistics. *New Literary History,* 2(1), 123–162. https://doi.org/10.2307/468593

Fish, S. (1976). Interpreting the *Variorum. Critical Inquiry,* 2(3), 465–485.

Fish, S. (1980). *Is there a text in this class? The authority of interpretive communities.* Harvard University Press.

Haruna, A., & Abd Aziz, N. H. (2019). Understanding how romance novels shape identities of female readers: A transactional reader-response approach." *Asian Journal of Multidisciplinary Studies, 7*(2), 33–37.

Holland, N. N. (1975). *The nature of literary response: Five readers reading.* Yale University Press.

Husserl, E. (1982). *Ideas pertaining to a pure phenomenology and to a phenomenological philosophy.* Springer.

Milton, J.. (2005). *Paradise lost: Authoritative text, sources and backgrounds, criticism* (G. Teskey, Ed.). W. W. Norton & Company.

Morrison, T. (2020). *The bluest eye.* Vintage Classics.

Percy, W. (2000). *The message in the bottle: How queer man is, how queer language is, and what one has to do with the other.* Picador.

Phillips Exeter Academy. (2006, November 10). *History of Harkness: The men behind the plan.* www.exeter.edu/news/history-harkness

Probst, R. (1994). Reader-response theory and the English curriculum. *English Journal, 83*(3), 37–44.

Richards, I. A. (2003). *Principles of literary criticism.* Routledge. (Original work published 1924)

Rosenblatt, L. M. (1988). *Writing and reading: The transactional theory (*Report No. 416). Center for the Study of Reading.

Rosenblatt, L. M. (1995). *Literature as exploration.* Modern Language Association of America. (Original work published 1938)

Tuchman, B. (1979, December 29). Papyrus to paperbacks: The world that books made. *The Washington Post.* www.washingtonpost.com/archive/entertainment/books/1979/12/30/papyrus-to-paperbacks-the-world-that-books-made/43c411da-2bf7-4e5f-8869-caaac5422e9e/

Weir, P. (Director). (1989). *Dead poets society* [Film]. Buena Vista Pictures Distribution.

Chapter Twelve

Un-Disciplining the Terrains of Literatures' Possibilities

Ruth Vinz

I receive an email from Darius Landon asking for the title of a Mark Doty poem—"Remember the one where he is walking his dog?"—right before Lizzie Mensa sends a text message reminding me to connect her to teachers who facilitate after-school book clubs. Both messages arrive before Kai-Ni Fu walks into my office and asks if I have time to read essays her ninth graders wrote on Sherman Alexie's *The Absolutely True Diary of a Part-Time Indian*. This moment of intersecting requests from three student teachers serves as a reminder of the complexities of planning for literature study: choosing texts; creating structures for discussions; determining how, when, and what types of skills, strategies, and responses to facilitate. These are contested "fields" of literature education and a reminder that even in the minutiae of daily planning, there are questions and beliefs about both purposes and practices that can't be understood by stitching together a curriculum through text selection, interpretive activities, or modes of discussion. In a moment of hopefulness, I imagine each teacher as a creative actant, charting courses *with* their students, coproducing deeply performative and fulsome participation in whatever approaches of *inventio* serve for deep engagement in and exploration of literary texts. And then I wonder, too, if hope is enough.

Literature Bound: Entering A Regime of Interpretive Practices and Mandates

I finish browsing the student essay: "Anything particular you want to talk about?"

Kai-Ni shakes her head. "It's frustrating to see kids take fiction or poems and write without any emotion. They perform a task set by the teacher. My cooperating teacher says that students must cite textual evidence so they are prepared for exams. That's most important."

I continue leafing through the stack of essays and count five "direct quotes" from the novel in each. Over and again, Arnold Spirit Jr. is identified as the main character. I ask myself: "Why would anyone need to argue that Arnold is important?" Sherman Alexie's wonderfully vibrant character is named as a "primary" character because he is the central character. The circuitous logic is mind numbing. No characterizations of Junior as a determined, talented young artist who yearns for more out of life than his present conditions.

I wonder if any of the student readers feel the tension in the jaw of Junior's resolve? Do they feel surprise or awe when Junior's artistic talents are revealed? Do they hold their breath as they await Junior's next move? They seem so intent on searching for quotes to support the idea that Junior is a "primary" character that they forget to experience *with* him. No laughter. No tears shed. No empathy for Junior in his struggle to straddle his Salish culture and a predominantly white culture that encroaches and compels him toward different values and actions. If students have a *felt-sense* of Junior's life experiences or find resonances to others' lives or their own, it is not evidenced in their essays. This form of disciplining literature relies on interpretive practices that emphasize critical and technical interpretations at the expense of affective or social dimensions that might open infinite possibilities for experiencing and imagining the terrains and contours of the novel.

Kai-Ni waves her hand across the pile. "I give students the opportunity to discuss their reactions and questions, invite multimodal responses, use tableau, and ask them to write short fictional scenes. They know their *real* teacher thinks these are frivolous activities. The goal is always that they state a thesis and support it with quotes. Their worth is inscribed in test results."

Kai-Ni, palms of both hands upward, "What am I to do? The first question students ask before they read is what argument they need to write about. Then they read to support that position."

When Kai-Ni leaves, I email Darius to let him know that I can't find the poem. I send him links to three other Doty poems. "These are too hard for eighth graders," Darius writes back, almost before I've hit send. "Mark Doty's dog poem would be perfect. It's accessible. Remember when we were talking about *horizon of expectations*? These kids expect poems to be hard. They expect the teacher to have the answer to *the* meaning. They give up too soon."

Message back to Darius: "I'll find the dog poem and other choices later tonight. One day soon let's talk about what 'accessible' means to you and to your students."

Accessible for an autonomous reading and interpretation? *Accessible* as a space for imagining and exploring? *Accessible* as fertile ground to throw light on our capacities to elicit responses *for* and *with* others? Traversing the terrain of literature's possibilities raises questions about how interpretive practices, each encouraging particular types of traveling *with* and *into* a literary text, frame and shape student readers' experiences.

When Literary Texts Become Objects

Just as I am texting Lizzie to suggest a time to talk, she leans into my office door. "My kids aren't excited by the reading we do for class. The department chair expects mostly nonfiction texts, and my cooperating teacher feels students need to write short, analytical essays when they read literature. I'm afraid my kids are losing literature in their lives. They write explications and concentrate on those rather than *think with* the text. I thought just maybe I can form an after-school club. Or a virtual one?"

My mind flashes into the corridors of my twenty-three years of high school teaching that began in the mid-1960s—no mandates, no scripted curriculum, no test preparation driving teachers' decision making. I have no victory narratives of teaching from these years, but the relationship with literature was . . . *not this*. No test preparation or "find three quotes to support a thesis." Classroom discussions, performances, interpretive projects, and writing poems, stories, scenes were *performative ways* to engage and demonstrate student readers' experiences with literature and *for them to learn with and through their own and others' interpretations and imaginings*. In this view, literary texts are not *objects* of study but *subjects* with multi-terrains to explore as avenues to cultivate multiforms of response.

Perhaps an example of how a literary text is "framed" *as an object for scrutiny and critique* will help demonstrate this point. Lizzie shares a copy of an assignment given by her cooperating teacher *before* students read Sandra Cisneros's story "Barbie-Q." The assignment:

> This story's theme is about the successful brainwashing of the girls and how their enthusiasm for dolls covers up their anxieties about physical imperfections. What are examples in the story that support this? What does this theme teach you about what these girls considered beautiful?

Cisneros's story becomes an *object* of a predetermined theme, and, before reading, the story has been "told." Students are on a laborious journey to search for quotes that support the teacher's reading. The assignment does not invite readers to enter into the textual world with all its animating qualities of events, perceptions, and sensations or to live with others' experiences. It might be viewed as transgressive if a student reader, responding to the "Barbie-Q" assignment, entered the text in ways that led to a different theme than the one stated by the teacher.

* * *

Lizzie's words bring me back: "I feel like I'm fighting for the survival of literature!" We walk in silence from my office into a gust of wind and rain. Neither of us is able to find the next sentence, so we talk weather and lament that we didn't bring umbrellas before we go our separate ways.

Just what does it mean to "teach" literature? There are hybrids of strategies-based approaches, versions of short literary criticism emphasizing thesis with exemplification, and/or "framed" readings that attend to key elements or devices—plot, character, theme, images, or figurative language. In each, the literary text is *an object* to be examined and dissected. In our desire to "teach" literature, we have "disciplined" literary texts and shaped the relationalities between text and reader. What types of un-disciplining might allow *texts to become subjects of exploration rather than objects of study*? What if the text is *the subject*—an opening for readers to experience and journey through a text? Serendipitous wanderings, the sensations of immediacy or vividness in description, stepping into an unfamiliar landscape, walking at the side of a writer who points to dimensions of the world that have gone unnoticed before—these are the interpretive practices that encourage a nearly impossible-to-put-into-words flicker and glow of a meaningful reading experience.

As I walk home, *remember when* becomes a steady thrum with each step. I think back on high school teaching—*remember when* Pete Billings wrote a diary from Raskolnikov's perspective, explaining his motivations and pleading with Dostoyevsky to change his (Raskolnikov's) motivations and actions? *Remember when* Becky Weeks choreographed a modern dance version of T. S. Eliot's *Cats* (before its Broadway debut)? *Remember when* a group of tenth-grade students wrote a collective poem "13 Ways of Looking at Janie" as a way of describing their understandings of Janie Mae Crawford in Hurston's *Their Eyes Were Watching God,* using Steven's thirteen stanzas to challenge their own varying perspectives of Janie? *Remember when* Jaylyn and Raul, both eighteen-year-old activists for the seasonal migrant workers in our community, took an idea from the twenty-year-old James Baldwin's *Notes of a Native Son* and wrote a collection of short essays based on interviews with migrant students, *inhabiting* the terrains of these literary texts, repositioning the *texts as subjects rather than objects* of exploration? The challenge as teacher was to pique anticipation, activate the fullness of bodies and minds, encourage a full-throated willingness to adventure into the text.

My first priority: *literary text as subject rather than object.* If literature is conceived of as a site for opening up worlds for experiential encounters, then potentially our teaching practices lean away from disciplining the reading, controlling the stance and viewpoints of readers. Too many prompts, assignments, discussions, synopses, and explications keep a reader at some distance from the text itself.

Think of the literature that stays with you, that resides not only in your mind but your body—Morrison's *Song of Solomon*, Jeanette Winterson's *Oranges Are Not the Only Fruit*, Ezra Pound's simple image "In a Station of the Metro," Mary Oliver's question for becoming in "The Summer Day," or the power of longing in Ocean Vuong's *Time Is a Mother*. I imagine, dear reader, you might list others as I continue listing, but the point is: think about one novel, play, or poem that has never left you, the traces of felt-sense, the roar of sensations that unmoor and unsteady your complacencies, the potential of words to lift you from the words, the page, and move you across space, time, and circumstance. This *is* my hope in facilitating engagements with literature—even just one such poem, one text that has *staying power,* vibrantly alive in the body/mind *to matter* in one's life. This poem or story, its words, images, imaginings, does not exist, but its very tissue is a *mattering* produced when reader and text converge. I am cautious about putting such feeling into words, fearful that naming what I have been trying to accomplish for more than fifty-years, what resides in my bones-cell-heart work might dissolve in a flicker of language *if* I try to explain.

With students and texts, we might *gaze* into images such as Cathy Park Hong's *Dance, Dance Revolution*'s "neon hibiscus bloom" and *hear,* trapped inside the petals of her flower, a pastiche of languages and creolization, *feel* the emerging sonic vibrations of languages and images surface, jostle, intersect, and *experience* a crosshatch of sensorium, perspective, and wonderment. My hope is to be part of experiences where literature *matters,* where reading *matters*, where a poem or a story causes us to float out of our shoes, to rise from *terra firma* to imagine, feel, and experience (other)wise. This means freeing literature from interpretive practices that, as Billy Collins (2006) reminds us, "tie the poem to a chair with rope/and torture a confession out of it" (p. 56).

Literature freed into *becoming* part of our world making and world understanding, as *subject* rather than as *object,* requires interpretive practices beyond the typical forms of disciplined scrutiny. William James reminds us ". . . the concept dog doesn't bite" (p. 48), but I worry that young readers who rely on interpretive practices where text is object will never feel the "dog's bite" of affective dimensions essential to mind/body reading experiences. Many interpretive practices distance readers from texts and encourage readings into particular and often narrow terrains, as Kai-Ni, Lizzie, and Darius remind us. Our common reading practices belie attempts to expand modes of being and thinking and often reinforce rather than critically challenge the interpretive practices of sameness.

When Holden Is No More than His Red Hat

And, just as I think this, my granddaughter opens the door with a "What's for dinner?" look on her face. Suddenly the drag of decades of *remember when* and *what if* and *shouldn't we try* stare me in the face. Samantha studies my eyes, turns hers away for only a moment. "Why are we reading *Catcher in the Rye*?" Her eyes spark and then squint, and I have the feeling she thinks this is my fault. I almost say: I don't know if it is the novel or how you read it, but I veer toward a question instead: "What did you do in class?"

"We read." I detect her eye roll. "Then we wrote a paragraph about why it was significant that Holden bought the red hunting hat for one dollar. How would I know? I'm *just getting to know* Holden."

I nod toward the kitchen. "Let's take Holden with us to heat up leftovers."

Samantha sighs. "YOU are so weird."

Little does she know in this moment that we will provide a place setting for Holden at the dinner table. "What are some questions you have for Holden three chapters in? Go ahead, ask him!"

We laugh. Samantha looks at the empty chair, the place setting: "I could make a scarecrow Holden to join us for the next month while he is under my teacher's microscope."

She sighs, grabs a large overstuffed bear from the bedroom and plunks him in the chair. "This will do for now." Her first words to him: "I hope you will become more interesting before this book ends. You are so dark. Will you ask our teacher to just let you *be*?"

As we finish our little interrogation of the opening chapters, I suggest, "Let's write a poem to Holden. It will be the dessert he can take back to his dorm room."

Samantha grins, "Can we ask him to do the dishes before he leaves?"

* * *

It's almost midnight. I scan shelves for Doty's dog poem or others Darius might find *accessible*. Why do we believe it is important for students to have exposure to poetry? What are the purposes? To ease the ardent wish for answers to these questions, I continue searching for poems. I think of Holden—the hand and mind of Salinger puzzling out next moves, creating this character, Holden, who haunts my memories of teaching adolescents of nearly his age and of this Holden who is now in-the-process-of-becoming for Samantha. I think this as I attach five poems for Darius. *Sent*—with that fleeting feeling that the accessibility lies in the reader's motivation and intention when poem is *subject* rather than *object*.

I end this night with a book and notebook in hand. The wind shudders the window glass. One lone siren conjures an image of a night walker making his way across the rain-marbled sidewalk, a show of light from tiny apartment windows high up off the ground. Is that a red hunting cap he wears? I squint. The window creaks against a gust.

Toni Morrison (1987) is my late-night companion, and I write this quote from *Beloved*: "Some things you forget. Other things you never do. But it's not. Places, places are still there. If a house burns down, it's gone, but the place—the picture of it—stays, and not just in my (re)memorying, but out there, in the world" (p. 88). Tomorrow morning, I'll take the subway step off at Gun Hill Road Station in the Bronx and walk to a high school where a first-year teacher, her students, and I are entering the worlds of *Beloved*. I fall asleep in the chair, the wind tapping at the window. *Beloved* slips away, the notepad grows an ink blossom on Morrison's word "rememory."

Morrison bends to whisper these words from *Playing in the Dark*: "I want to draw a map, so to speak, of a critical geography and use that map to open as much space for discovery, intellectual adventure, and close exploration as did the original charting of the New World—without the mandate for conquest" (p. 3). Rain batters the window. For now, skeins of rememorying quiet the world, the radiator's hiss atrophies, and the mind hums a rehearsal for tomorrow—Sethe's hauntings, Sweet Home's legacies and textures and, somehow, Holden is there, too, and Alexie and Kai-Ni Fu and Doty—all entangling into a knot of connectedness, opening spaces to feel, reach beyond, imagine, and discover. In this moment of near-dreaming, Morrison whispers again, "and use that map to open as much space for discovery, intellectual adventure, and close exploration as did the original charting of the New World—without the mandate for conquest." Literature is a map for discovering and imagining *with* and *for* others.

Literature Unbound: Wandering off Sanctioned Pathways

Perhaps Sheridan Blau should make an appearance in this moment. He burrows into my late evening planning along with the conundrums of teaching literature that linger from the day. Over many years, Sheridan advocated for a National Literature Project to support teachers in ways similar to the National Writing Project. Sheridan took the lead in organizing a keynote talk at NCTE's Annual Convention each year to highlight both intent and need for such a project. Sheridan asked me to give the keynote in this moment when I was steeped in the conundrums of how our student teachers and my granddaughter were struggling with schooled interpretive practices.

"Send me a title as soon as you can" was Sheridan's parting request.

"Let me think on it."

* * *

I mull; I pace; I read. I make a list of potential titles and settle on "Un-Disciplining the Terrains of Literatures' Possibilities." I imagine Sheridan in the audience—on the edge of his chair nodding at times, furrowing his brow of skepticism in other moments, or calling out points for clarification or questions when he cannot resist—*always* a willing partner in thinking through the dimensions and dilemmas of pedagogies to build communities of literate practices. Sheridan and I both work to reimagine vibrant approaches, but distinct are the foundational territories upon which those pedagogical principles and approaches rest. And, as it should be, then, Sheridan becomes my provocateur-muse and my imagined audience in all the fits and starts of drafting the opening of this keynote in-the-making.

If literature is to matter, I suspect there are four *matters* that entangle to explain and demonstrate what I mean by un-disciplining literature education: (1) *matters* of readers *becoming*; (2) *matters* of practice; (3) *matters* of participation; and (4) *matters* of purpose. I want to pause here, maybe to catch my breath and yours, to remind us that this keynote/this chapter is exploratory and ruminates on how un-disciplining literature might offer a rich terrain of exploration.

Matters of Readers Becoming: "Go Inside a Stone . . ."

I begin with a consideration of how readers *take shape and substance* literally and figuratively through the ways they are *disciplined*. Readers *becoming*—present progressive, in process, always-in-motion, never fully formed or finished. How do our practices in literature education encourage, or not, readers-in-the-making? Sheridan Blau (2003) writes about his belief in the power of interpretive communities of practice to provide spaces for readers of literature to engage in exploratory talk as they develop what he coins *performative literacy* which he defines as "the kind of knowledge that enables students to perform as autonomous, engaged, readers of difficult texts . . ." (p. 210). Blau goes on to suggest that developing performative literacy will "constitute the foundations for a related set of literary actions or an intellectual discipline that expert adult readers characteristically exhibit or readily recognize as the discipline" (p. 210). Sheridan's thoughtful articulation of seven characteristics of *performative literacy* is preparation for students for something they are not yet, "expert adult readers" (p. 210).

Sheridan's articulation set me thinking about what defines "expert." Is "expert" when student readers become more adept at the interpretive practices taught? Or is expert when they go beyond, surprise us with engagements far different than we teach or use ourselves—recasting a text into new meaning, demonstrating empathy or ethical longing, or responding with silence to avoid diluting the embodied experience? What if "expertise" read something like this: *to read* into contradictory beliefs with openness; *to read* in order to become *relationally involved* with the unfamiliar and/or to see the familiar differently; and *to read* into the terrains of literatures' possibilities as a way to enlarge the logics and sensorium of experiencing?

We might expand interpretive practices by collapsing the ontological separation between reader and text in order to experience a form of thinking/feeling embodiment. I. A. Richards (1929) articulates the fear that "the increased prestige of science encourages readers toward attaching emotional belief only to intellectually certified ideas" (p. 278). Richards suggests giving more significance to "uncertifiable" language negates this tendency. Ninety years later, we might argue that the logic machine of criticism still predominates over aesthetic and affective responses and offers only "a few clumsy descriptive names for emotions, some scores of aesthetic adjectives" (p. 216).

In part I blame our distrust of the subjective—*literary text as object rather than subject*—on the production of readers who are taught to remain at some distance from a text. How might we encourage readers to become performatively entangled, walk into and around in the text, breathe when characters breathe, draw in the same air of doubt or joy in a textual moment, allow the faculties of mind and body to imagine, experience, feel, listen, and see more and differently? *Inside* the text, a reader might reside in spaces of contradiction and experience *relationally* to enlarge both the logics and sensorium of the encounter. How might the terrains of experiencing the text change if we move inside, and how might this change readers' habits in reading literary texts?

Charles Simic's (1971) wonderful poem "Stone" begins with the line "Go inside a stone. . ." and in his beautiful three-stanza, twenty-two-line poem, Simic invites readers to enter the stone, to move around inside and feel the outside world acting upon being encased-in-stone-selves—a cow's weight on stone, a child throwing stone/us through air into water, and, as we sink to the river bottom, we hear fish knocking on our stone walls. Throughout the poem, Simic continuously reminds us that we are *inside* the stone, experiencing and finally coming to see dim light on the walls of our temporary home where strange writings and star charts ignite our imaginings. This is the encounter, the literary experience—held inside the stone, touching cool walls, feeling ourselves hurdled through air and sinking to the river bottom, and the final discovery of just enough light to see the writing inside our new cave walls.

The art of literary experience IS held inside a stone, a text. I often read Simic's poem with students to remind all of us that his invitation, "Go inside a stone," is a way of reading that *matters* experience. Then, a diffractive invitation to students and teachers—"Now, remember Simic's voice and perspective. *Go inside the stone* becomes shorthand for a way of reading, one that positions us as readers in ways that make it difficult to claim distant and generalized insights."

Choosing texts like Simic's poem, ones that overtly draw the reader into the materialities of the experience, focus attention on particular ways of attending differently without prescribing how to feel or compose meaning. Text choice provides an immediate provocation for expanded types of responses from readers and, I conjecture, for creating readers. The challenge is to (re)commit ourselves to conceive readers as "always-in-the-making." *What if* we offer provocations that encourage readers to imagine their own methods, processes, and imperatives—to resist the production of sameness through control over interpretive practices for how readers encounter texts?

Whether explicit or not, Sheridan and I are both conceiving/ *inventing readers* through our practices of *(re)casting readers into multi-relationalities*: with texts, each other, and interpretive practices that bring them to texts in particular ways. Immersion into any complex set of cultural activities will condition their understanding of what readers "do" with literature. Sheridan's and my differing articulations make visible our preferences for particular interpretive practices and what we anticipate as results of the underlying logics of the discursive and material ways of *being in and with* the literary text. Working toward a pedagogy that expands interpretive possibilities requires upending structures enacted most commonly. Un-disciplining readers requires imagination and focus on the complexities and differences that are part of the fabric of twenty-first-century readers' lives where expanded technologies of reading are already un-disciplining the terrains of literature education for fuller participatory engagement.

"We are responsible for boundaries; we are they," writes Donna Haraway (1988, p. 180). Haraway provides a stark reminder that we must make it a priority to imagine and interrogate the borders and boundaries of the long-held beliefs that shape what we value. We are responsible. And, just now, as this first part of my keynote is drafted, I imagine Sheridan lingering on the word "responsible" for a moment before suggesting that he would focus more on *learning* rather than *teaching*. I nod agreement but remind him that as long as we advocate for and adopt approaches such as his commentary project (Blau, 2023, pp. 299–314) or our articulation of a "geometries of attention" (Pindyck & Vinz, 2022), we are implicated in the invention of particular types of readers. The responsibility is to keep challenging and questioning our current thinking and outcomes of practice.

Matters of Practice: Failure Is a Favor to the Future

The poet Rita Dove (2016) reminds us in "The Fish in the Stone" that "to fail is/to do the living/a favor . . ." (p. 74). To un-discipline interpretive practices offers readers an opportunity to explore new terrain but also leads to a dreaded feeling of indeterminacy. All the "*what ifs*" of uncertainty surface: *what if* students are not interested in expanding interpretive practices; *what if* students don't pass the tests requiring them to use sanctioned interpretive practices; *what if* literature is really dying because we have not figured ways to make it relevant? All of these *what ifs* might signal failure to us rather than serve as generative iterations.

As Sheridan might ask from his perch on the imaginary chair in the front row as I deliver these sentences: "So what is your approach then, the practices?" Sheridan's voice, just on the edge of frustration, for I did dwell too long on matters of becoming readers.

"Let me describe three conditions of practice and hear your thoughts," I say to my on-the-edge-of-his-chair Sheridan.

Immersive Experiencing

Susan Sontag (1963) writes, "In place of a hermeneutics we need an erotics of art" (p. 7). This might begin with time and space for readers *becoming with* the text, as suggested in the previous section. Counter to many practices for facilitating reading experiences for students, I see my role as supporting *staying power*, inviting student readers to stay alert to the voluminous possibilities, contexts, and ways in which each word or image or action moves to keep the reading experience alive and vital. Part of facilitating students' readings (and my own) is to create the energy and desire to journey through the terrains of a literary text and offer provisions along the way, complete with rest stops to pause, invitations to gaze back at where we have traveled, and time to imagine what is ahead. These provisions require space and time for readers to find their way, stumble into missed and misreadings, fall into a rabbit hole, or kneel down at an oasis that has an elixir to quench the thirst for certainty.

Consider this example. What type of readers are encouraged through this way of coming to Wallace Stevens's "Thirteen Ways of Looking at a Blackbird"? Try this for yourself, dear reader, to see where it takes you. Read the first stanza aloud two or three times:

> Among twenty snowy mountains,
> The only moving thing
> Was the eye of the blackbird. (p. 99)

Pause and consider. What stays with you? Hovers? Repeats? Read the stanza again. Invite the stanza into your body or take your body into the stanza. Where do you find yourself? What sensations, words, images, or sounds travel into your body and stay with you? Next invitation: Let's hear words or phrases that linger. Say those aloud into the air. Now, write or draw or attend in whatever ways make sense to capture this encounter with the first stanza of "Thirteen Ways."

If we were together now, I would project that stanza on a wall and just let the stanza *be* with us in this space. We would talk in small groups. We would read the rest of the poem aloud, with multiple readers reading each stanza in and out of order. To be *in and with* the poem requires lingering through rereadings, pausing, pacing, visualizing, feeling, and letting loose the language of the poem's first stanza. Working both as a lone traveler and then as a traveling companion with others.

With one group of high school students, we took three days with various iterations of the poem. Students' central impulse was their desire to understand how what seemed abstract in perspective was solidly concrete with blackbird, snow, mountains, icicles, glass coaches, and so forth. Our discussion led to a decision to work in groups or individually to "make material/to matter," through performances, *how* the abstract/concrete of the poem might materialize.

On the day of the great reveal, Stephen Reusser walked through the classroom door, a rustle of multi-sized fragments of paper and interwoven ribbons with words and phrases adorning his body. Pinned (*as if* feathers) to his shirt, pants, belt, socks, and black skull cap (intended to be a blackbird's head) were words from Stevens's poem, and we would come to learn, Stephen's original thirteen-stanza poem on John Lennon. He stitched his own stanzas as overlays to Stevens's stanzas, sketched images from both his and Stevens's poems, again as overlay or underlay to written lines and stanzas. Intricate, temporary tattoos of images and words covered his cheeks, forehead, and hands. His makeshift pair of glasses "filmed' his view with the right-eye notation: *Thirteen Ways*. On the left: *Of Seeing*. When he walked into the room, I was reminded of Bradbury's *Illustrated Man*. He was one of thirty students, each with either group or individual ways to express provisional and playful understanding of their reading experiences through "performance/participation." I wonder what type of readers might result from an experience similar to this. The cynic might ask how Stephen Reusser will fare in traditional literary analysis assessments. I suspect better than most. His mind won't be numb to the challenge, and he will have multiple pathways to find his way into and through a literary text.

Immersive experiencing highlights the plasticity of interpretation as well as emphasizes opening spaces in which to (in)form/perform/participate and enrich our capacities for emotional intelligence and empathy and to hone social perception and affect. Sheridan takes this opportunity as Stephen Reusser's image fades to say to me and my still imagined audience of this keynote that his Commentary Project is another version of what I describe. For Sheridan, commentary/discussion is what we *do* with literature. Mine may be a bit more material/performative, but in either case, I assure Sheridan, we both hope to avoid interpretive practices that block the light given off from a literary text, to work toward an evocation of the fluidity between being and seeming, sensations and experiencing the world anew—*doing* and *discovering* with literature.

Foregoing Knowing for Wondering

If students' textual experiences are controlled and overly structured, does this leave space for the exhilaration of discovery? As Eco (2004) reminds us, "Literary works encourage freedom of interpretation, because they offer us a discourse that has many layers of reading and place before us the ambiguities of language and of real life. But in order to play this game, which allows every generation to read literary works in a different way, we must be moved by a profound respect for what I have called elsewhere the *intention of the text*" (p. 4). Teaching freedom, trust in multiple and ambiguous readings, open spaces for a reader to wander and wonder—all are taught through doing and experiencing, being *in-the-making* with text.

I came to teaching high school seniors in 1966 as a twenty-going on twenty-one-year-old with a B. A. degree with majors in English and history. Two years their senior, we journeyed, *together*, through Shakespeare, Orwell, Bradbury, Hurston, and Wolfe. I was not an expert guide through this terrain of literary texts. Those first years invested an indelible habit in me of exploring literary texts *with* students. My experiences left me questioning the rigidities of more formal/technical practices of literary criticism and instead to work toward nurturing curiosity, staying power, and ways to encounter texts that would support a desire to read. Not always in the moment of teaching, but in looking back, I (re)cognize the principle at work here: The *poietic* power of literature resides in the creative capacities of composing. Both the writing (by author) and the reading (by reader) are composing and imagining processes, allowing both/and *to write and to read* into and through literary texts.

As Eco (1994) suggests, a text hints at possibilities and "asks the reader to fill in a whole series of gaps. Every text, after all (as I have already written), is a lazy machine asking the reader to do some of its work" (p. 3). If such explorations and the journey into a text are worthy goals, then an obvious question: If the text is asking the reader to work, are the types of sanctioned instructional practices that teachers are asking of students augmenting or disrupting their abilities "to work" the terrains of the text?

In the spirit of wondering rather than knowing, I want to share a few questions from sixteen-year-old Luna's response to reading the opening paragraphs of Morrison's *Song of Solomon*:

> It is an odd collection of people who have gathered to witness. Is it coincidence that the woman with the basket of rose petals distracts people from Mr. Smith's fall? This woman is in labor so why is she there and why the basket of rose petals? I can almost smell them. Something about the sweetness when she bursts into song? Sugarman? Guitar? Sweetness and song? I feel like I'm standing with them and we are feeling together Mr. Smith's leap?

After finishing the novel, Luna writes six short poems of one stanza each to offer a glimpse into her experience. I offer two:

#3

She's a wide-open sky
    singing,   astounded
by flight—her mouth wide open
    to the back of breezes—dust
  dances and feathers ruffle
    in the quiet
forgotten corners
    of her Sugarman mind.

#6

Wise folks take to the mountains
not the air when they need distance.
But we fly like fingers waggin' in the sky
and up   above we dance and shout
as currents grab at us like fate. Each
tender touch whirls our feathers, and
we are left moist and grinning.

Reading with wonder is a way of reaching into the open-endedness of a literary text. In this moment, my imagined Sheridan is engrossed with writing notes and questions. I know we will continue our conversation of our different ways of encouraging discoveries and the power of wondering rather than knowing. As Sheridan (2014) writes, experiences "devised viscerally or intuitively or discursively" (p. 42) lean toward action/the doing of literature. I touch Luna's "back of breezes," "fingers wagging," and the "tender touch" as the doing.

The Ending as a Beginning

The last word of the last stanza of a poem, the last sentence of the novel, the closing words from a character in a play—all are endings. Closure, perhaps. Pleasure in the finality? Thousands of words and sentences read. And where does this leave the reader? The ending is only a beginning, the near *simultaneity* of temporal and spatial collapse——all swirl in a vortex of space and time. I am reminded of Umberto Eco's description in *The Role of the Reader* (1979) of "the sensitive reader, feeling something unusual in the disposition, tries to make abductions (that is, to single out a hidden rule or regularity) and to test them. . . . That is why in reading literary texts one is obliged to look backward many times . . . and read back from the end" (p. 26). *Conjecture in reading* is something akin to Eco's description of reading by "forecasts and inferential walks" (p. 31). Reading backward while reading forward captures this sense of the limitations of conceiving of reading as a linear progression.

A pedagogical experiment might go something like this. When reading the last paragraph of a novel, the last stanza of a poem, or the last scene of a play, invite readers to drift backward across the terrains of experience and meaning, pausing, holding, taking in what seems in the moment to have "ended" but what is really only the *beginning*. The text defies its linear presentation of words, sentences, paragraphs, pages, stanzas, or other linear structural components. The end *might be* the beginning. The text bends backward on the experience of reading, then leans forward, sideways, and skips across events, words, actions of characters, feelings, then holds momentarily on an image or into the haze of meaning. Wisps of sensation, of meaning, of image, of idea are all left as part of the *lasting* dimensions, (in)forming the mind/body of the reader.

At this moment when delivering the keynote, I would stop and ask the audience to remember a moment when reading the last line of a novel was only the beginning. I would pause and give time to conjure that image. Sheridan might go along with this moment, too, but might choose his beloved Milton's *Paradise Lost*, where the ending has played out in his dreams, imaginings, and logics many times: "They hand in hand with wandring steps and slow,/ Through Eden took thir solitarie way" (p. 305, 1674 version).

The grandeur of literature enriches our capacities to feel that we can no longer live without literature. Just how do we facilitate such experiences? In *The Literature Workshop* (2003), Sheridan points to a moment of recognition early in his teaching career as a TA and speaks to the intensity of preparing himself "to teach" a story to his students. He describes how he put so much thought, reading, and study into the text before the class session and then during class realized that the students had "an experience of witnessing and possibly recording the teacher's learning, and not an experience of learning for oneself" (p. 3). Sheridan's realization is yet another example of how a too thorough preparation of a text might potentially work against students' learning and experiencing the text for themselves. Sheridan suggests that we may not trust ourselves or our students to "access the resources that are yours. I am speaking, of course, first, of the most powerful resources at your disposal: your own concentrated attention and capacity to think. Nor should we forget the resource we are to each other . . ." (p. 12). Sheridan's statement is worthy of a long pause.

As I write into the end of this keynote-turned-chapter, I pose an invitation for each of us to remind ourselves of how we might articulate our purposes in teaching literature.

Matters of Purpose: Teachers' Dreaming

Maybe only in dreams or when we have a weekend for beach reading does literature feel undisciplined and freed from the regime of schooled practices. The problem with dreams is they are hard to recount when we wake from the haze. Working through possibilities for this keynote, I determine it might be best to end in dreams. Sharing my dream is an invitation to create a dream of your own, one that doesn't crumble when exposed to the light or the classroom—a dream that begins or continues as articulation of your purposes for teaching literature. My imagined Sheridan looks at me with doubt, but when I suggest to the audience, "just close your eyes and travel with me," his shoulders loosen as his eyes close.

* * *

I am sitting on the floor in my classroom, not exactly my classroom, but more like a family room filled with adolescents and books and they are reading and suddenly we are outside. I am with Jamal Landry and Emily David, from fifth period, talking about—I can't remember—but Holden Caulfield walks toward us, shouting that readers should be allowed to pour *themselves* into books.

Jimmie Harris is reading aloud from *The Handmaid's Tale,* and Paul Peterson (from a class almost thirty-five years ago) is reciting the opening lines of *Twelfth Night.* Something like: "If music be the food of love, play on." He forgets the next lines and asks me, and I can't remember what's next, but I think how we've lost the art of memorization, and I haven't asked students to memorize lines they love in a long time, but I do believe the body is an instrument of reading. *Reading is shelving books into the library of the mind and body.* I pull one from the mind's shelf, open it, and Raskolnikov appears and then like flat Stanley, he wriggles out of the pages before I can close the cover of *Brothers Karamazov.* I realize he was in the wrong book, and then I think: Why would I correct myself in a dream? And Raskolnikov, who really belongs in *Crime and Punishment,* has time to say before he disappears: "I'm going back into the shadows of meaning."

Near an old stone wall, Robert Frost points at that proverbial fork in the road where kids sprawl across both roads, reading and arguing, and one group places the finishing touches on masks created to portray the five faces of *Hamlet* from the play's soliloquies. Johnny Wilkerson's little brother comes in with flippers and a snorkel mask. He is reading *Old Man and the Sea,* but Dirk Riley is there with that look on his face . . . even under the mask I can see his grin. He slams the book shut. "Life is too short." And he laughs, Dirk laughs, and I laugh with them and think about Susan Sontag's (1963) opinion that "interpretation is the revenge of the intellect upon art" (p. 7). There are slips of paper littering the ground as if a box of magnet poetry had been upended, and I make out words like inference, main idea, prediction, explication. Suddenly, I feel very tired.

Einstein taps me on the shoulder: "Mystery is the most beautiful thing in the Universe." I think how all this pulling apart and ravaging a text moves it a wider distance between reader and text. The throb in my right temple keeps time to my concern that I'm not spending enough time "undoing" habits. Polonius enters with fanfare and wisps of cloud. I share my desire toward undoing. He nods agreement, which makes my head hurt less, but then I remember he eagerly followed Hamlet, who said the clouds were "very like a whale," although Polonius had agreed earlier they were very like a camel and before that a weasel (I think). I realize Polonius falls into any interpretation and is a *slipping trope* himself.

I see a heavy stack of literature anthologies gathering dust in the corner of our classroom, those from publishing houses that gain wealth off schools *and* shape experiences with literature. This image brings Mr. Houghton into view with the reminder that he comes from a lineage of great lovers of books and his great-great grandfather purchased a unique manuscript of the Persian "epic of kings." Arthur Houghton Jr. gazes at his purchase of 258 folio-sized paintings, 759 illuminated pages of text, and an illuminated rosette, held intact by a 450-year-old binding.

I recall he dismembered the manuscript and sold it in parts. So, what credibility does Houghton Publishing House have as a protector of the heritage of reading literature? Images of engraved tablets, scrolls, parchment, and papyrus come into my mind. I think of the materiality of reading and how a book smells and feels in the hand, and I wonder if my students ever feel that pleasure or if their interrogation lamps burn too brightly on the text and they miss the feelings and experiences of what they read. I long to see their commonplace books, like that in the *English Patient*, filled with texts on texts that cover Herodotus's *The Histories*—and the stack of texts starts growing higher. Students add one text on top of the other. It's like they're *binge reading!*

Words, images, and characters begin to ooze out of books, and some Victorian lady starts knocking down the stacks and pulling books from hands. She shouts that novels lead to constipation, flabby stomachs, eye disorders, and idleness if not madness. Edgar Allan Poe sulks off into the corner with Bobbie James and Jason Edelson, who usually likes only computer games but Poe's darkness overtakes their resistances. And Chinua Achebe is arguing with Emily Dickinson, reminding her that "There is no frigate like a book/To take us lands away." If we don't teach students to read with a critical eye, they won't see the racism in Conrad or question the canon or representations of difference, and they will grow into complacent readers who are critically unaware of their ideologies, identities, or the power to shape new ones. By the time I've dreamed these thoughts, Emily shakes her head and sighs that she is feeling a little like she might hope death would stop for her rather than listening to me recount again how we have disciplined literature. With Emily's departure, Joy Harjo evokes her image that we are like fish in a bowl and do not know we are in waters of social, cultural, and political reading practices unless we make those visible. The tensions between all the competing beliefs hold me down. How do I help students examine cultures and difference from multiple and unstable perspectives and yet avoid another type of tyranny? How do we avoid interpretive practices that create binaries? How do students learn to examine themselves as a text, reflecting on the cultural influences that compose them?

Just now, Toni Morrison (1992) pats me on the shoulder with a reminder that part of the critical project of teaching is "to avert the critical gaze from the racial object to the racial subject, from the described and imagined to the describers and imaginers; from the serving to the served" (p. 93). And then Atticus Finch takes my head in his hands and says: "You never really understand a person until you consider things from his points of view . . . until you climb into his skin and walk around in it" (Lee, p. 32).

"That's what I'd hope for students," I whisper as I catch my breath.

"Your dream is getting really long," Atticus remarks.

Then Mr. Houghton leans against Atticus, looking smug, and Herodotus slips up beside him along with Ray Bradbury. Ray is the one to speak, and he says don't forget how dangerous reading is. Don't forget *Fahrenheit 451*. Kids need to know that books are dangerous, and, if they do, they may not take reading for granted. I can smell the fear and taste it now and the smell of ashes. A date comes into my mind: August 25, 1992. Serbian nationalist soldiers trained artillery on Sarajevo's National and University Library. I see the flames and start to count the 1.5 million volumes that smoldered for three days. Just as the sadness washes through my body, I see the human chain that fought to save books, and 100,000 were saved, and I am crawling forward through the ashes to find just one book. I look up to see students staring at me, and I ask them if they have any books they would save.

Before they can answer, the images of Baghdad flash across the screen of dream: April 14, 2003. The National Library in Baghdad loses historical documents from the Ottoman era and books that survived the Mongol conquest of 1258 . . . cuneiform tablets from Sumerian, Akkadian, Assyrian, and Babylonian eras . . . and it goes on. I see the tablets exploding into fine dust and my students are still sleeping . . . they haven't been convinced. I think I need to remember to teach them about all this. Mandela talked about Shakespeare circulating secretly among prisoners at Robben Island in South Africa and Terry Waite in Beirut for 1,763 days kept his sanity by composing a memoir in his mind and by reading books his captors doled out. Imagine how all they have read as lived experience is with them in their libraries of the mind, to come back to encounter and experience again from inside their prison walls.

"What then?" I'm saying. "What now?" and I know I've co-opted these lines again, "But louder sang that ghost What Then? What Now?" I sigh and feel confounded. What confounds me is the realization that the language upon which I am completely dependent for expressing this dream is incapable of conveying something I experienced vividly in the dream but cannot put into words. Isn't that, too, what we want from the experience of literature?

We all face the loss of language, language to capture, to (re)member, to re-experience, to read or think (other)wise. To name what we do or dream. But ideas shared in words sometimes distort and alter the vision, especially in dreams. We change the dream to make sense in the language available to us.

I think this statement is important enough that I want to write it again: We change the dream so it makes sense in the language available to us. And, as is often true with dreams, our efforts to make sense of what seems to be nonsense—so often the dreams that drive powerful and visionary experiences—are lost in the use of the only words we can say to describe the moment: "I had this dream." Sadly, the visionary experience is carried away in wisps as the sleeping brain awakens to different legacies from the language of dream and vision.

Desire to read, to experience, to travel through words, pages, stanzas, scenes, and books. Desire to experience anew and otherwise and to read unsatiated. Eco comes to mind again. He owned a library that housed near 30,000 books. The beauty of the library is a concrete manifestation of the desire to read, to explore and encounter all the riches of the unknown, to journey into a story or poem or essay and to have books surrounding us. Books waiting with words, ideas, myths, histories, stories, and speculations.

Eco himself calculated that if he were to read a book a day every day from age eight to eighty, it would total 25,200 books. Books, readers, authors—caught in a web of desire. Desire is what I hope for students by making certain not to fill all the spaces in the terrains of reading but leaving empty space for imagining and experiencing.

I imagine Eco walking around in his library, touching book spines gently with an index finger, taking out one then another, the gold lettering burned on the spine brings back memories of stories read or the desire to read one not opened or finished. Eco opens, reads a first paragraph, promising to come back later. He takes another book from the shelf, moves to his chair, the small lamp beside him burning. He settles into the terrain of the story and leaves us and all the other books in the room in this moment.

The physicality of reading—bodies with books of paper, ink, and the flesh and blood of words and cobwebs of books in the library of the mind. The community of readers—readers in the presence of other readers and writers. As our libraries become more and more virtual, I am already missing the materiality of paper, glue, and ink that is the scent of desire, but I know those have possibilities to encourage new practices, new ways of reading, new collaborations with others. If literature is to beguile, entertain, amuse, horrify, anger, and help us experience others' lives, we must keep searching, experimenting, and imagining.

Hannah Arendt (1961) wrote: "And, education, too, is where we decide whether we love our children enough not to expel them from our world and leave them to their own devices, nor to strike from their hands their chance of undertaking something new, something unforeseen by us, but to prepare them in advance for the task of renewing a common world" (p. 193). To help students undertake something they desire, to assist them in their task of reinventing the worlds for the future, is a vivid description of the essence of this dream of un-disciplining literature that I tell in my way, that Sheridan has committed a life to living and articulating, and that Kai-Ni, Lizzie, and Darius will grapple with in their teaching in ways we have yet to imagine.

Works Cited

Arendt, H. (1961). *Between past and future*. Viking Press.

Blau, S. (2003). *The literature workshop: Teaching texts and their readers*. Heinemann.

Blau, S. (2014). Literary competence and the experience of literature. *Style*, *48*(1), 42–47.

Blau, S. (2023). On not teaching college-level reading in order that students might learn it: Honoring our pedagogical legacy in the composition classroom. In P. Sullivan, H. Tinburg, & S. Blau (Eds.), *Deep reading, deep learning* (Vol. 2, pp. 299–314). Peter Lang.

Collins, B. (2006). *The apple that astonished Paris*. University of Arkansas Press.

Dove, R. (2016). *Collected poems: 1974–2004*. W. W Norton & Company.

Eco, U. (1979). *The role of the reader: Explorations in the semiotics of texts*. Indiana University Press.

Eco, U. (1994). *Six walks in the fictional woods*. Harvard University Press.

Eco, U. (2004). *On literature*. (M. McLaughlin, Trans.). Harcourt.

James, W. (1979). *Some problems of philosophy*. Harvard University Press.

Lee, Harper. (2014). *To kill a mockingbird*. Harper.

Milton, J. (1674/2005). *Paradise lost: Authoritative text, sources and backgrounds, criticism* (G. Teskey, Ed.). W. W. Norton & Company.

Morrison, T. (1992). *Playing in the dark: Whiteness and the literary imagination*. Harvard University Press.

Morrison, T. (2004). *Beloved*. Vintage.

Pindyck, M., & Vinz, R., with D. Liu & A. Wittchow. (2022). *A poetry pedagogy for teachers: Reorienting classroom literacy practices*. Bloomsbury Academic.

Richards, I. A. (1929). *Practical criticism: A study of literary judgment*. Kegan Paul, Trench, Trubner & Co.

Simic, C. (1971). *Dismantling the silence*. George Braziller.

Sontag, S. (1966). *Against interpretation and other essays*. Farrar, Straus & Giroux.

Stevens, W. (2015). *The Collected Poems of Wallace Stevens: The Corrected Ver*sion. Vintage Books.

IV

"I had three or four heroes. . . . They were all self-taught—they were all autodidacts."

—Blau interview, 2021

Chapter Thirteen

Memoir and Valediction

Sheridan Blau

I have been overwhelmed, I must confess, by the feeling that nothing I might write for this volume could serve as an adequate response to the honor bestowed on me by the distinguished colleagues and gifted former students who have edited this volume and written essays for it to celebrate my own meager contributions to our field and my very long career of teaching three generations of students who were exemplary learners and a constant source of inspiration and learning for me. I have taught as long as I have because I couldn't think of a more personally gratifying or intellectually exciting way to spend my limited time on Earth.

What I will now present as my utterly inadequate response to the embarrassingly generous contributions offered by the writers and editors of this volume are some memories and reflections largely on my early years of teaching—years that allowed me to develop into the patriarchal, if not venerable, teacher I have become for the generation of students who have known me over the past twenty years or so, which is to say from about the time when I reached the usual retirement age but felt compelled to keep going and to continue learning mostly with and from graduate students and veteran classroom teachers. The story of my development until that point will, I hope, serve three purposes. First, it will allow me to portray a history of the field of English education and of a university teaching culture largely unknown to the generations behind my own and for which the number of potential memoirists is rapidly diminishing. Second, it will enable me to offer a possibly instructive account of how the experiences of those years transformed me into the teacher and writer about teaching that I have become. And finally, the history I recount will represent the grounding in lived experience that gave rise to the postulates or maxims printed below about English education and learning more generally—maxims I am inclined to share with my students and younger colleagues as the necessarily tentative product of my long career as an English teacher and teacher educator in English. I think of these now as part of my legacy and valediction to my student heirs:

1. Teaching is the enemy of learning (usually).
2. Learning derives only from what can be called "experience," though the experience can be an interior one as well as one that entails a transaction with the world.
3. Learning is a natural and essential trait of human beings, as indicative of mental health as breathing is of physical health.
4. While traditional schools with their emphasis on teaching and on the measurement of student knowledge are hostile to learning, communities of persons committed to a common project are almost always productive sites for learning individually and collectively.
5. Knowledge is a problematic aim and achievement: it is often valuable, always provisional, and frequently an illusion; authentic knowledge is impossible to transmit to someone else, and for the entire span of human history, knowledge has served as a dangerous temptation and object of idolatry, leading to an incapacity to learn, a devotion to illusion, and an abiding sense of fraudulence and self-hatred.

My First Experience of Teaching as the Enemy of Learning

My first postulate may seem problematic at the outset, at least for its grammatical ambiguity, which renders it a sentence that is both true and false. Most experienced and thoughtful teachers know that the opposite is true in the sense that teaching is a powerful occasion for learning for the teacher but, unfortunately, not for the learner, who is the presumed beneficiary of the act of teaching. I had my first glimpse of this principle early in my teaching career when I was a graduate student in English and American literature at Brandeis University (having come to Brandeis after two years of teaching English in my hometown high school where, I am ashamed to say, I learned nothing of value about teaching except that I liked doing it). In my second year of grad school, in the fall of 1963, I was given a TAship to teach the first-year English course, which was taught exclusively by English graduate students. I remember one bright morning early in the semester when I came to class after having spent some hours the evening before carefully reading and preparing stimulating discussion questions on some typical anthologized belletristic essay I had assigned for my students. In class, expecting a lively discussion, I was disappointed to discover that although my students assured me that they had read the essay, they had almost nothing to say about it, though they were alertly poised to take notes on what I would say, and I, of course, had plenty to say. I was filled with ideas and questions. So, why were my students so empty? I felt confident that there was nothing in my experience or education that gave me greater access than my students would have to the ideas in the assigned essay. Why then was I able to find the essay rich in ideas and questions worth discussing, while my well-read and highly articulate students in this extremely selective university had nothing to say about the same essay?

I don't remember how long it took me to figure out an answer to this pedagogical problem, but when it finally came to me, it seemed obvious. I learned much from the essay and had potentially illuminating questions about it, because I had to teach it. The students learned almost nothing from the essay, and had no questions about it, because they merely had to read it and wait for me to teach it to them, largely by asking them questions about it. Hence, the one who has the responsibility to teach is the one who learns what he is presumably teaching. From that experience, I came to the tentative conclusion that if I wanted my students to learn, I had to find ways for them to function as teachers. But how that could happen I hadn't yet worked out. Nor had I come to understand the larger significance of my discovery about the pedagogical dangers of teaching. Still, that initial recognition in 1963 of the problematic impact of teaching awakened me to the need for new thinking about my responsibility as an instructor and thereby prepared me for the experience of additional pedagogical realizations that came to me gradually over the course of my early years of teaching as a young professor of English.

Not Quite Learning to Teach: Becoming a Teacher at the University of Michigan

The years I spent as a newly-hatched English professor at the University of Michigan (my first year at the rank of lecturer, while I completed my dissertation; then three more years as assistant professor), immediately after graduate school, seem to me now, as I reflect on my teaching journey, perhaps not the most transformational years of my teaching career but utterly essential years for the degree to which I underwent teaching and learning experiences that occasioned and refined the questions about teaching and learning that I would subsequently articulate and more systematically explore for the remainder of my teaching life. Those years also marked my initiation and beginning self-identification as a faculty member in the field of English education and not merely as a young scholar with a PhD in English and American literature.

My Michigan years began with teaching experiences for me that were accidentally good learning experiences for my students and ended with some dubious learning experiences for my students that, for me, were better learning experiences about my teaching. Those years also launched me on the two initially parallel and eventually intersecting tracks I have taken in my scholarly life as a specialist in English education and the teaching of Milton. They also taught me some needed lessons about the politics of departmental life in a university community. I'm going to give more attention in this essay to my Michigan years and my first few years in California than to subsequent years, mainly because they were so formative for me but also because as I have been summoning memories of those years, I realize how much they reveal about the early years of the field of English education and also present a picture of university English department life (especially at Michigan) that was very distinctive yet representative of a time and academic culture that few colleagues are still available to report on.

A Lesson in Self-Righteousness. I have several teaching and learning stories to recount about my Michigan years that, in retrospect, mark those years and that place as an important way station in my pedagogical development. And my first story is about my first years at Michigan when I found myself teaching an introductory course in prose fiction that served as one of the optionally required courses for first-year and sophomore students who had already declared or were planning to declare English as their major. The course was supervised by a faculty committee that regulated the four introductory English courses from which English majors were required to complete two or three (the others were drama, American lit, and poetry). To my dismay, the faculty committee governing these courses specified approved reading lists for each of the courses, not exactly writing the course syllabus but naming texts and authors that could be chosen by the faculty teaching each course and strictly forbidding the teaching of any texts except those listed. In my youthfully arrogant idealism, I regarded that limitation as an unprofessional insult to faculty and a serious compromise of our academic freedom, and I complained bitterly to any colleague who would listen. Some sympathized with me. More often, I was advised to get myself appointed to the committee (after a few years of experience as a faculty member) and then get the books I wanted to teach on the approved list. That, I insisted, was beside the ethical and professional point I was righteously trying to make.

My passion for textual liberation did nothing, of course, to advance the cause of academic freedom, but it did result in an admonition from my department chair, the venerable Professor Warner Rice, who at the end of my first year of teaching sent me a letter evaluating my first year's performance as a member of the faculty. He began his letter approving of my teaching (he had actually observed one of my classes himself) but admonishing me to be mindful of my lowly status within a rigid departmental structure and to remember that there is a time for a new and untenured faculty member "to speak up and a time for his silence," and that, during my probationary period, when decorum demanded my silence, I had shown "an unseemly business about departmental affairs."

I believe I am remembering his exact words (including the echoes of Ecclesiastes), which I took as the serious reprimand they were meant to be, though I didn't know if I should also assume that he was warning me to help me succeed as a young faculty member or to alert me that I was likely to be fired at the end of the next year. It turned out that he was actually trying to help me (in spite of how I must have tried his patience) as became clear when I approached him that summer to ask his advice about buying a very inexpensive house that was for sale not far from campus. The down payment was $750.00, of which I was going to borrow $500 from the mother of a friend, to be repaid from my anticipated salary for a summer school class I had requested and been assigned. Colleagues a few years ahead of me had told me that in the English department, no untenured faculty member should make an offer on a house without first talking to Mr. Rice, as one might talk to one's father about the prudence of buying a home in Ann Arbor at that moment, given the location, and price, and condition of the house, and one's position in the department. Mr. Rice's response would then indicate with a high degree of certainty whether he saw you as likely to be reappointed after the following year or likely to get fired. Fortunately, Mr. Rice thought that the house and the price were reasonable, and he offered to help me put a much-needed new roof on the garage, an offer I tactfully declined.

Teaching as Learning. If my teaching deserved his commendation, however (he had visited my class in prose fiction), it was not because I managed to teach the texts I wanted to teach, but because I found myself forced to teach many texts and authors I had never studied and never even read and could therefore learn with my students in a classroom community that functioned as a true community of learners, where I served less as a traditional teacher than as a model learner. But I didn't recognize any pedagogical principle in that experience or know how to create such a learning community when I was later able to teach in an area of my own specialized expertise, most notably in my first opportunity (and last at Michigan) to teach a course in Milton. What I did notice in the pattern of my classroom practice, however, was a sequence that I remarked upon one sunny noontime in the fall of 1967 as I walked back from some literature class I had been teaching, on my way to my office in the company of a colleague with whom I was discussing the problem of teaching literature. I remember the moment vividly for an observation that became especially important to me years later when it occurred to me for the first time that one might engage in research and writing about the teaching and learning of literature, as well as about critical and interpretive issues. Thinking about the class I had just taught, I observed to my colleague that it seemed to me that the reading and teaching of literature could be described as an inquiry consisting of three questions: What does it say? What does it mean? and What does it matter? It would be another seventeen years before I began to make those questions explicit in workshops that I was by then conducting for preservice and inservice teachers in California and in my own earliest attempts to write about the teaching of literature.

First Opportunity to Teach Milton. In my second year at Michigan (1967–68), our feared and revered department chair, Professor Rice, who had taught the undergraduate Milton class for the previous forty or more years, was scheduled to retire in the summer (after serving for over 20 years as chair). But before he retired (to be replaced as chair in the fall by an outside appointee), Professor Rice laid out the full teaching schedule for the academic year 1968–69 and made me, to my amazement and that of most of my colleagues, the heir to his Milton course. He had been impressed by my publication of an article on "Milton's Salvational Aesthetic" and of my obvious strong interest in Milton, and sometime in the spring before his retirement, in a conversation on some other matter, he had casually asked me if I would ever want to teach the Milton course. I assumed he meant in the distant future, and I said of course I would. So, I was stunned and grateful for the unimaginably early opportunity for me to stand in for him in the Milton class, which, as it happens, I taught only once at Michigan but have continued to teach fairly regularly and with much greater satisfaction for my students and unflagging interest for me over the ensuing fifty-five years. I estimate that by the time I retire, I will have taught Milton and *Paradise Lost* forty-five times. For forty-four of those times, I was a learner with my students and learned much, as they did, too. My first-time teaching Milton, however, I was the teacher of my students and learned little, and they did too, as the story below will reveal.

Apparently, by the end of my second year at Michigan, I had corrected my unruliness sufficiently to win Mr. Rice's approval as his heir to the undergraduate Milton course, which I was assigned to teach in the second semester of my third year as a faculty member. The assignment itself improved my status among the older faculty, one of the oldest of whom advised me of my responsibility to carry on Warner Rice's tradition of honoring Milton and my new teaching responsibility by memorizing all twelve books of *Paradise Lost*, as Mr. Rice had done. I was told that he managed to accomplish that feat fairly early in his teaching of Milton by carrying around with him small cards, each with about 20 lines of the epic typed on them, and memorizing a new card every day. At that rate, I would have been able to memorize the poem in 525 days. I should have done it.

Nevertheless, I was finally able to teach what I had been wanting to teach and with no external constraints to compromise my own decisions about what and how to teach this advanced undergraduate course, where the students were all junior or senior English majors, along with a couple of graduate students. I remember none of the students except one international student who eventually became a professor and sent me an article on Milton she had published in a Japanese journal on English literature. What I do remember is that I felt liberated to call upon my own expertise in Milton and seventeenth-century religious poetry by selecting the most historically important minor poems and most significant prose selections to be studied before we turned to Milton's great epic, *Paradise Lost*. I also remember that I spent enormous amounts of time preparing for each class, mainly in rereading Milton's texts and consulting major critical works about each poem or prose tract I assigned so that I could deliver well-informed lectures and lead or direct discussions designed to yield the critical and interpretive conclusions I had already determined or borrowed from authorities about the texts in question. My students, at least the most conscientious of them, learned something about what I thought or knew about Milton's poems, but they surely didn't learn what Milton's poems might have taught them. My teaching was, no doubt, the enemy of their learning. Why didn't I know better? Hadn't I seen that danger as an undergraduate in classes where I found lectures boring and simply stopped going to class? I may have, but I didn't understand the problem as a teaching problem until I experienced it as a teacher. And then I didn't know what to do about it. At least not until I got to California.

Before I tell of my more enlightened approach to teaching Milton in California, let me tarry a while more in Michigan for two other stories that now seem to me formative in a way that I didn't begin to recognize until I found myself composing the pages I am now writing about my pilgrimage as a teacher of literature and teacher of teachers. The first of these stories is the story of my first opportunity to teach a methods course in English education. The idea of my teaching the course was raised for me by our new department chair (the distinguished Renaissance scholar Russell Frazer) in the spring of 1969, when he told me that for the coming academic year, I had the choice of once again teaching Milton or else teaching the English methods course for English majors preparing to become secondary English teachers. I assume that Mr. Rice had prepared documents for his successor's guidance, labeling each faculty member by areas of expertise.

My Induction into English Education

The idea of teaching the methods course was attractive to me (quite aside from my first unsatisfactory experience teaching Milton, which I was inclined to do again sometime but perhaps better), because from the time of my arrival at Michigan, I found myself drawn to and welcomed into the small coterie of English department professors who identified themselves as English language and literature scholars with special interests or special expertise in the preparation of English teachers. This included people like Dan Fader, who was a Shakespearean, who by chance became involved in advising teachers at a Detroit area reform school and ended up writing a book called *Hooked on Books* that became one of the most widely read and influential books of the decade of the '60s on the problem of getting students to read. Our small group also included Steve Dunning, who held a joint appointment in English and in the School of Education and who was widely respected as an expert in contemporary poetry and an extensively published author and professional leader in the fledgling field of English education, eventually to serve as the chair of the Conference of English Education and subsequently as president of NCTE. It also included the then young and eventually distinguished linguists Jay Robinson and Dick Bailey. Our senior member in age and experience was Alan Howes, who had been deeply involved in the NDEA Institutes and spent much of his career developing programs to enrich the preparation and professional development of English teachers.

It was no accident that these faculty members took me under their wing from the time I arrived at Michigan. Warner Rice told them that I would be a good addition to their group, since I had two years of experience teaching English in an urban high school in New Jersey when I was fresh out of college before I went to graduate school in English. Mr. Rice told me at the time he interviewed me for the Michigan job (prophetically, at the 1965 NCTE Convention in Boston in November, while almost all my other eight interviews were at MLA in January) that a substantial percentage of the undergraduate English majors at Michigan were planning to become secondary teachers of English while virtually none of the faculty who taught them in English courses had any experience in teaching secondary English, and he asked me if I might be interested in becoming part of the small group of professors who were actively involved in thinking about preparing interested English majors for the work of teaching English in secondary schools. Michigan was my first choice among all the many attractive openings for new assistant professors in English in 1966, and I was thrilled to feel that I was needed there, though I had never had a real course in the teaching of English myself.

So, from the time I arrived at Michigan, I found myself being groomed as a member of the teacher preparation group, initially by being assigned (unhappily on my part) to teach the course in grammar for English teachers with Jay Robinson and Dick Bailey to whom I was, at first, as much an apprentice as a colleague and eventually became a much appreciative colleague with a lifelong interest in linguistics. Now, in my third year at Michigan, the year I was allowed to teach the Milton course, I was offered the opportunity of teaching the English methods course in the following year but at the cost of giving up the Milton course for that year. Fortunately, I accepted the offer.

However, not ever having taken such a course, I could hardly imagine what it might entail to teach it, and I discovered to my dismay that nobody I asked had any advice to offer me about it. Maybe I didn't inquire widely enough. I certainly didn't know where to look in the professional literature, as I would have a few years later, though I don't understand now why Steve Dunning, who had become my dear friend and a sometime mentor to me (and had surely taught the course himself), didn't offer to help me. Perhaps he did, and I didn't want to follow his example.

On the State of the Field of English Education. Part of my problem was that the field of English education as a distinct academic field was itself in its infancy. The journal *English Education* didn't begin publication until that very year, 1969, which was five years after the founding of the Conference on English Education (of which I knew nothing and my colleagues never mentioned), which means that the very idea of English education as an area of expertise for university faculty was itself quite new. It was generally the case that methods courses in English taught in colleges and universities in the decade of the 1960s and before, if they were taught at all (it was common at the time for courses in teaching methods in departments of education to cover all disciplines), were taught by some veteran high school English teacher hired for the job as a temporary instructor.

That was surely the case in most colleges in California, including the University of California at Santa Barbara, up until my arrival on that campus in 1970 to serve as an assistant professor of English to teach literature courses (including Milton) and also direct the Program in English Education. In fact, it was also the case at UC Berkeley, where Jim Gray (who would become the founder of the Bay Area Writing Project in 1974) had been hired away from his position as a much-revered classroom English teacher at San Leandro High school in 1961 to take a non-faculty position as "supervisor of student teachers" on a year-by-year contract to run the teacher education program in English and to teach the English methods course and the course in the teaching of writing in the UC Berkeley Graduate School of Education, as well as to supervise the English student teachers in their secondary school assignments. He was still holding that position at that rank when I arrived in Santa Barbara in the late summer of 1970 as an assistant professor, soon to be promoted to associate professor with tenure.

Meeting Jim Gray. I didn't meet Jim in person until the fall term of 1974, shortly after he had conducted the first summer institute of the Bay Area Writing Project. We were at a statewide meeting of specialists in English education sponsored by the California Department of Education, and Jim was invited to report on the first summer of his innovative professional development project known as the Bay Area Writing Project. We had each heard of the other from former mutual students and knew that we were philosophically compatible; so, at the first break of the morning, after introductions of all the folks at the meeting were completed, we managed to catch hold of each other and make plans to have lunch together. I knew well before the end of that lunch that this man, twelve years my senior, without a doctoral degree, and serving in a non-faculty position on a year-by-year contract at Berkeley, was light years ahead of me in what he understood and knew how to do in teaching inservice and preservice English teachers about the teaching of writing and the teaching of English more broadly. I had found my true mentor in the field of English education, though that mentorship was not fully realized until I was ready to organize and direct my own site of the California and National Writing Project in 1979, and Jim became my constant friend and valued mentor for the next twenty-six years until his death in 2005.

My Problem in the Context of the History of Our Field. If I had been able to consult Jim in 1969 on the question of how to teach the English methods course at Michigan to students who were planning to become secondary English teachers, he would have told me exactly what to do, and I would have done it, but perhaps I would not have been entirely ready for it myself. He would have told me to use the book he was going to use that year as the major text in his methods course. It had just been published by Houghton Mifflin and was titled *Student-Centered Language Arts, K–13: A Handbook for Teachers* by a young scholar-teacher named James Moffett, who had taught English for a decade at Phillips Exeter Academy and had recently held an appointment as a researcher in the Harvard Graduate School of Education and who, a year later, would be recruited through Jim Gray's efforts by the Graduate School of Education at Berkeley to come to Berkeley as a visiting lecturer to teach English education courses to MA students in the secondary English teaching credential program. But I had never heard of Moffett until I moved to California and UCSB in 1970. Apparently, Steve Dunning didn't know about Moffett's new book, either. Maybe I never asked Steve. Perhaps I wouldn't have realized how valuable Moffett's handbook could have been, even if I had been told about it.

Teaching My First Methods Class. My solution to the problem of how to teach my first English methods course, as I remember it, was that I began to read and then assigned my students to read a substantial number of the unprecedented flurry of popular new books, written for the public rather than for educators, on teaching and literacy and schools that were published in the mid and late '60s, almost all of them highly critical of the bureaucratic indifference of schools to the lives and learning of children. These included, most notably, Jonathan Kozol's *Death at an Early Age* (1967) about the author's first year of teaching children in the spirit-killing culture of a Boston public school; John Holt's *How Children Fail* (1964), a critique of schooling in general, and *How Children Learn* (1967), an account of his extensive observations of young children, showing how they learn best through their own efforts to figure things out and how teachers and teaching almost always interfere with genuine learning; Herb Kohl's *36 Children* (1967) about his year of disheartening teaching of a sixth-grade class in a NYC Public School; James Herndon's *The Way It Spozed to Be* (1968), a shocking expose based on his year of teaching in a virtually segregated inner-city junior high school in California; Paul Goodman's *Compulsory Miseducation* (1964), in which he argues (as I remember) that in our text-saturated society, every child would learn to read by age six or seven, if they hadn't already been ruined for reading through instruction in school; and Postman and Weingartner's inspiring volume (for me), *Teaching as a Subversive Activity* (1969). I'm fairly sure I didn't and couldn't teach all of these books in any single semester. But I read all of them, and I'm quite confident that I taught most of them.

We read these books, talked about them in class, and I suppose I had students write papers about them as well. I can't imagine that my course served very well to prepare my students to teach English in a secondary school, but the reading surely had a powerful impact on my own attitude toward schooling and the new imagination I acquired about the kind of teacher I hoped my Michigan students would become and that, perhaps, I too needed to become.

Learning to Teach (Once Again) as a Fellow Learner of My Subject

In the fall of 1970, I embarked on my new position as an assistant professor of English at the University of California, Santa Barbara, where I was hired to direct the teaching credential program in English and to teach the English methods course and whatever literature courses I chose to teach, all with a guarantee that I would be able to teach the Milton course every year as long as I wanted to (it was a required course for UCSB English majors and was taught twice a year). Thus, upon my arrival in the fall, I taught the English methods course to our cohort of over 20 English teaching credential candidates, and that spring I taught Milton (and other classes as well, each with a syllabus entirely determined by me). What is relevant to the story of my pedagogical development, however, was that I taught my English methods course in the fall of 1970 in Santa Barbara entirely differently from how I had taught the same course in the spring of 1970 at Michigan; and in the spring of 1971 in Santa Barbara, I taught my Milton class entirely differently from how I had previously taught it in the spring of 1969 in Michigan. More importantly, I taught both courses in a way that focused on learning rather than on knowing, which is to say they were not conceptually informed by the idea that as the teacher I was responsible for transmitting knowledge to my students. Rather, both classes were focused on inquiry, on the questions that arose for the learners (including me as the head learner) of the subject matter that defined each course.

In my methods course, I therefore began the class by asking three questions that would serve essentially as the syllabus for the course: *What is English? What do we want our students to learn?* and *What can we do to help them?* The class would then proceed to try to answer these questions (and the additional questions that arose from their answers) through our in-class discussions and through our assigned and subsequently discovered readings and just as often through our own educational experience and our observations in classrooms (where all my students were both observing classes and engaged in student-teaching).

In my Milton class, I asserted that the premise of my class would be that Milton was wiser than we and had much to teach us and that our responsibility was to try to understand him. Which in practice would mean that we (including me) were all responsible for doing our best to understand the assigned texts for each week and to bring to our classes (which met twice a week) any questions we had about what we had been reading—but only genuine questions representing what, after a good faith effort, we couldn't understand either in the sense that we couldn't figure out what the textual passage was saying or that we could figure out the plain sense of what it said but couldn't understand what it meant, which is to say, how to interpret it. I did not yet include in that first year the more radical and important question that came to appear on the guidelines I subsequently printed for my students on "How to Read *Paradise Lost*," which also enjoined them to question any moral or philosophical or prudential claim or value advanced by the text that they couldn't understand as true. The principle behind that addition derived from Milton's aim in *Paradise Lost* to "justify the ways of God to man." Since "justify" must mean demonstrate the reasonableness of God's actions (toward humans) in a way that is comprehensible to human beings, then we should be able to understand how the universe and the human condition as given to mankind (and represented by Milton) are consistent with an originating creative force that is both reasonable and loving.

Accounting for My Demonstrable Progress in Teaching: Learning as Experience

I have often wondered over the past half-century how to explain the dramatic shift that took place in my two signature courses between the academic years of 1969–70 in Michigan and 1970–71 in California. The story of my teaching history that I have been excavating in this chapter has helped me to solve some of that mystery. The first explanation is that all of the reading I assigned for my English methods course in Michigan helped me to understand the importance of shifting a classroom from a teacher-centered teaching space to a student-centered learning space, and the Postman and Weingartner book convinced me of the power of a course centered on inquiry. My shift to an emphasis on questions in my Milton course may also have been influenced by my pedagogically radical reading, but I suspect it owed as much, if not more, to what I was privileged to experience, outside of the classroom, reading a difficult Renaissance poem in the company of friends and colleagues.

If I remember correctly, it was in the summer of 1969 when my officemate and closest colleague at Michigan, Bill Ingram, who was several years older than I and already an accomplished Shakespearean and Renaissance scholar, and his wife, Elizabeth "Betty" Morley Ingram, who was also a respected literary scholar and specialist in Medieval and Renaissance iconography, proposed that they and my wife and I meet weekly to read Book I of Spencer's *Faerie Queene* (1590) aloud, simply for our own enjoyment and edification and with none of the pressure of time that would require us to move on from any passage or section before we were finished discussing it. Our pattern was to take turns reading aloud, pausing when any one of us had a question or felt that we didn't fully understand any stanza or any portion of the text. We would then stop the reading to discuss the problematic passage or word or whatever question we had about the narrative in progress. Then, we would try to answer whatever question we had before we proceeded further in our reading, sometimes moving ahead without having resolved all our problems but with a good sense of what questions remained for us to solve with further study or consultation. Hence, our progress through the text was slow, but our reading was enjoyable and even exhilarating, largely because our method was focused on our own questions and ensured that we would arrive at an enriched understanding of everything we were reading, including lines that we may have understood only partially, but with a better-informed sense of what problems we were still unable to solve in a particular passage or episode.

This experience in the summer of 1969 must have influenced my approach to teaching Milton in the spring of 1971, when I taught Milton for the second time so differently from the way I had taught the course two years earlier at the University of Michigan, where I taught *Paradise Lost* and the other texts we read by lecturing and leading discussions toward interpretations I judged to be correct. At UCSB two years later, I taught the same course with a focus on the lines and passages that my students or I didn't understand, limiting my role in dealing with passages that I thought I understood but my students had identified as problematic by taking their questions seriously and assisting them in their effort to make sense of the problem passage (usually in small groups), refusing to impose my understanding as the answer. Yet I have no memory of ever before consciously linking those delightful evenings with the Ingrams in the summer of 1969 with the distinctive method I employed for the teaching of Milton in 1971 and have continued to employ (with some additional efforts to decenter my role) to this day, a method that has also influenced the way I teach other literature courses and that shaped many of the workshops I conduct (and articles I have written) on the teaching of literature for inservice and preservice English teachers.

The Cultural Context for My Development as a Teacher

As much as I would like to think of my development as my own individual achievement and the product of what I was learning as an individual, it would be misleading to decouple my learning experience from the cultural, political, and broader intellectual context in which it transpired. In my case, the changes I am describing in my thinking and teaching took place in the late sixties, in the midst of the Vietnam War and nationally influential protests against that war and widespread questioning of the political and cultural values that spawned it. That questioning was surely reflected in many of the books about schools that I was reading and teaching, and it extended to the hierarchical structures of academic life and the traditional roles of students and teachers. And nowhere was the cultural crisis of the late '60s more visible and vocal than on university campuses across the country, including Michigan while I was teaching there and with historical notoriety at UC Santa Barbara as I was preparing to move there. These protests were accompanied on both campuses by sit-ins, where faculty and students together conducted anti-establishment versions of classes outside of the official spaces for classes and engaged in various forms of counter-cultural discourse, particularly eschewing the differences in authority and expertise that characterize regular academic classes.

By the time I arrived at Michigan in 1966, the campus community was already a vibrant center for radical groups and revolutionary action and the site where Tom Hayden and Dick Flacks (who was later my colleague at Santa Barbara) had organized the historically important SDS, Students for a Democratic Society. Meanwhile, at UC Santa Barbara, student protests against the war were growing in strength in numbers and violence in actions. A staff member was killed when a bomb went off at the Faculty Club in April of 1969. Then, on February 25, 1970, after I had already accepted an offer to join the UCSB faculty, a mob of UCSB students burned to the ground the branch of the Bank of America that served the student community of Isla Vista, adjacent to the campus. (I watched the event on TV from Ann Arbor, noting that the rioting students were dressed for spring, while we were freezing in Ann Arbor.) A "police riot" ensued in Isla Vista, with sheriff's department officers breaking into student apartments and clubbing and arresting students who resisted unauthorized searches for marijuana or evidence of participation in counter-cultural activity. Shortly after I arrived on the UCSB campus in the late summer of 1970, I was invited to a party at the beautiful home of one of the senior English professors who had been heavily involved in sit-ins, and there I met a dozen students who had been traumatized by the events of the previous spring and couldn't stop telling stories of how they were brutalized (and consequently radicalized) by a crazed student-hating police force.

While the future of the university was being questioned in the press and legislature, faculty members on the campus were questioning their traditional teaching practices. In my own department, my colleague, Homer "Murph" Swander (1921–

2018), was experimenting (eventually with national influence) in his Shakespeare classes with performance teaching, insisting that his students come to understand crucial scenes not merely through textual analysis but through the physical and emotional process of acting them out. Murph became an early mentor to me at UCSB, and we shared a sizable group of students who took his Shakespeare course and my Milton course (in that order), many of whom, after graduation, entered the UCSB English teaching credential program, where they took my methods course. Years later, many of these same former students who had become exemplary secondary teachers of English became active participants in the Writing Project site I established at UCSB in 1979, and they continued to learn with me as colleagues for another twenty or thirty years and remain close to me intellectually and emotionally to this day.

In the UCSB Graduate School of Education, the Confluent Education Program (with generous funding from the Ford Foundation) was experimenting in 1970–71 with ways to bring together cognitive and affective experiences for students to promote a more authentic kind of learning, and while I found their experiments in English education mostly trivial or misguided on the cognitive side and inauthentic on the affective, I observed workshops involving emotional and cognitive experience in values clarification and workshops modeling Gestalt therapy but also constituting dramatic conflicts acted out in words and movement. My experience as a participant and witness to these workshops set me on my own journey to develop workshops to enable students to have intellectual and personally meaningful (dramatic) experiences that would engender deep and authentic understandings of texts and concepts important to the study of literature and to the teaching and learning of literature, a journey that shaped much of my teaching and virtually all of my professional development work with teachers for the rest of my career. It also led to my 2003 book, *The Literature Workshop: Teaching Texts and Their Readers*.

New Thinking about Teaching Writing and about the Writing Project. In the late fall of 1978, I was alerted to a call for proposals for funding to establish new sites of the California and National Writing Projects, the networks that had been created to extend statewide and nationally the work initiated by the Bay Area Writing Project at UC Berkeley, under the direction of Jim Gray, to provide a new model of professional development for teachers of writing across all levels of education. I had turned down Jim's invitation to establish a Writing Project site at UCSB some years earlier, mainly because I couldn't then see myself working with the typically traditional and closed-minded teachers (who turned out not to be entirely representative of the district) I had met in the schools where we had placed our English student teachers.

Fortunately, in the summer of 1976 or '77, I had attended a series of workshops sponsored by the county education office for secondary English teachers, where the eminent composition scholar Ross Winterowd had been invited to present current research and research-based practices in the teaching of writing. Winterowd was professor of English and head of the Program in Rhetoric, Linguistics, and Literature at USC and had written important books on modern rhetoric and the teaching of writing. I started attending the workshops after a teacher-friend from a local high school had called me to say that she had been at the first session and thought I would want to see what Winterowd was doing. And she was right. I attended the remaining four or five workshops in the series and was inspired both by Winterowd's research and the practices it generated, as well as by the excitement he shared as one of the pioneering figures in what amounted to the creation of a new academic discipline focused on newly developed research on writing and the teaching of writing.

During the breaks and after the formal sessions, I managed to engage in follow-up conversations with Winterowd, and I found him a very compatible colleague and generous source of practical professional wisdom. He was also intimately familiar with one of the earliest expansion sites in Southern California of what was becoming the National Writing Project, and he persuaded me that I would enjoy and learn much from directing a Writing Project site. He also assured me I could find a cadre of teachers for the Writing Project Summer Institute that I would enjoy working with. After all, my project, if it were funded, would probably serve all of Santa Barbara County and perhaps neighboring counties as well.

The Writing Project: Learning in a Community of Learners

The South Coast Writing Project (SCWriP) was officially founded and funded under my direction early in 1979 to conduct its first five-week Invitational Institute in the summer of 1979 with twenty-five participants who were designated UCSB/SCWriP "fellows" and recipients of a modest fellowship stipend. All of our fellows were veteran teachers, collectively representing all grade levels, from six different collaborating school districts in Santa Barbara County. By our second year, our service area was extended to include all school districts in Santa Barbara County and neighboring Ventura County (a total of roughly forty school districts), plus two community college districts (of four colleges) and my own university, so that our fellows by our second year included teachers at virtually every grade level, from early elementary through the community college and the university. Our participants in those first couple of years and ever after tended to be veteran teachers with at least 6–15 years of teaching experience and typically included some very senior faculty members with twenty or more years of experience. We rarely accepted applicants with fewer than six years' experience except for university doctoral students who were TAs in the UCSB composition program. Our careful selection process, which became increasingly reliable over the years, allowed us every summer to create a community of talented and experienced teachers who were themselves accomplished enough to command the respect and admiration of their colleagues and who were confident enough to be receptively open to learning from each other and equally ready to support and encourage each other.

It was an ideal community of learners, and my role was first to ensure that our Writing Project site observed the essential principles and practices of the original Bay Area Writing Project while sustaining the spirit of collaboration, inquiry, and dialogue, which would continually contribute to the learning and professional development of all of our members. Basically, that meant selecting open-minded teachers of all grades, having them demonstrate and reflect on their best practices for teaching writing, providing them with rich opportunities for writing during the institute, and having them share their writing and respond to the writing of colleagues in small groups on a regular basis throughout a five-week summer institute. It also meant that I was responsible for ensuring that our fellows had the opportunity to read and discuss some seminal articles representing current thinking and research in the field of writing studies and that they had available to them the physical space and material resources they needed and deserved for their five weeks of work in what we characterized as a combined think-tank and professional seminar. In the intensive day-to day activity of the summer institute and during the academic year, I was assisted by trusted colleagues whom I had invited to serve as co-directors and associate director: one was a high school teacher of legendary professional stature in our region; a second was a widely respected faculty member who was a reading specialist in the School of Education; and a third was a veteran English teacher with a PhD in Confluent Education and expertise in the evaluation of learning. The motto of the National Writing Project is "teachers teaching teachers," and that process began for our professional community of Writing Project fellows in the Summer Institute and was enacted thereafter in the professional development programs that our fellows were well paid to conduct for teachers in schools that contracted with our project for inservice programs for their teachers at schools and colleges in our two-county service area and sometimes beyond.

I would need to write another and longer essay to adequately cover what I learned from my experience in the Writing Project from the teachers I worked with and from the mentors (most notably Jim Gray and Miles Myers) who advised me about my role. But what I learned or more precisely acquired in my development as a teacher and teacher educator was an altered sense of my role and responsibility in the classrooms where I had been teaching. What I witnessed and experienced in the Writing Project in virtually all of our activities was the phenomenon of learning. I witnessed growth in most participants in their understanding of the nature and process of writing and of learning to write, and, more importantly, I saw them develop a new conception of their own capacity as writers, a virtual transformation in their sense of themselves as professionals, and a new sense of respect for the importance of their work. Nor was the learning I saw illusory or temporary. It constituted a powerful and transformational change in identity, a change that is carefully and convincingly documented and explained by Anne Whitney's widely cited research study conducted at my Writing Project site at UCSB (2008). And all of this powerful new learning seemed to take place by virtue of the learner's membership and participation in a community of learners, where it could be said that no individual or every individual functioned as the teacher.

While I didn't become familiar with the work of Lave and Wenger (1991) or situated learning theory for at least a dozen years after I became a Writing Project site director, I recognized the power of communities of learners (as did many of my writing project colleagues) and looked for ways to create such communities in the undergraduate and graduate classes I taught. I believe my development and dissemination through workshops at NCTE and throughout the NWP of the "Commentary Project" (Blau 2010; 2023) represents an effort on my part to make ordinary English classes at the secondary and college levels into communities where all members are contributors to the making of knowledge (by writing and posting online weekly commentaries on the assigned readings and by responding online every week to the postings of classmates) and thereby become the producers and not merely the consumers of knowledge in a classroom. But it wasn't until I found myself teaching seminars for doctoral students specializing in English education in my last few years at UCSB (where we had started a small PhD program in Language, Literacy & Composition, with a sub-specialty in English ed) and over the past sixteen years at Teachers College that I managed to fully replicate in my classes the spirit of learning that characterized a Writing Project institute. Of course, by that point, virtually all of my students were themselves experienced teachers, and some of them had actually been Writing Project "Fellows."

Nevertheless, the foundational principle of such a teaching practice and the unstated principle presupposed by a theory of situated learning or a community of practice is that every participant can learn and will learn if not blocked by any of the obstructions we ordinarily associate with teaching and teachers. And this brings me to the most advanced point I seem to have reached in the course of my thinking about teaching and learning, which, embarrassingly, seems to me the most appropriate first principle for anyone who is preparing to become a teacher: It is the assumption that all human beings are by nature learners and that learning is the most natural of all human activities, from birth through old age, unless blocked by illness or education. The evidence of this proposition is abundant in our experience and understanding of when learning happens and when it doesn't and especially in the magnificent achievement of language learning by every child. It is also wittily and dramatically expressed in the humorously accurate definition of craziness as doing the same thing over and over while expecting a different result. That piece of folk wisdom, which accurately describes every form of neurosis and mental illness, implicitly asserts that human mental health is manifest in the capacity to learn. Or we can say that healthy human beings are always learning. This is undoubtedly true for infants and young children. Why should it not be equally true in every stage of life? Perhaps because learning becomes obstructed at about age six with the onset of school and teaching.

Miltonic Wisdom on the Problem of Knowledge

But why should the institution of schooling, so intent on the education of the young in virtually every civilization we think of as advanced in literacy and technology, engage in state-sponsored educational practices that seem to do more to obstruct rather than enhance the learning of their youth? The most compelling answer, I believe, takes us back, as most questions about human nature do, to the poet John Milton and *Paradise Lost* and the foundational story of the human condition (for the Abrahamic religions) in the experience and fate of our first parents, Adam and Eve, as Milton represented the biblical account in his classic epic. In Milton's seventeenth-century account, which is entirely consistent with, though more elaborated than, the original Hebrew version, the universe was created by a loving and just Creator for the growth and freedom of an original human couple, who are designed for learning, for love and procreation, and for eternal life on the condition that they remain obedient to a single law forbidding them to eat of the fruit of the Tree of Knowledge, while they may freely eat of all the other trees and delicious plants in their Garden Paradise.

But our first parents choose to disobey that one easy requirement for preserving their happiness and continuing their healthy growth as progenitors and learners. And they do so through a process of temptation and ultimate revolt against their Maker and their nature that starts with our general mother Eve, who, believing the lies of the enemy of mankind, Satan, allows herself to be tempted into eating the attractive aromatic fruit of the Tree of Knowledge in the expectation that by taking the fruit of knowledge into herself, she will grow in knowledge and wisdom and thereby become equal in knowledge to her partner Adam or even superior rather than inferior, as she had experienced herself to be by virtue of his earlier creation and longer experience. In other words, Eve's desire for knowledge equal to Adam's seems to make her vulnerable to the temptation to eat the forbidden fruit, which will presumably confer knowledge. And upon eating it, she imagines herself wise, as if she were an angel rather than a human. Then, not wanting to be so different from her beloved husband (or to risk punishment by herself), she tempts him to likewise betray their Creator by also eating the forbidden fruit. Together, they experience an illusion of new power and heretofore unimagined pleasure before they realize that their eating of the fruit of the Tree of Knowledge gave them no actual knowledge except knowledge of what they have lost—their former sense of their own righteousness and honor, while what they have gained is a new sense of shame and unworthiness.

Milton's portrait of our first parents after their fall reminds readers of his earlier depiction of the despair of the rebel angels who, through their rebellion against their Maker, had been cast down to hell, a place where nothing lives except death itself. Now, Adam and Eve too seem to inhabit a spiritually dead psychological space as they blame each other (and even their Maker) for their individual disobedience, while they seem bereft of all capacity for love. They also demonstrate their despair by wishing for an immediate physical death for themselves and consider suicide as a means to escape the legacy of death they will otherwise bequeath to all their offspring.

If we take Milton's account of the fall seriously as a cautionary tale for all readers—as I think we are obliged to do, given his focus throughout the epic on the problem of learning and knowledge and the role of teachers and stories—I think we will find this story of the root cause for human misery to be a story, first, about how and when human beings are created (which is to say by God and nature) as beings designed for learning. But it is also a story about how knowledge (which is also a product of learning) can constitute a temptation insofar as it can become the object of desire that supersedes the process of learning and thereby becomes the aim and end of human attention, an object, as it were, of idolatry and therefore indicative of an act of rebellion against God and nature and against the nature of human beings as beings who are most essentially learners.

That God is in no way responsible for the fall of our first parents is evident first in His promise that if they remain obedient to the only rule He imposes on their otherwise absolute freedom, they will inevitably grow in knowledge and wisdom by "degree" or gradual steps until they are able to eat and converse as equals with angels and reside as comfortably in heaven as on earth. In other words, the key to heaven and life eternal is to continue in a life of learning and to reject the temptation of knowledge as something that can be ingested or otherwise taken into oneself from the outside without the effort and time required for learning through one's own experience. To reject the requirement of learning through human experience is to reject the nature of human learning, which constitutes a rejection of the self and thereby entails the hellish misery exemplified by Satan himself, whose governing passions are his baseless hatred of his Maker and an unending fury at his own spiritual or mental position in the hierarchy of the universe, while he endlessly refuses to repent or show any inclination to learn or acknowledge the reality or justice of his position.

I hesitate to refer to my explication of the fall as an allegorical reading of the problem of learning and knowledge in the world of our experience, because the language of Milton's great epic is far too literal and literally applicable to the mistaken conceptions of learning and teaching and knowledge that are operative in our own lives and in the human world we inhabit. What could be more literal than the warning to human beings that learning is what happens to us gradually, by degree, and in steps through our lived experience, as long as we don't turn away from our task of learning to an imagined shortcut of swallowing knowledge whole, unlearned and unearned in the refusal to learn through experience, as if knowledge could be contained in a fruit that could be eaten? Knowledge may be a fruit, indeed, but it is the fruit of one's own experience and therefore it can't be taken from anything or anybody else.

Such is the last of the postulates or principles I have identified as my valediction and legacy for my students and the fruit of my 63 years of teaching. Those same principles, of course, require me to assert that I offer them provisionally to my teaching colleagues and heirs, since they too are subject to modification and clarification if and when new learning renders them inadequate for some learners, even as it might confirm them for others.

In the meantime, must I now ask forgiveness for tempting my readers to accept a set of principles or propositions about learning and knowledge even as provisional truths, if those propositions don't arise from their own experience and understanding as I claim that they arise from mine? Why should readers put their faith in my words, even if I speak honestly in words that arise from my experience, largely including my experience of reading Milton? The answer, I trust, is that I am not asking readers to allow my experience to give authority to ideas they have not experienced. Rather, I have spent most of my discourse telling stories about my experience, stories that exemplify the abstract principles I offer as the lessons to be reasonably drawn from my narrated experience and that (to the degree that my stories are convincing) invite readers to undergo my experience vicariously, thereby legitimizing through "aesthetic experience" and the tentative authority of reason the abstractions articulated by my principles. That is how we learn from our experience of literature, and why we can't learn legitimately from literature when the interpretation or experience offered to us is not our own, but that of a teacher or other authority who doesn't convincingly share his or her experience with us. It also explains why good teachers are almost always inveterate story-tellers.

Index

Note: A page number followed by "f" denotes a figure. One followed by "n" denotes a note.

Editors

Kathleen (Buchan) Kelly has been an educator for over twenty-five years in public and independent school settings. She has taught at the middle school, high school, college, and graduate school levels on the east and west coasts. Along the way, she has earned two master's degrees and a PhD. What it means to think, read and, write *with* and *alongside* others defines her work in the ELA classroom. Kelly's writing has appeared in journals such as *English Journal* and *Knowledge Cultures*. She has also recently coedited two books on James Moffett. Kelly has chapters forthcoming within *The Legacy of James Moffett* and *What is College Writing 2.0?* She took up this Festschrift project so that others in the field would come to know the magic of Sheridan Blau. Kelly currently teaches English at a small independent school in Southern California.

Ruth Vinz is the Morse Endowed Professor in Teacher Education and professor of English education at Teachers College, Columbia University. She is the author of seventeen books and numerous articles, written over the fifty-seven years of her teaching career. Vinz taught high school English and humanities courses for twenty-four years, where she came to understand teaching and learning as restless cartography, journeying *with* students through landscapes filled with possibility, promise, and poignancy. In her thirty-three years at Teachers College, she continues to learn *with* others through coursework, collaborative (re)search/writing projects, and community engagements. She suggests that her writing is intended as an invitation to others and a reminder to herself of the need to continuously move beyond familiar boundaries and to (re)cognize that we are always in the making, always *becoming* through a process of learning, un-learning, questioning, and revising ourselves anew. Vinz calculates that she has provided feedback to at least 38,500 students'

poems, essays, stories, research reports, and dissertation drafts, from which she continues to learn and—thrilled by the power of imagination in combination with the resources of language—to craft writing into exhilarating and intimate portrayals of our hopes, fears, and dreams.

Paul M. Rogers is an associate professor of writing studies at the University of California, Santa Barbara. He is the former director of the Northern Virginia Writing Project, a cofounder and former chair of the International Society for the Advancement of Writing Research, and the coeditor of eight collections, including *International Models of Changemaker Education* (2022), *Toward a Re-Emergence of James Moffett's Mindful, Spiritual, and Student-Centered Pedagogy* (2023), and *Writing as a Human Activity* (2023). He is a recipient of the K. Patricia Cross Award for leadership in higher education and a corecipient of the Janet Emig Award for research in English education.

Contributors

Deborah Appleman is the Hollis L. Caswell Professor of Educational Studies at Carleton College. Professor Appleman taught high school English for nine years before receiving her doctorate from the University of Minnesota. She is the author of more than a dozen books on literacy education, including *Critical Encounters in Secondary English: Teaching Literary Theory to Adolescents*, (winner of the Richard A. Meade Award); *Adolescent Literacy and the Teaching of Reading; Adolescent Literacies: A Handbook of Practice-Based Research* (coeditor with Kathleen Hinchman); *Teaching Literature to Adolescents* (with Rick Beach, Robert Fecho, and Rob Simon); *Uncommon Core;* and *Reading Better, Reading Smarter.* Her book *Words No Bars Can Hold: Literacy Learning in Prison* draws from her experiences teaching in a high security prison for men. Her most recent book, *Literature and the New Culture Wars*, examines current political challenges in the teaching of literature.

Richard Beach is Professor Emeritus of Literacy Education at the University of Minnesota, Twin Cities. His recent research focuses on fostering languaging activities and teaching about climate change in the ELA classroom. He has published thirty-two books, including *Languaging Relations for Transforming the Literacy and Language Arts Classroom, Teaching Language as Action in the ELA Classroom* (http://languaging.pbworks.com), *Drawing on Students' Worlds in the ELA Classroom: Toward Critical Engagement and Deep Learning* (http://adolescentsworlds.pbworks.com), *Teaching Climate Change to Adolescents: Reading, Writing, and Making a Difference* (http://climatechangeela.pbworks.com), and *Youth Media Creation on the Climate Change Crisis: Hear Our Voices* (http://youthclimatecrisismedia.pbworks.com). He served as former president of the Literacy Research Association and received the 2022 John Gumperz Distinguished Lifetime Scholarship Award from the Language and Social Processes SIG, AERA.

Faythe Beauchemin is an assistant professor at the Lynch School of Education & Human Development at Boston College, specializing in the areas of language and literacy. Drawing upon the fields of anthropology, linguistics, and literacy studies, her academic research is grounded in theories that recognize teaching and learning as a social and cultural process that is historically and politically situated. Her current research examines how young bi-multilingual children experience multilingual literacy learning in English-medium schools located in emerging immigrant destination towns. Additionally, she explores how teachers in these towns who share and do not share the cultural and linguistic background of their students enact humanizing, culturally sustaining literacy instruction in their classrooms.

Sheridan Blau is Professor of Practice in the Teaching of English at Teachers College, Columbia University, and Professor of English and Education (*Emeritus*) at the University of California, Santa Barbara, where he directed the South Coast Writing Project and Literature Institute for Teachers and the UCSB Composition Program. Beyond the university, he has served as director of the National Literature Project Network, a member of the National Writing Project Advisory Board, and senior advisor for the development of California's literacy assessment. He is a former president of the National Council of Teachers of English and the recipient of awards for his teaching, for his scholarly and professional contributions to the discipline of English, and for his published research. He has published widely on the teaching and learning of composition and literature, on seventeenth-century British literature, on professional development for teachers, and on the ethics and politics of literacy.

Suzanne S. Choo is an associate professor in the English Language and Literature Academic Group at the National Institute of Education, Nanyang Technological University, Singapore. Her research has been published in various peer-reviewed journals such as *Harvard Educational Review, Reading Research Quarterly, Research in the Teaching of English*, and *Critical Studies in Education*, among others. Her book, *Reading the World, the Globe, and the Cosmos: Approaches to Teaching Literature for the Twenty-First Century* was awarded the 2014 Critics Choice Book Award by the American Educational Studies Association. Her most recent books are: *Teaching Ethics Through Literature: The Significance of Ethical Criticism in a Global Age* (Routledge, 2021) and a coedited volume titled *Literature Education in the Asia-Pacific: Policies and Practices and Perspectives in Global Times* (Routledge, 2018). In 2016 and 2021, she was awarded the Excellence in Teaching Commendation award by the National Institute of Education. Her website is https://suzannechoo.com/.

Ralph Adon Córdova, PhD, has worked as a school site leader, university professor, elementary school teacher, and educational researcher. In his teaching career spanning almost three decades, he has taught at La Patera School in Goleta, CA; served K–university students and teachers at the University of Missouri-St. Louis as a tenured professor in the College of Education; and recently served as principal of the Rio Del Sol Elementary School in Oxnard, CA. Dr. Córdova's work is concerned with seeing and hearing the authentic voices and lives of learners and teachers. His scholarship is grounded in an Interactional Ethnographic Perspective to create an interdisciplinary nexus where complementary theories from anthropology, critical discourse analysis, and literary theory intersect with principles from art and design. Córdova is a trained educational ethnographer with numerous peer-reviewed publications. He is the founder and director of Cultural Landscapes Collaboratory.

At the time of publication, **Dominic Nah** is a PhD candidate at the National Institute of Education (NIE), Nanyang Technological University, Singapore. His doctoral research focuses on examining student responses to ethically oriented literature pedagogies at the secondary school level, with a focus on representations of otherness. His research on ethical criticism and Literature education has been published in *Changing English* and is forthcoming in *Australian Journal of English Education*. He has also coauthored publications on the sociological analysis of education policies, literature education, dramaturgy, and literary criticism, which have appeared in *Pedagogy, Culture & Society, The Routledge Companion to Literature and Social Justice, (Asian) Dramaturgs' Network: Sensing, Complexity, Tracing and Doing,* and *Journal of Practice, Research and Tangential Activities*. He previously worked as a research assistant at NIE, and was associate faculty teaching literature at the Singapore University of Social Sciences.

Peter Elbow is Emeritus Professor of English at the University of Massachusetts Amherst and author of numerous books and articles focusing on how everyday spoken language can make writing more feasible, lively, and clear—even formal writing. His larger theme is the democratization of writing, and books originally intended for a lay readership transformed the way writing was taught from grade schools through the university, among them *Everyone Can Write, Writing without Teachers,* and *Writing with Power.* He was director of Writing Programs at SUNY Stony Brook and UMass Amherst and was on the founding faculty at two experimental colleges: Franconia College and Evergreen State College. He has also been the recipient of several prestigious awards: the Braddock Award; the James A. Berlin Award; the James R. Squire Award "for his transforming influence and lasting intellectual contribution to the English Profession," and the CCCC Exemplar Award for "representing the highest ideals of scholarship, teaching, and service to the entire profession."

Noah Harris Gordon, PhD, completed his undergraduate studies at the University of Vermont and earned his master's and doctoral degrees at Teachers College, Columbia University. His dissertation advisor was Professor Sheridan Blau. Gordon founded the high school English department at Special Music School—a public school that serves a diverse community of gifted musicians in New York City—in 2013. He continues to teach at SMS, where he continually revises his teaching and reinvents his curriculum by returning to the practices and principles he learned through his work with Professor Blau. He was a Blackboard Award Honoree in 2016 and a finalist for the FLAG Award for Teaching Excellence in 2023. He considers Sheridan his mentor, his trusted collaborator, his dear friend, and his intellectual forebear.

In 2019, **Jeff Hudson** packed a teaching career spanning three decades, two cats, and a dog into a small pickup truck and left the Midwest for California with his wife Leslie. They each work now in the Rio School District of Oxnard—Jeff as a seventh-grade teacher and now TOSA and Leslie as an elementary school principal. Jeff first became a fellow of the Mississippi Valley Writing project in 1997. In 2007, he founded and directed the Piasa Bluffs Writing Project with Dr. Ralph Córdova. Today, he is excited to be reconnected with the National Writing Project at SCWriP.

Carol Booth Olson is Professor Emerita in the School of Education at the University of California, Irvine. After directing the UCI Writing Project for forty-two years, she became the director of the WRITE Center, an IES-funded national research and development center focused on improving writing outcomes for secondary students and principal investigator of the EIR Expansion project, the Pathway to Academic Success. She is the author of numerous journal articles and author of *The Reading/Writing Connection, Helping English Learners to Write,* and *Thinking Tools for Young Readers and Writers.*

Andrew Rejan has taught English at Darien (Connecticut) High School since 2011. He has facilitated workshops for teachers throughout the US, contributed to the development of curriculum for educational programs around the world, and taught at the graduate level at Teachers College, Columbia University, where he received his PhD in English education. Rejan regularly publishes articles for English teachers and teacher educators, and his work has appeared in *English Education*, *English Journal*, and *Changing English*. His current research focuses on attempts to reimagine or reframe the place of writing in the literature classroom given the rise of generative artificial intelligence.

Peter Smagorinsky is Distinguished Research Professor, Emeritus, at the University of Georgia, and Distinguished Visiting Scholar at the Universidad de Guadalajara, Mexico. His work has drawn on cultural-historical theory to explore a variety of questions in literacy practice, literacy education, teacher development, teacher education, service-learning, mental health, character education, and other topics. Recent recognition has come through his election to the National Academy of Education, the AERA Cultural Historical Research SIG Lifetime Contribution to Cultural-Historical Research Award, the AERA Division K Exemplary Research in Teaching and Teacher Education Award, and runner-up status for the LRA Edward B. Fry Book Award and United Kingdom Literacy Association Academic Book Award. Recent books include *L. S. Vygotsky and English in Education and the Language Arts* (Routledge & International Federation of Teachers of English) and, with Allison Skerrett, *Teaching Literacy in Troubled Times: Identity, Inquiry, and Social Action at the Heart of Instruction* (Corwin).

Cheryl Hogue Smith is a professor of English and the Writing and Reading Across the Curriculum Certification Coordinator at Kingsborough Community College of the City University of New York. She is a past chair of the Two-Year College English Association and a fellow of the National Writing Project (SCWriP). She has published articles in *TETYC*, *JBW*, *JAAL*, *English Journal*, *JTW*, *California English*, and *Midsummer Magazine* (Utah Shakespeare Festival) and chapters in *What Is "College-Level" Writing?* (vol. 2, NCTE), *Deep Reading, Deep Learning* (vol. 2, Peter Lang), *Challenging Antisemitism: Lessons from Literacy Classrooms* (Rowman & Littlefield), and the forthcoming *When Challenge Brings Change: How Teacher Breakthroughs Transform the Classroom*, (TC Press/NWP).

Patricia Lambert Stock is Professor Emerita of English and Writing, Rhetoric and American Cultures at Michigan State University. She has served as associate director of the Syracuse University Writing Program and founding director of Michigan State University's Writing Center as well as of two National Project sites. A former president of NCTE and recipient of the council's Distinguished Service Award, she has written books and articles about literacy teaching and learning, teacher research, the scholarship of teaching, writing programs and centers, and contingent faculty in higher education. Her published work has been recognized with the James

Britton, Richard A. Meade, and Janet Emig Awards; with Hofstra University's National Research Award; and with the CCCC's Outstanding Book Award (with Eileen Schell).